PO

WIT

PRAISE FOR

NO GO ZONES

HOW SHARIA LAW IS COMING TO A NEIGHBORHOOD NEAR YOU

"Raheem Kassam is one of the most fearless and insightful journalists on the scene today, and he pulls no punches in *No Go Zones: How Sharia Law Is Spreading in America* as he boldly exposes what most of his peers and colleagues would rather pass over in silence or, even worse, actively deny in the face of an ever-increasing mountain of evidence. All that evidence is in this book, presented with the candor and realism that is so urgently needed on this increasingly serious issue. *No Go Zones* is a unique look at a phenomenon that is growing under the noses of our politicians and law enforcement officials, who are too busy pursuing 'outreach' to Muslim communities to notice."

—**ROBERT SPENCER**, director of Jihad Watch and author of the *New York Times* bestselling books *The Politically Incorrect Guide® to Islam (and the Crusades)* and *The Truth About Muhammad*

"An important and eye-opening look inside the Islamic enclaves that dot Europe and are now cropping up in America. Kassam takes us on a tour that is both enlightening and frightening. If you want to understand why radical Islam is spreading in the West and why so little is being done to stop it, this is the book to read."

—**WILLIAM KILPATRICK**, author of *The Politically Incorrect Guide® to Jihad*

"What the West calls 'No Go Zones' are Islam's way of building a territorial shield of separation and a firm line of demarcation between "Dar Al Islam," the House of Islam, and "Dar Al Harb," the House of War—the rest of the world, with which Islam is at perpetual war. The Islamic community is saying 'We will never assimilate.' Thank you, Raheem Kassam, for alerting the West of this purely Islamic phenomenon of rejection that will inevitably lead to a bloody confrontation between the Islamic and the Western way of life."

—**NONIE DARWISH**, director of Former Muslims United and the author of *Now They Call Me Infidel: Why I Renounced Jihad for America, Israel, and the War on Terror* and *Wholly Different: Why I Chose Biblical Values over Islamic Values*

NO GO ZONES

NO GO ZONES

How Sharia Law Is Coming to a Neighborhood Near You

RAHEEM KASSAM

FOREWORD BY NIGEL FARAGE

REGNERY
PUBLISHING
A Division of Salem Media Group

Regnery® is a registered trademark of Salem Communications Holding Corporation

Cataloging-in-Publication data on file with the Library of Congress

ISBN 978-1-62157-680-8
e-book ISBN 978-1-62157-694-5

Published in the United States by
Regnery Publishing
A Division of Salem Media Group
300 New Jersey Ave NW
Washington, DC 20001
www.Regnery.com

Manufactured in the United States of America

10 9 8 7 6 5 4 3 2 1

Books are available in quantity for promotional or premium use. For information on discounts and terms, please visit our website: www.Regnery.com.

Distributed to the trade by
Perseus Distribution
www.perseusdistribution.com

*This book is dedicated to all those who have given their
lives for liberty. From dissenters in the Middle East,
to dissidents in the Soviet Union, from our military
heroes who fought to preserve our way of life in the West,
to the filmmakers, satirists, and cartoonists brave enough
to confront would-be tyrannical theologies.*

This is for all of you.

CONTENTS

FOREWORD

BY NIGEL FARAGE

When Raheem told me he was writing this book on No Go Zones in the Western world, my first reaction was "Thank goodness someone is doing this job." My second thought was, "I hope he's careful."

The reason for my first response is probably self-explanatory. This is an issue that is so contentious mainly because no one has yet documented these areas as comprehensively as Raheem does in this book. It's a topic that is marred by half-truths, full denials, slips of tongues, and an attempt to reject the notion of such areas in such a brazen and unfounded manner that much of the establishment media that spends its time in denial can truly wear the title "Fake News" proudly.

Now, I'm pleased to say, they have a very good starting point by which to judge the merits of the debates on integration, assimilation, and the scale and speed of migration into the West.

My second thought on the book was multifaceted.

Firstly, people who speak out against radical Islam, highlighting issues such as Sharia law, terrorism, and indeed things that shouldn't be contentious like integration are often targeted, abused, endure massive attempts at being discredited, or even find themselves on the receiving end of threats or violence. As a personal friend, I am sincerely concerned that such brave truth-telling on the subject might find Raheem on the receiving end of some of this.

But as a professional colleague, I was also concerned at the scale of the task.

How can you, I wondered, summarize so much, over so many decades, in so many places around the Western world in just one book?

I'm delighted to say after having read this book that Raheem has done an excellent job in balancing hard data and statistics, and using multiple areas from around Europe and the United States in his attempt to fairly portray the issues facing majority Muslim areas in the West.

And it's not just that, either.

From Molenbeek to Malmö, from Brooklyn to Hamtramck, each of these areas has its own, unique characteristics. Its own players. Its own resistance movements.

The personal stories and interviews contained in this book shine a much-needed light on how actors, from residents to local officials, politicians, and pressure groups, all play into the massive discord taking place in areas across Europe and America.

Truly, the final product is one that bears reading, citing, and even corroborating by other journalists, who I implore to follow Raheem's lead in getting to the bottom of these issues.

Of course, with any book of this length, there is so much more to tell, and I hope Raheem can follow up with more information, more trips, more investigation, and more documentation of what is going on in our towns and cities.

I also want to take the opportunity to commend his fair mindedness on this issue.

Raheem has been careful not to portray—as someone more alarmist might—these communities as marauding, out of control groups intent on the decline of the West. In a lot of instances in fact, the people who find themselves ghettoized and demonized from all sides are victims themselves of their community leaders and actors who want to drive a wedge between migrant communities and native populations.

The work concerning poverty and socioeconomic factors is pivotal. The work on Deobandism and the Tablighi Jamaat movement is seminal. And the work contained in this book on the aggravating factors—usually the establishment, the political Left—is a warning sign to America to stand up and assert its identity, enforce its laws, and demand integration before it is too late for many places in the United States.

There will of course be plenty of critics of this book. They'll ask questions like, "If these places are really 'No Go', how come you were able to go there?"

The answer should of course be obvious if you read the text. Raheem timed his visits carefully, didn't seek to antagonize locals with video cameras, and in some cases—already reported by news organizations across the board—managed to luckily avoid mass incidents of violence and rioting by a matter of hours. In short: it was due to the studiousness of his approach that he managed to fairly document his experiences and put together a piece of work that will stand the test of time both academically and from a philosophical perspective.

It should be required reading for conservatives, Republicans, liberals, teachers, students, reporters, editors, and activists alike. And I'm delighted he has managed to resist tabloid-style presentation, and painstakingly sought out reliable sources, high-level interviews, and even hard-to-come-by data on topics like crime, imprisonment, and more.

If you do one thing after picking up this book, I recommend this: buy it for, or recommend it to, someone else too, and do your part to help settle the debate we shouldn't even be having—whether or not these areas exist. Only by leaping this hurdle can we get onto the real debate: what should we do about it, now that it is on our shores?

ONE

THE UNSETTLED DEBATE

When I heard this, frankly, I choked on my porridge and I thought
it must be April Fools' day. This guy's clearly a complete idiot.

—FORMER BRITISH PRIME MINISTER DAVID CAMERON,
SPEAKING ABOUT STEVE EMERSON'S COMMENTS
ON BIRMINGHAM, UNITED KINGDOM[1]

I t was just after the *Charlie Hebdo* terror attack in Paris
when Steve Emerson appeared on Fox News. During the
interview, while discussing where extremism-fostering
enclaves exist, he described the city of Birmingham in the
United Kingdom as "totally Muslim" and a "No Go Zone."[2]

The claim was manifestly false. While Birmingham is a
city not without its multiculturalism-imposed problems—and
as you'll find out later in this book, especially as regards one
particular area called Sparkbrook—there is not much besides
the area's horrific architecture that would give me pause
before visiting. Emerson, of the usually reliable Investigative
Project on Terrorism, had clearly misspoken. He eventually
admitted his error, took to the airwaves again—this time in
the United Kingdom—apologized, and the matter was forgotten for the most part.

But watching that moment live, I realized just how scarce the facts are when discussing No Go Zones, or as the French call some of them—as only the French would—"sensitive urban areas." At the time, former British Prime Minister David Cameron described Emerson as "a complete idiot" for his comments about Birmingham. But in my experience, Emerson was only off by a couple dozen miles at worst, and a couple hundred miles at best. This was the debate that was lost in the maelstrom of attacks on Emerson's character that followed his mistake.

A commonly heard trope from the Left, especially on the issue of climate change, is that "the science is settled." And despite the science being settled on the question of whether No Go Zones exist, there is still a reluctance—borne perhaps out of an unholy alliance of misplaced "tolerance," philosophical vacuousness, and perceived electoral advantages—to tackle the issue head on.

No Go Zones are, in effect, a microcosm of the debate surrounding Muslim immigration and Islam, areas where few people will dare to venture. And can you blame them? The pioneers of the subject matter in the late twentieth and early twenty-first centuries have all ended up either dead, with prison sentences, with fines for thought crimes, or had their lives reduced to skulking around public areas with their hats pulled low and their gazes averted.

From Ayaan Hirsi Ali—herself a victim of female genital mutilation—to her colleague Theo Van Gogh, the *Charlie Hebdo* satirists, Geert Wilders, Robert Spencer, Pamela Geller, Douglas Murray, and others, entire livelihoods and careers have been ruined (or almost ruined) because these people dared to speak the truth or at least ask tough questions.

It is, in large part, fear that drives people away from the subject matter. But for big, establishment media outlets that seek to create harmony on the Left and division on the Right, it is expedient to ignore No Go Zones. The combination of fear and ignorance surrounding this topic has begun to manifest itself in tragic ways. Islam itself has become a No Go Zone for many. One can easily see why.

The Pew Research Center has found that Muslims in the West are not integrating as well as CNN or the BBC would have you believe. The endless scare stories—many demonstrably fake—of women having their hijabs ripped off in Western cities or being verbally abused are scarcely balanced with the troubling hard data on how Muslims in the West think, feel, or behave, especially toward one another.

The figures for how many Muslims believe in Sharia law, or death for apostasy, are staggering to say the least. On March 22, 2016, I wrote an article entitled "DATA: Young Muslims in the West Are a Ticking Time Bomb, Increasingly Sympathizing with Radicals, Terror." I reported that 20 percent of British Muslims sympathized with the 7/7 bombers who killed fifty-two people on the London transport network;[3] that 27 percent supported the attacks on *Charlie Hebdo*; that 12 percent of young Muslims in Britain said that suicide bombings can be justified, and that 26 percent of young Muslim Americans felt the same.[4] At some point, this mindset ceases to be on the "fringe" or "radical" and becomes an integral and significant part of the demographic concerned. It also becomes part of what the rest of the world expects from it.

The BBC, hardly known for its ability to talk tough on Islam, was forced to include a man who was arrested in 2014 for possibly wanting to travel to Syria to support the Islamic State in a reality TV show called *Muslims Like Us*. The British Broadcasting Corporation admitted at the time, in December 2016, that Abdul Haqq—who was subsequently acquitted—"represent[s] a voice" in the Muslim community. Despite Haqq's comments excusing the actions of Islamic State, the production company for *Muslims Like Us* said, "People who have monstrous views aren't always monsters."[5]

Separating emotion from this debate is difficult, especially for someone like me, born and raised in a Muslim family, who still has many practicing Muslim friends and family members. That's why data was the key to writing this book. It allowed me to assess this situation objectively and see what most participants in the debate ignore or cover up.

It's impossible to turn a blind eye to cold hard facts—at least for me. Data reveals that 18 percent of young British Muslims would not report details of a planned terror attack to the police, 40 percent of British Muslims want Sharia law in the West, and one in five prison inmates in the United Kingdom are now Muslim,[6] despite the religion making up only 5 percent of the population as a whole.[7]

The situation in the United States is equally dire. Nearly 10 percent of prison inmates in America are Muslims, despite adherents of Islam making up around just 1 percent of the total country's population.[8] A 2015 poll published by the Center for Security Policy—run by President Ronald Reagan's former Acting Assistant Secretary of Defense for International Security Affairs Frank Gaffney—found that 51 percent of Muslims in America believed they "should have the choice of being governed according to sharia [law]." Nearly one quarter of those polled said they believe there should be violent punishments for those who insult the Muslim prophet, Muhammad.[9] All this is deeply troubling given the prevalence of Islamic enclaves and No Go Zones.

Younger generations of Muslims in the West may be more susceptible to extremist tendencies because they are ghettoized, segregated, and radicalized. This often occurs due to foreign money being pumped into mosques and madrassas around the West. But it has also been a consequence of this being a unique situation, and thusly both their immediate support networks—friends, family, imams, colleagues—turning a blind eye or not knowing what to do when faced with hardline views.

When Europe's migrant crisis was in full flow in 2015, instead of welcoming Syrians into Saudi Arabia, the Saudi government pledged to build two hundred mosques in Germany.[10] These mosques and their leaders often promote anti-Western sentiment, anti-Jewish sentiment, and push a hardline interpretation of the Quran and Islamic jurisprudence, which we have come to know as "Wahhabism" or "Salafism."

This attracted almost no media attention when it was announced. The *Independent*—once a newspaper and now an online platform—published two articles on the matter. The *Daily Mail* published one. *HuffPost*, *International Business Times*, and *Breitbart News* all published articles on it too. But in terms of the massive global news sources, there was zero coverage. Nothing from the BBC, nothing from CNN, nothing from ABC, NBC, or CBS.

When searching Google for this story, by the second page of search results, the reader is now looking at news sites from Pakistan, India, and a small denial of the story tucked away in a Reuters article on page three. This is indicative of how Western media failed to live up to its basic obligations to its readers to cover the story. Whether true or not—and I suspect the original source in the Lebanese newspaper that broke the story was telling the truth—most established media organizations in the West did not want to broach the subject. It was too tricky to explain. Too inconvenient while they were pushing an open borders narrative.

The same applied to the Cologne sexual assault scandal story from New Year's Eve of 2015. On that night, over one thousand men—some sources even claim up to two thousand[11]—of varying migrant backgrounds were reported to have sexually assaulted, raped, or mugged German women in front of Cologne's Central Station. Overall, around 2,000 sexual assaults and robberies were reported across major German cities, leading even the most promigration German officials to concede this was a new phenomenon perpetrated by recently arrived migrants and refugees.

Despite reading about this atrocity on German news websites, I could find nothing about it for several days in the Western media. It was only when my colleague Oliver Lane, now one of my reliable deputies at *Breitbart London*, brought it to me himself, certain that he could accurately represent the facts of the case, that we set about figuring out how to cover the story.

I was perplexed by the lack of coverage—the most "telling" reports claimed the incident involved multiple robberies and rapes—and my disbelief that this could happen almost led us to miss it entirely. But between Lane and I, we figured it out: this topic was a sensitive issue that no one wanted to touch. Still, when Oliver came to me with his final story, I almost hit "Delete" immediately.

"There's no way this is true and no one else has written about it yet," I thought. It simply couldn't—in an era of smartphones and twenty-four-hour news—be of the scale Oliver claimed. But it was.

We broke the story later that day, much to the panic of my bosses, who insisted that my head would roll if we had bungled any details. I gulped, and kept refreshing my Google search page over the next few hours, hoping someone else would corroborate our work.

Phew.

Shortly afterwards, major news organizations started to report the incident, with an op-ed in the *Times of London* even crediting us for the fact that the news had been reported at all.

"Cover-up" would be a strong word to use when discussing the broader attitude of the media on this incident. "Disbelief" and an unwillingness to pursue the story would perhaps be more accurate. I almost had the very same reaction. It is the same disbelief that pushes journalists away from the topic of No Go Zones. Most of them probably think, "It's 2016 in western Europe and in the United States. These things cannot possibly be happening. These places cannot possibly exist. These are the fantasies of Islamophobic right-wingers seeking to target and abuse Muslim communities out of sheer bigotry." None of that is true.

The establishment media and political complicity—cowardice— behind a failure to accurately report an almost psychological and physical enslavement perpetrated upon Muslims—young Muslims especially—is far more damaging than what the most bigoted West-erners could imagine as a punishment for the adherents of Islam. It is more unfortunate for the Muslim communities that are being targeted for ghettoization and radicalization than it is for the Steve Emersons of the world who experience mild reputational damage as a result of missing the mark by a few miles.

Otherwise normal people, who go to their jobs every day, who pay their taxes, who want to, as Ayaan Hirsi Ali has said, "share in the mutual benefits" of Western nations, are being converted, perverted, and radicalized in the name of the world's fastest growing religion and the political goals that have been hitched upon it. So-called "progressives" should hang their heads in shame over this. In reality, they trumpet their "tolerance" for these people and blast critics, including critics from within the Muslim faith, as "Islamophobes."

In December 2016, a British group called "Hope Not Hate," which has received funding from the George Soros-backed Open Society Foundations,[12] insisted that practicing Muslim reformers like Dr. Zuhdi Jasser and anti-Sharia campaigner Raquel Saraswati were part of an "anti-Muslim" cabal seeking to promote "hatred" against Muslims in the West.[13] In reality, as Hirsi Ali noted in a video for Prager University, these people are the modern-day Aleksandr Solzhenitsyns—the famed Russian dissident who played a huge role in bringing down the tyrannical Soviet Union. Instead of spending their time in prison, however, reformers like Jasser and Saraswati live their lives under constant threats and harassment because of such groups, which also donate millions of dollars to projects supporting the eradication of national borders.

They are effectively being sacrificed at the altar of a political battle between nation-statists and globalists. Their plight—trying to salvage their religion from extremists and barbarians—is no more than an inconvenience to those in the establishment who would use Islam and "Islamophobia" as a stick with which to beat its philosophical opponents.

Over the course of this book, you will read interviews from the major players involved in this struggle, as well as those—including me—who have investigated "sensitive urban areas" on the ground. This is an international issue that, if left misrepresented, will continue to spread until it overpowers the establishments that oppose it. From Malmö to Molenbeek, from Dewsbury to Dearborn, the fight against No Go Zones—indeed the fight to settle the science and have it acknowledged that these places even exist—is as much a fight for the reformist Muslims of the world as it is for the heart and soul of Western civilization.

It has not been enough that major government figures from around Europe have conceded there are now areas that cannot be normally policed. It is not enough that the Belgian Home Affairs minister has admitted his country's authorities do not "have control of the situation in Molenbeek [Brussels]."[14] It appears to not be enough when journalists who actually report on this issue are beaten within an inch of their lives in Sweden, or when 'Muslim Patrols' are set up,[15] or when the British government has to lay on extra policing in areas like Tower Hamlets in East London in a bid to tackle Pakistani- or Bangladeshi-style electoral corruption.[16]

These things scarcely prompt mass headlines or investigations. But when Steve Emerson mentions the name of the wrong city on Fox News, the former British Prime Minister feels compelled to rebuke and ridicule him publicly. Unfortunately, Emerson was not the only one who had his knuckles rapped over No Go Zones.

CNN went after Governor Bobby Jindal after he mentioned No Go Zones in a 2015 speech in the Houses of Parliament. The network's reporting focused primarily on the fact that Governor Jindal was unable to name a specific No Go Zone area, and the reporter asserted that No Go Zones were such because of crime rates rather than demographics. The problem is that a CNN journalist, Dan Rivers, had just two years prior broadcasted a report on Muslim Patrols in East London—a story I originally broke—which revealed that homosexuals and women were being accosted, threatened, and hectored in high Muslim population areas in the city.[17]

The hypocrisy is abundant and clear. When it serves the needs of a left-leaning news outlet, that outlet will turn a blind eye to this issue. Governor Jindal's appearance in the House of Commons was one of these moments.

I have traveled to Molenbeek. I have spent extensive amounts of time in Tower Hamlets. I have dispatched colleagues to Malmö and Rosengård, and I have interviewed filmmakers and journalists who have been to other such areas across Europe. I can tell you beyond a shadow of a doubt that No Go Zones are real.

The important questions, as far as I am now concerned, are not as evident as whether these places exist, or whether Islam plays a major role in this ghettoization. Rather, the crucial questions are those that I answer in this book. What are the parameters of a No Go Zone? To what extent can one not go there? What is one susceptible to in doing so? And how is this phenomenon now manifesting itself in the United States of America?

Before most of my trips to these areas around Europe and the United States, I hoped, I wished, I prayed that I would be unable to finish this book for a lack of evidence about No Go Zones.

I fear this was not the case.

TWO

WHAT HAPPENS IN EUROPE

You have territories in France such as Roubaix, such as northern
Marseille, where police will not step foot, where the authority of state
is completely absent, where mini Islamic states have been formed.

—FABRICE BALANCHE, ASSOCIATE PROFESSOR AT THE
UNIVERSITÉ LUMIÈRE LYON 2 AND VISITING FELLOW AT
THE WASHINGTON INSTITUTE[1]

The adage "when America sneezes, the world catches cold" remains true when discussing financial markets and Hollywood culture. But if the irrational debate surrounding Syrian refugees and 2016's Brexit vote are anything to go by, it is safe to assume that American politics are now sneezing along to the tune of Europe's cold.

It has been some time since this was the case. The Cold War was perhaps the last time it happened, though arguably that was as much an American phenomenon as it was a European one. You would probably have to go back more than a hundred years to the world wars for another concrete example of this.

The lecturing from across the Atlantic, be it from newspaper columnists, German Chancellor Angela Merkel, or European Union apparatchiks, is designed to do one thing:

make America as sick as Europe is. This ploy is actualized through the exportation of problems created by the establishment within my home continent in an attempt to normalize the ailment internationally instead of cure it.

In January 2015, Carol Matlack published an article in *Bloomberg*, claiming in her subheading: "Stories about big Western cities surrendering neighborhoods to control of Islamist extremists are shocking—and totally false." Matlack attempted to "debunk" the idea of No Go Zones, spending over 10 percent of her 800-word article on Steve Emerson, and the rest on drawing a distinction between an area that police find difficult to respond within and a place people cannot visit. But despite her aforementioned derisive subheading, Matlack concedes in her conclusion:

> As with many urban legends, there are grains of truth in this one. Many French Muslims live in tough, isolated neighborhoods and have faced discrimination in housing and employment. Sometimes, police are afraid to respond to calls from dangerous neighborhoods in France and elsewhere. A few years ago, an Islamist group in Britain demanded that the government establish autonomous sharia-governed zones in some cities. The government swiftly outlawed the group, and it hasn't been heard from since.[2]

In effect, the article suggests that while a document prepared by the French government claims there are 750 No Go Zones in the country, many of these areas are in fact just deprived neighborhoods. Daniel Pipes, the head of the Middle East Forum in Philadelphia, agrees. He noted in an interview with Matlack that, "for a visiting American, these areas are very mild, even dull. We who know the Bronx and Detroit expect urban hell in Europe, too, but there things look fine…hardly beautiful, but buildings are intact, greenery abounds, and order prevails. … Having this first-hand experience, I regret having called these areas no-go zones."[3]

Pipes's regret reveals a problem: what is a No Go Zone? No one seems to know. The name would suggest, obviously, that these are areas where one cannot, or should not, risk visiting. That at least would be my interpretation of it. A good working definition would perhaps be this:

> An area in which the likelihood of being attacked, accosted, or otherwise abused on the basis of your appearance, or the bigotry of locals, is higher on average than elsewhere in the city or country in question. A 'No Go Zone' may refer to an area in which police require authorization or acceptance from a religious figure or community leader before entering, or indeed where the rule of law has either broken down or been supplanted by a foreign set of rules.

It is sensible to realize that there will be a gradation of No Go Zones in the Western world. Do I feel unable to enter Molenbeek? No. Do I feel that I am risking my safety as a result of the bigotry and ghettoization of its locals by doing so? Yes.

So in a sense, Mr. Pipes is correct. Many of the "sensitive urban areas" can be equated to 1980s Harlem, or the Bronx, or other ghettos around the United States. But many cannot. In any case, are such areas to be ignored? Is such deprivation, which is commonly cited as causing violence and high crime, to be dismissed or even accepted across the Western world simply out of fear of offending the "at risk communities"?

It was just eleven months later that Pipes wrote again about the phenomenon, noting:

> My visits establish that non-Muslim civilians can usually enter majority-Muslim areas without fear. But things look very different from the governmental point of view. On a routine basis, firefighters, ambulance workers, and even social workers meet with hostility and violence. For example, days after I visited the Marseille slum, its residents shot at police preparing for a visit by the prime minister of France. Thus does it and its ilk represent a no-go zone for police, a place which government representatives enter only when heavily armed, in convoys, temporarily, and with a specific mission.
>
> The term *no-go zone* is informal (apparently deriving from American military argot); dictionaries ascribe it two meanings in line with my conclusions: either (1) ordinary people staying away from an area out of fear or (2) the representatives of the state entering only under exceptional circumstances. [Sensitive Urban Areas] do not fit the first description but do fit the second.
>
> Whether or not Molenbeek, Rinkeby, and the Marseilles slum are no-go zones, then, depends on what aspect one chooses to emphasize—their accessibility to ordinary visitors at ordinary times or their inaccessibility to government officials in times of tension. There are also no-go gradations, some places

where attacks are more frequent and violent, others less so. However one sums up this complex situation—maybe partial-no-go zones?—they represent a great danger.[4]

But this level of nuanced analysis appears to have been lost on traditional or establishment news outlets. U.S. news organizations attempting to illustrate the worst cases of the argument, usually on both sides, have failed to reflect on the importance of these areas for the United States—its immigration policies, its internal cultural issues (otherwise deemed 'social cohesion'), and its security. As a result, areas that resemble Europe's No Go Zones, or indeed compounds, have begun to spring up in the United States.

The counter-extremist think tank the Clarion Project has documented at length the rise of the Muslims of the Americas group—a Pakistani-funded, Islamist sect otherwise known as Jamaat ul-Fuqra—which claims to have twenty-two Islamic villages across twelve states in the U.S. A coalition of reformist Muslims have called for the group, known as Fuqra for short, to be designated a terrorist organization based upon the organization's motivations and ideology.

The Clarion Project reported that a 2007 FBI document stated:

> The MOA is now an autonomous organization which possesses an infrastructure capable of planning and mounting terrorist campaigns overseas and within the U.S.
>
> The documented propensity for violence by this organization supports the belief the leadership of the

MOA extols membership to pursue a policy of jihad or holy war against individuals or groups it considers enemies of Islam, which includes the U.S. Government.[5]

Fuqra is one of the most extreme examples of Islamic fundamentalism manifesting itself in the United States. Its methods, including the creation of compounds such as 'Islamberg' in New York state,[6] are both extreme and hardly commonplace. Far more prevalent is the tactic of creating introspective, ghettoized communities, such as in Tower Hamlets in East London. And we have seen such strategies, whether organic or planned, take root in the United States too.

The most frequently quoted example of a dominantly Muslim area in the United States is Dearborn, Michigan. During the presidential election campaign of 2016, the *HuffPost* published an article that can only be described as a public relations piece on behalf of the city of Dearborn. Illustrated with a picture of hijab-clad women serving food, the article, written by self-described "LGBT advocate" Brian Stone, states: "Arab Americans make up about 44% of Dearborn residents, but make up a smaller proportion of the active voters—and many Arab Americans are not Muslim, *a common misconception*." He adds: "Just think of how far ahead we'd be as a country if we were following Dearborn's lead!"[7]

The political element in all this is of course crucial. Stone notes that the city is overwhelmingly Democrat in its voting intentions, and that (then candidate) Donald Trump would have no chance of being elected in an America that looked like Dearborn. The phrase "Sherlock," prefaced with an expletive, comes to mind. Stone also listed his occupation as "Communications Director" for Dr. Anil Kumar, who failed in his bid for Congress in Michigan's Eleventh District in 2016. Party politics, especially implementing tactics imported from the Middle East and South Asia, play a large role in the establishment of ghettos—even though Stone claims an Arab American or Muslim American demographic remain in the minority. This was certainly the case in Tower Hamlets in London.

Though Stone seeks to ease the mind of his reader with the population statistic of 44 percent Arab Americans, a 2011 census in Tower Hamlets revealed that just 41 percent of residents were "Asian" or "Asian British," which in Britain means they were originally from South Asia—Pakistan, Bangladesh, India, etc.[8] Despite this "minority" status, the area still saw the rise of the Islamist-sympathizing demagogue Lutfur Rahman, who became the borough's mayor in 2010 before being unceremoniously removed and banned from office in 2015.

Although the U.S. political system affords third parties relatively restricted access at the ballot box, Mr. Rahman was able to start his political career as a Labour Party member in a similar fashion to how Stone describes Dearborn when he claims, "Oh, and they're Democrats through and through." It was three years after Mr. Rahman left the Labour Party, having been linked to the Islamic Forum of Europe, that he founded the Tower Hamlets First organization. He gained support by leveraging the area's unique Bangladeshi Muslim demographics, using banana-republic-style politics of corruption and inducements to bolster his position. He swept into power in 2010 with 51.8 percent of the vote. He was re-elected in 2015 with a reduced 43.4 percent share.[9]

In the same year, the city of Hamtramck, which is northeast of Dearborn, elected a "Muslim majority" council. The *Wall Street Journal* described Hamtramck as the "first U.S. city with the distinction."[10] It wrote: "A city of 22,000 that is surrounded on all sides by Detroit, Hamtramck was once a haven for immigrants who were mainly Polish and Catholic. But more recently, churches have given way to mosques. The Polish population has dropped to about 11% today from 90% in [the] 1970s. Since 2004, the Muslim call to prayer has been broadcast to the city's streets."

So much for Stone's claims that the area's voters are scarcely Muslim, or even the suggestion that locals who are Arab Americans pose little threat to assimilation given the area's long history with immigration. One area of the city is now known as "Banglatown" due to its high Bangladeshi population. Considering that younger Muslims in the West tend to be more fundamentalist than their immigrant mothers and fathers, the trend would suggest that rather than integrating, these towns' Muslim populations will become further segregated.[11]

The harbinger of East London looms large considering that when Mr. Rahman leveraged his power with the local Bangladeshi community, he rose to a position whereby he controlled a local budget of over two billion dollars a year. When he was removed from power, the judge presiding over his court case found him guilty of corruption, bribery, and abuse of public funds. Judge Mawrey noted at the time: "It is guaranteed Mr Rahman will denounce this judgement as racist and Islamophobic. It is nothing of the sort...the natural sense of solidarity (of the Bangladeshi community) has been subverted."[12]

When even a High Court judge in the United Kingdom—a position typically inclined toward political correctness and establishment thinking—can successfully identify the forthcoming "Islamophobia" backlash, you know something is seriously awry.

The court's conclusions also underscore how, despite what some may claim about the case against No Go Zones, the communities that fall prey to the exploitative "leaders" of such policies are victims. If those on the liberal Left and in the political establishment really cared about these immigrants, they would fight tooth and nail against this kind of segregation and lack of integration. Instead, they support and propagate it.

Further conclusions from the court documents back this up: "The Bangladeshi community might have thought itself fortunate to have been the recipient of the Mayor's lavish spending but in the end the benefits were small and temporary and the ill effects long-lasting. It was fool's gold."[13] The court added:

> The real losers in this case are the citizens of Tower Hamlets and, in particular, the Bangladeshi community. Their natural and laudable sense of solidarity has been cynically perverted into a sense of isolation and victimhood, and their devotion to their religion has been manipulated—all for the aggrandisement of Mr Rahman. The result has been to alienate them from the other communities in the Borough and to create resentment in those other communities. Mr Rahman and Mr Choudhury, as has been seen, spent a great deal of time accusing their opponents, especially Mr Biggs, of 'dividing the community' but, if anyone was 'dividing the community,' it was they.[14]

So clear is the case against No Go Zones, partial No Go Zones, or indeed demographically un-diverse areas purported as being "diverse," you would think such ideas would be anathema to every thinking liberal across the Western world.

THREE

FROM MOLENBEEK, WITH TERROR

We don't have control of the situation in Molenbeek at present. We have to step up efforts there as a next task. I see that Mayor Françoise Schepmans is also asking our help, and that the local police chief is willing to cooperate. We should join forces and 'clean up' the last bit that needs to be done, that's really necessary.

—**JAN JAMBON,** DEPUTY PRIME MINISTER AND MINISTER OF SECURITY AND HOME AFFAIRS, BELGIUM[1]

O
n March 18, 2016, Belgian counter-terrorism police raided the home of the Aberkan family, located at 79 Rue des Quatre-Vents in the heavily Arab populated neighborhood of Molenbeek. Cops, in huge numbers, intercepted and arrested Salah Abdeslam, one of the two surviving, alleged terrorists who took part in the November 2015 Paris attacks in which 130 people were killed and around 400 were injured. Abdeslam had evaded capture for over four months, fleeing from France through the Schengen border-free area into Belgium, eventually finding refuge in Molenbeek.

Molenbeek, within spitting distance of the "political capital of Europe," namely, Brussels, is often described as one of Europe's most notorious No Go Zones. However, if you look like me, or rather, if you don't look like a white blonde woman or an undercover police officer—you *can* indeed go there. So I did.

At 79 Rue des Quatre-Vents, Molenbeek does in fact appear to be not much more than a deprived little town, as Daniel Pipes has noted, not dissimilar to the Bronx or Detroit in the 80s. You can flit and slip quickly between the better and worse parts of Brussels, though to the west of the city such movement becomes almost pointless. Vast swathes of the city's westerly borders are becoming—to the chagrin of my tour guides—"Arabized." From Schaerbeek to Molenbeek, to Anderlecht, to right outside the Brussels Midi station, it is not uncommon to see Arabic graffiti, or graffiti lauding "Arab nationalism."

Counterintuitively, like on the peripheries of Schaerbeek, you can still walk down streets filled with brothels. Young, usually eastern European girls glare at you in their bras and panties, beckoning you in, almost shaming you for not gawping at them or succumbing to their low, low prices. On the other side of these very same buildings are Arabic shops selling Qurans, cafes with hijabi women drinking mint tea or "tea nana," and men trying to sell you new iPhones from within their coat linings.

Schaerbeek is perhaps an example of multiculturalism done better than usual, but this is because, unlike Molenbeek, the residents of the area are Turkish rather than Moroccan or Tunisian. A few hundred miles makes a world of difference, within just a fewm miles, apparently.

While much of Schaerbeek is scarcely diverse, it is an upbeat and welcoming neighborhood. Locals will smile at you and joke with you in their cafes. Visitors, especially on a Sunday when downtown Brussels is a ghost town, are of mixed origin and dash from shop to shop looking for the best deals. No one seems to mind their presence. Molenbeek is entirely different.

A huge, imposing, grey slate and glass police station sits right in the center of Mr. Abdeslam's former refuge. Twenty police cars line the streets. But not a policeman or woman is to be seen when you walk around the neighborhood. One of my guides told me that when she was in a car accident in the area late in the afternoon, she was advised to move her car outside the police station and leave the area before dark. If I had been in her situation, I probably would have been fine. But an unaccompanied white woman with her hair down and a nice vehicle in Molenbeek at night? That is a target.

As we traversed the neighborhood—not for my first time, mind you—it became clear the locals were not fully comfortable with our arrival there. No one said a word, unlike my last visit. But this time I didn't have young blonde women in my company.

On a visit to Molenbeek in 2015, just days after the Paris massacres, our group was jeered at and heckled and the women were told to cover their heads. Unmistakable tension rode high. The suspicion of the locals manifested itself in hateful, jingoistic, and barbarous ways. This wasn't Europe. This wasn't Brussels. This was what they call Little Marrakech. Where you must act accordingly, or leave.

A whisper of that mindset still lives. It is easy to see how and why such a neighborhood would provide refuge to someone like Abdeslam. In an "us or them" world, they will always choose themselves and look after their own. Their protestations about not knowing his whereabouts are as likely to be true as his own claims of ignorance regarding his accomplices, their identities, and the entire Paris massacre planning.

Men stand outside cafes—cafes with only men inside too—smoking, gossiping, all too happy to offer deathly glares to perceived outsiders. Nativism obviously runs rampant in these communities—far worse than in those the political Right gets accused of—but it is largely ignored or swept under the carpet by local politicians, most of whom belong to what would be considered far-left and even communist-sympathizing political parties in Brussels.

While Molenbeek's streets are dominated by halal butchers, Arabic signage, and Islamic bookshops, estimates of the area's Muslim or Arab demographics vary significantly. Writing in *The New York Times* in April of 2016, Roger Cohen claimed that 41 percent of Molenbeek inhabitants were Muslim.[2] *GQ Magazine* claims a figure of 25–30 percent,[3] and *The Guardian* reported that "In lower Molenbeek some 50% of the inhabitants are of northern Moroccan provenance."[4] These figures vary drastically because of local governance failures—seemingly intentional—to know who is living where. Census estimates in 2015 placed the local population figure at around 95,000, though locals insisted to me that it is closer to 110,000 today.[5]

Many immigrants, empowered and entitled by Belgium's laws that allow families from abroad to live with their loved ones, settle in Molenbeek and take a pension from the state. Dilapidated structures in the town center are said to house up to ten or fifteen people inside three or four bedroom apartments, and the fertility rate of these locals is said to be far higher than their Belgian counterparts. This certainly seems to be the case when you arrive in the neighborhood on a weekend, just as the market in the town square opens. But the flood of people is not the only remarkable thing one sees in the market.

Chadors and hijabs are sold alongside fruit and vegetables, as residents avert their faces for photographs. This "privacy," in the middle of a street, in what is supposedly twenty-first century Europe, is something you don't experience in other areas. "What are they afraid of?" I wonder. Being implicated? Being in a news-paper? Nothing is normal to me about such a reaction. Indeed if you travel to more integrated immigrant communities around the Western world, children will scurry around cameramen demanding to have their pictures taken, or pulling faces for live television cameras. Not here.

Perhaps they feel targeted, or vulnerable. But without much police or state action in the area, how could they? Who would be targeting them? An Englishman with an iPhone camera? It continues to boggle my mind.

Brussels is increasingly becoming this way. "The politicians, the bureaucrats, the elites, they spend all their time in the Euro-pean quarter," one Brussels native tells me. "They don't see anything wrong because they don't see anything at all. For them life is Dolce and Gabbana and H&M and cafes and bars." That sounds familiar. Whenever I invite politicians or journalists to visit Tower Hamlets in East London with me, they refuse or suddenly fall silent. One such example was when *Elle* magazine decided to goad me on Twitter, asking if they could "job swap" with me for a day so they could see what working for a "far right" website is like, and so that I could see what a "feminist" publication looks like. I refused, instead offering to escort them to Molenbeek. They never got back to me, which was unsurpris-ing considering what day-to-day life in Molenbeek is like.

In Molenbeek, women shuffle through the streets with unease. "Why do they all look miserable?" I ask my guide. He replies, "They don't want to wear the veil. This is new. At home [in their countries of origin] this was not the case, when they grew up, not the case. Now they are made to do it. It is the Salaf-ist influence. The Saudi money and youngster[s] who are more strict with Islam." The older men don't seem to mind or care.

They may even prefer the dominant position they have in the household that perhaps they didn't have in Morocco or Turkey, though none were keen on discussing the matter.

It's possible they were too blind to see it. I was constantly advised during my visits to No Go Zones across Europe not to take pictures. "They don't like it, they will come after you," one Parisian guide warned me. But some scenes are just too poetic to miss, and you have to take your chances. In Molenbeek, I couldn't help but snap a photo of a piece of graffiti that read "GIRL POWER" positioned on an electrical box adjacent to a cafe populated only by men both inside and out. I noticed this phenomenon in almost all the neighborhoods I visited. But I may have been the only man who did.

"[Apologists] say it is just like how we in the West were fifty years ago. This is not true, first. But even if it was, why do they want us to go back? Aren't they supposed to be the 'progressives'?" notes one of my guides in the French suburb of Saint-Denis.

———————

At an awards ceremony lampooning the mainstream media—the Bobards d'Or in France—a host semi-jokes that the real name of Molenbeek is "Sint-Jans-Molenbeek" or Molenbeek Saint-Jean, named after St. John the Baptist. They are, he claimed, trying to erase the area's Christian history by changing its name to simply "Molenbeek." Whether this is true or just a convenient truncation is unclear. But what is clear is that all around Europe, regardless of what they call it, people talk about Molenbeek in hushed tones. Interestingly, with my audience-member vote included, the "fake news" story about Molenbeek won the award for mainstream media lie of the year.

A French camera crew from *Le Petit Journal* had hand picked interviewees for a short segment on the town following comments from then presidential candidate Donald Trump on the security situation in Brussels. Trump described Brussels as an "armed camp" after the March 2016 attacks, which came just days after Abdeslam was apprehended in Molenbeek. During my November 2015 visit, his comments were accurate. They remained so in March 2016 and continue to remain true today, when the first thing you notice after exiting the Brussels Midi station are two carefully positioned armed police trucks.

In November 2015, soldiers and policemen armed to the teeth stood at almost every street corner. Heavily armed vehicles toured the city as a matter of course. The size of their weaponry would put even the most enthusiastic Second Amendment supporter to shame. The situation had calmed by early 2017. This is in no small part thanks to the continued raiding of addresses across the city and other European cities, as the hunt for jihadists continued.

After just one week of traveling in Europe, we had heard of arrests of four Islamic State supporters in the South of France planning an "imminent" Paris attack, a British national arrested at London's Gatwick Airport for the same charge, anti-terror raids in Germany, and a spate of riots, protests, stabbings, and shootings in associated neighborhoods across the continent. German police raided fifty-four different properties, including mosques, homes, and businesses, in their attempt to uncover a serious terror plot in the nation.

The news comes so fast and hard that it is no wonder traditional media outlets struggled to cover it all; it is unprecedented and they have no expertise to report on such matters. They also lack the will to do so. *Elle* magazine didn't avoid coming to

Molenbeek with me because it wasn't an interesting proposition. They avoided it because it *was* an interesting proposition.

The unholy alliance of political inconvenience, cowardice, and willful ignorance has created fertile ground for statements like Donald Trump's to be lampooned. Mainstream journalists in France called Mr. Trump's comments on Molenbeek "bullshit," which set *Le Petit Journal* off to interview residents of the area on the street. One hijab-clad girl remarked, "Here, we live in a community of Muslims, non-Muslims, religious, non-religious. There is no concern about that."[6] Except, as the Bobards d'Or conveners noted, this is a place deeply associated with the November 2015 attacks. It is also where Mehdi Nemmouche, who attacked the Jewish Museum of Belgium in Brussels, and Amedy Coulibaly—who killed a number of people on behalf of the Islamic State and was a close friend of the *Charlie Hebdo* attackers—all found themselves at some point in their jihadist careers.

Perhaps this is of "no concern" to the hijab-clad girl on the street, or to the journalists interviewing her who spend most of their time in the posh, up-market areas of Paris and Brussels. But for much of the population it is of serious import, as reflected by recent polling numbers from across the continent confirming rapidly changing attitudes toward Muslim immigration and associated jihadism.

In January 2017, the largely establishment Chatham House think tank in London found that the majority of populations across ten major European countries want a full and total shutdown of Muslim immigration into their countries. Majorities in Belgium (64 percent), Germany (53 percent), Greece (58 percent), France (61 percent), Italy (51 percent), Austria (65 percent), Hungary (64 percent), and Poland (71 percent) all supported the statement: "All further migration from mainly Muslim countries should be stopped."

More interesting still is the number of people who disagreed with the statement. Across all countries polled, an average of just 20 percent disagreed. In the two countries which did not express majority support for the "complete and total shutdown," as Donald Trump once expressed it, there was still more support than opposition for the proposal. In the United Kingdom, 47 percent of people supported it with 30 percent unsure and 23 percent in opposition. In Spain, 26 percent were unsure, 32 percent disagreed, and 41 percent agreed.[7]

Again, the convenient anecdotal video interview with the hijabi girl in *Le Petit Journal* does not appear to reflect reality. Nor does the show's follow-up interview inside one man's house, where he claims Molenbeek is a "normal area, like every area in Europe. Belgium, Holland, France, it's the same." The broadcast of the video of the original segment drew howls of laughter from the crowd at the Bobard d'Or awards, who were positioned in their seats just a few hundred yards away from the now infamous Bataclan theatre, in an act of sobering defiance.

The presentation of the Bobard d'Or award to the creators of the massaged Molenbeek video may have been celebrated as a "gotcha" moment in a room of a few hundred French right-wingers, but the impact of such misinformation can be seen around the world. Journalists and politicians, rather than informing themselves about these areas, rely increasingly on the testimonies of liberal-left journalist-cum-activists. They end up accepting these accounts as true instead of forming their own opinions about this issue, and so the false idea that No Go Zones do not exist still pervades in establishment media circles.

This was most evident when, in February 2017, President Donald Trump broached the topic of Sweden at a rally in Florida. "We've got to keep our country safe," he said, "You look at what's happening in Germany. You look at what's happening last night in Sweden. Sweden, who would believe this? Sweden. They took in large numbers. They're having problems like they never thought possible. You look at what's happening in Brussels. You look at what's happening all over the world. Take a look at Nice. Take a look at Paris."[8] And of course I did look. First-hand. And in person.

But most of the establishment journalists who criticized the president's comments just seconds after he made them have never been to Rinkeby, or Husby, or Molenbeek, or Saint-Denis, or Barbes, or Tower Hamlets, or Savile Town. These are the places "journalists"—like those from *Elle* magazine—don't want to visit. It would break their narrative in half if they saw first-hand how pro-mass-migration policies have wrecked entire suburbs and large parts of cities.

This is the sort of view I sought to vindicate when I visited Brussels in 2015. There I interviewed both Jimmie Akesson of the poll-topping Sweden Democrats Party and now UKIP leader Paul Nuttall MEP. All of us were clearly stunned by what we saw back then in Brussels. The situation has not improved since. "It looks like parts of Malmö in Sweden," Akesson told me at the time. "It's the same. The Arab signs and Arab people everywhere. The big problem is that we are getting used to it. I've heard a lot about this part of town in the last few days. I'm quite uncomfortable walking here because of what I've heard on the news. We have these places in Sweden too."

Your average journalist would balk at the statement "The big problem is that we are getting used to it." "Why SHOULDN'T we get used to it?" they'd ask. "Why this prejudice against Arabs?" they'd insist. But for someone willing to take even a perfunctory look at the situations unfolding on the streets, the reasons are many.

Certain policies actually impede the progress they are designed to create in these areas. Signposting in Arabic, offering Arab language classes paid for by the state, and placing all these immigrants in government housing buildings in far away suburbs all run contrary to the notion of integration. In fact they create states within states. But for the Left, a lot of these policies are electorally satisfying. Across all the No Go Zones I visited, election posters, flyers, and stickers for socialist and communist parties littered lampposts and local notice boards. The underlying message of this propaganda is "Keep voting for us, and you can keep not working. Keep voting for us, and you'll get more free stuff."

I didn't know how accurate Akesson's assessment of the situation was until I visited Malmö and Stockholm myself. Malmö enjoys and endures both the benefit and danger of having the Islamic elements of its Arab-dominated neighborhoods pushed further underground than they are in Stockholm. This is not the case in Molenbeek or Barbes or Tower Hamlets. Each of those areas is at a unique milestone on the journey to ghettoization and Islamification. The differences between the stages of their decline are partially due to the type of Islam that is popular with their respective residents. Where their inhabitants immigrated from makes all the difference. The divergences between Turks and Pakistanis and between Moroccans and Algerians are massive. And their internecine warfare that spills out onto the streets and within asylum centers often underscores this.

In Tower Hamlets we saw "Sharia Patrols" in 2013. This is less likely to happen in places like Beziers or Aulnay, but Molenbeek is more susceptible to a similar wave of extremism.

In Molenbeek, Islamic bookshops are scattered throughout the municipality, carrying material by Islamist sympathizers and supporters such as Tariq Ramadan and the infamous Egyptian cleric Abdal-Hamid Kishk, whose pronouncements include opposition to music, promotion of polygamy, and the idea of "greater jihad"—the idea of purging oneself of human desires and fashioning the reader in the image of Muhammad. I found one store that sold a Kishk DVD with a cover that bore a striking resemblance to one of Manhattan's former Twin Towers getting struck by a plane, bleeding smoke. On closer inspection, the image depicted a building, covered by some black scribbles, with a moon over the top of it. In other words, it was gibberish intended to invoke the scenes of 9/11 without actually doing so. The headline on the DVD read, "Stories of the prophets." Who could possibly be surprised that the area hosted jihadists when material of this nature is openly available in broad daylight?

"Look at this, is this what I think it looks like?" I asked one of my guides.

"Come on, of course it's that. But they get away with it like this," he replied. "They use our liberty against us," he opined, wary that book banning or burning would scarcely be encouraged in a Western capital.

The failure to identify and proscribe Islamist paraphernalia is one of the major causes of the rise of extremism and jihadism in the West, otherwise known as "homegrown" terrorism. The fear of trampling free speech in the process of banning extremist propaganda is understandable. But we shouldn't shy away from a solution merely because it requires a delicate and complex implementation. If we did this every time a solution to this problem seemed difficult to carry out, we would have no effective solution at all—which is exactly what has happened.

————

Walking through the streets of Molenbeek didn't feel overtly or existentially dangerous. If anything went wrong, I knew I could immediately hotfoot it to the nearby police station. God knows I wouldn't typically find an officer on patrol on the street. I was never more aware of this than when I took pictures, which always stirred up hidden tensions. Groups of men would stare. Women would lower or turn their heads. Of course no pictures were allowed in the bookshops or the cafes, though I did try. The difference between Molenbeek and Schaerbeek—just a few miles apart—was pronounced on this point.

In Molenbeek, Moroccan and Algerian flags hang from windows. In Schaerbeek, no such nationalistic symbols are prevalent. It was also striking to note that in the corporate headquarters of the European Union—the City of Brussels—the EU flag is scarcely seen in these neighborhoods. I reckon I saw more European Union symbols in Tower Hamlets in East London than in these Brussels suburbs. Yet another example of how these areas are not viewed by the local population as being part of Brussels, part of Belgium, or part of Europe.

Perhaps the defining common trait that all No Go Zones share is that people throughout Europe are leery of them. Molenbeek certainly possesses this prerequisite; its reputation precedes it. From London to the South of France to Sweden, people say, "Oh God, you're going to Molenbeek? Be careful."

With such fear to recommend it, it is surprising that Molenbeek's neighborhoods are expanding across western Brussels. What was once confined to a few streets has now taken root and expanded, ironically in a crescent shape, to the nearby areas of Anderlecht and Schaerbeek. The last piece of the crescent, Uccle, is a wealthy and respected neighborhood, and residents are keen to keep it that way.

State policies of throwing money at this problem haven't worked, and the only option left is to refuse to leave the areas like most of Molenbeek's old natives did. Brand new glass and steel apartment buildings straddle the Canal Bruxelles-Charleroi that separates Molenbeek from the downtown district where the Grand Place and Palace of Justice stand. There are just minutes between the two areas, such is the expansion of the foreign enclaves. Yet scarcely do the Eurocrats or journalists or politicians trundle over into Molenbeek. Even in Stalingrad near the Gare du Midi, the central rail station for Eurostar arrivals as well as those from across the continent, Arab graffiti adorns shop fronts.

While most find these developments unnerving, some consider them very exotic and positive. A man in a beanie hat riding a fixie bike—clearly too old to be doing so—eavesdropped on a conversation between me and one of my guides, who was telling me stories about how car accidents descended into violence late at night in Molenbeek.

"This is bullshit. Complete bullshit," the cyclist insisted. "It is attitudes like this that are the problem," he said before adjusting his tortoise-shell glasses and cycling off. I called after him to explain to me what he meant, but he just shouted, "Bullshit!" again and rode off.

It is surprising that some view areas like Molenbeek as "foreign cities" they can vacation in without the inconvenience of leaving their native countries. They like the low prices of the cheap goods at the No Go Zone market stalls, and they sit awkwardly in the cafes—without their girlfriends or wives of course—drinking tea nana and feeling sophisticated and more worldly than those who concern themselves with the high crime levels or terrorist attacks in these places.

Consider the testimony of journalist Teun Voeten, as published in *POLITICO* in November 2015. Voeten lived in Molenbeek for nine years, and wrote the following about his experiences:

> I was part of a new wave of young urban professionals, mostly white and college-educated—what the Belgians called bobo, ("bourgeois bohémiens")—who settled in the area out of pragmatism. We had good intentions. Our contractor's name was Hassan. He was Moroccan, and we thought that was very cool. We imagined that our kids would one day play happily with his on the street. We hoped for less garbage on the streets, less petty crime. We were confident our block would slowly improve, and that our lofts would increase in value. (We even dared to hope for a hip art gallery or a trendy bar.) We felt like pioneers of the Far West, like we were living in the trenches of the fight for a multicultural society.
>
> Slowly, we woke up to reality. Hassan turned out to be a crook and disappeared with 95,000, the entire budget the tenants had pooled together for our building's renovation. The neighborhood was hardly multicultural. Rather, with roughly 80 percent of the population of Moroccan origin, it was tragically

conformist and homogenous. There may be a vibrant alternative culture in Casablanca and Marrakech, but certainly not in Molenbeek.

Over nine years, I witnessed the neighborhood become increasingly intolerant. Alcohol became unavailable in most shops and supermarkets; I heard stories of fanatics at the Comte des Flandres metro station who pressured women to wear the veil; Islamic bookshops proliferated, and it became impossible to buy a decent newspaper. With an unemployment rate of 30 percent, the streets were eerily empty until late in the morning. Nowhere was there a bar or café where white, black and brown people would mingle. Instead, I witnessed petty crime, aggression, and frustrated youths who spat at our girlfriends and called them "filthy whores." If you made a remark, you were inevitably scolded and called a racist. There used to be Jewish shops on Chaussée de Gand, but these were terrorized by gangs of young kids and most closed their doors around 2008. Openly gay people were routinely intimidated, and also packed up their bags.

I finally left Molenbeek in 2014. It was not out of fear. The tipping point, I remember, was an encounter with a Salafist, who tried to convert me on my street. It boiled down to this: I could no longer stand to live in this despondent, destitute, fatalistic neighborhood.[9]

For "bobos," the people causing the negative elements of mass migration are perverting what could otherwise be a paradise-like situation. And in some ways they are correct about this. Few would scorn the diversity of cuisines, fashion, even languages that immigration creates, provided the foreign counterparts of these cultural aspects do not become primary or "official" in the new countries they migrate to. But if the primacy of a foreign culture becomes endemic, if sympathy for radicalism reaches high minority, plurality, or even majority status, the romanticization of immigration and the state-driven policies that pervert it must cease. Unfortunately, the political Left doesn't understand this. In fact it seems to be intensifying its campaign against those who advocate for controlled migration.

During my trip I met some so-called "far Right" or "fascist" activists and politicians. Not one advocated mass deportation programs or a total halt to immigration. Instead they spoke passionately about integration and education, about defending the rights of Muslim women forced to wear the veil against their wishes, and about helping immigrants get real jobs so they can stop doing what many of them currently do in places like Barbes in Paris—stand on the street corners peddling hashish and stolen goods.

But what the Right advocates is lost on many, like Mr. Fixie Bike, who prefer lawlessness to order and open borders to control. "No Borders, No Nations," is a common chant among the George-Soros-funded campaign group activists. It was also graffitied across walls on the outer rim of Molenbeek, and in Tower Hamlets too.

Left-wing pressure groups target these areas systematically. They distribute anti-Israel stickers, race-baiting, divisive posters, and activists who convince locals that they are the perpetually oppressed. Fill in the following blank with any country I visited and you will find non-native residents there willing to suggest that "XXX is the most racist country in the world." If you ask them, "Why?" they reply with a diatribe about how "run down" the areas in which they dwell are, how they struggle to live off the already generous state benefits, how political parties that oppose mass migration are climbing in the polls, and how their governments have pursued "anti-Muslim" wars abroad.

In an interview with *Vice News*, a local clothes shop owner called Ahmed declared, "We should not have to sit here and justify to everybody the actions of a few radicals...Nothing needs to change here. The problem is with the political environment of Belgium, with France, and right here in the city."[10]

After the Molenbeek raids, as the neighborhood received the brunt of its negative attention, left-wing activists from Brussels gathered in the area to proclaim their love for the place. They held up "I <3 Molenbeek" placards, and a Facebook group with around 400 members declared, "'I love Molenbeek' aims to bring positive news about Sint-Jans-Molenbeek, in response to the negative news that is present in abundance elsewhere." Despite the activists' best efforts, no vestiges remain of their activism less than two years later. No shop windows carry the "I <3 Molenbeek" placards anymore. Things are basically back to normal. That is to say the new "normal."

However, a political and media schizophrenia about Molenbeek still remains. "Almost every time, there's a link with Molenbeek," Belgian Prime Minister Charles Michel said after the Paris attacks. He continued, "We've tried prevention. Now we'll have to get repressive. It's been a form of laissez-faire and laxity. Now we're paying the bill."[11]

These were tough words to swallow at the time, but Molenbeek remains "unrepressed." Security services are evidently cracking down, following more leads than ever. But the conditions that created the area's problems—including having over twenty undisturbed and often undisclosed mosques in such a small area—remain unchallenged. And the pressure on journalists to depict the suburb as something it is not—a fairly quiet, bohemian test-bed for mass migration—is enormous. Criticism of reporting from this area, as I am sure I will experience upon publication of this book, comes before anything else. Before reflection, before understanding, before critics even visit the place themselves.

Teun Voeten again had something to say about this in his November 2015 *POLITICO* article:

> But the most important factor is Belgium's culture of denial. The country's political debate has been dominated by a complacent progressive elite that firmly believes society can be designed and planned. Observers who point to unpleasant truths such as the high incidence of crime among Moroccan youth and violent tendencies in radical Islam are accused of being propagandists of the extreme-right, and are subsequently ignored and ostracized.
>
> ...Two journalists had already reported on the presence of radical Islamists in Molenbeek and the danger they posed—and both became victims of character assassination. In 2006, Hind Fraihi, a young Flemish woman of Morrocan [sic] descent published "Undercover in Little Morocco: Behind the Closed Doors of Radical Islam." Her community called her a traitor; progressive media called her a "spy" and a "girl with personal problems."
>
> In 2008, Arthur van Amerongen was tarred and feathered for "Brussels Eurabia," and called a "Batavian Fascist" by a francophone newspaper. When he

and I went back to Molenbeek in March and I subsequently described it as an "ethnic and religious enclave and a parochial, closed community" in an interview with Brussel Deze Week, that too provoked the wrath of progressive Belgium and an ensuing media storm.

I always thought as [sic] myself as a defender of human rights and human dignity, beyond left- or right-wing categories. Now suddenly I was painted as a right-wing firebrand. For some people I became an "untouchable" and I even lost a few friends, who refused to talk to me.[12]

Molenbeek has almost become a trigger word, a parody to some, of the whole debate surrounding No Go Zones. When discussing my trip with establishment journalists and leftists, I could feel them attempting not to roll their eyes skyward when I mentioned Molenbeek. Their attitude is perhaps best paraphrased as, "Yeah okay, one place in Europe is bad, what else you got?"

What else? A whole lot more.

FOUR

FROM SWEDEN, WITH RAPE

We have a number of no-go-zones in Sweden and they are expanding...police can go to these places, but you have to take precautions. Years ago you could go with two officers, no problem. Now you have to send four officers and two cars—if the fire brigade wants to go, they have to take a police escort. They throw stones and try to stop the firemen from putting out fires.

—**TORSTEN ELOFSSON**, FORMER POLICE CHIEF SUPERINTENDENT, MALMÖ, SWEDEN[1]

P ulling into the central station in Malmö, across the bridge from Copenhagen, is a delight. The trains are clean and run on time. The station is immaculate. And despite the bitter, sweeping winds that hit you from the Forstadskanalen in the winter, the town is picturesque beyond what a postcard—or I suppose, nowadays, Google Street View—can convey.

"There's no way this place has No Go Zones," I thought to myself, as I dragged my suitcase noisily between the cobbled pavements of the Great Square. To my left stood a Burger King, to my right, a "Schwarma King" which stands where the "Stortoget Gatukok" or "Great Square Snack Bar" once was. A sign of the times, I suppose. But also one of the benefits of immigration as far as I am concerned. I still regret not sampling the Schwarma King.

In downtown Malmö, American, Canadian, English, and German accents abounded. At the pub attached to my hotel, scarcely a word of Swedish was spoken. So I quickly polished off my drink—a "sharpener"—and set off with a local guide to the suburb of Rosengård. This, I was led to believe, was Malmö's primary No Go Zone.

We arrived by car. A nice one too, which made us even more nervous at first. But as I looked around, I noticed something peculiar. I had noticed it in Molenbeek too. "There are some *very* nice cars here!" I exclaimed. "How dangerous can this be?" BMWs, Mercedes, Range Rovers, you name it, you could find it in Rosengård. These luxury vehicles were dotted around the parking lots of the government housing projects and lining the streets, like traces of glitter skirting grey, soulless heaps of concrete and glass. The residents of Rosengård were clearly not hard up.

"They get a lot of welfare. And they spend it. Many of them share these cars," my guide told me. Not bad. I'm thirty years old, living on a London-D.C. editor's salary, and there's no way I can afford one of those things.

My mind shot back to when I interviewed the leader of the poll-topping Sweden Democrats Party, Jimmie Akesson. When Jimmie told me—as we walked through Molenbeek just days after the Paris terror attacks in 2015—"we have these places in Sweden too," I was skeptical. Sweden is supposed to be paradise-like, I thought. Isn't it all leggy blondes and Ikea and Abba and lingonberries? Well if you stay downtown in Malmö or Stockholm, perhaps it is. Even the elevator muzak had a whiff of "Fernando" about it. But the stereotypes and clichés, kept alive for the tourists no doubt, end when you leave the city centers and head out to some of the suburbs.

There I was, standing before these ugly, behemoth housing estates, as appalled by the architectural travesty as anything else I had seen so far. Yet we continued our trek and trudged along the scarcely lit, iced-over pavements, circling the estates before entering. We stopped two millennial girls hurriedly carrying food back to their houses. "Where is Herregarden?" my guide asked them. That was the name of a housing estate known for being particularly rough. Their eyes lit up in disbelief. A young, blond man and his English friend wanted to go to Herregarden at night?

They pointed us in the general direction of the estate before calling out, "Good luck there!" as we continued.

"Fantastic," I thought to myself, genuinely half-pleased we had found some locals who had confirmed a nervous attitude toward the area, and half-nervous about what we might find there. As luck would have it, for safety's sake, Herregarden was almost a ghost town that night. It was below freezing and a chilling wind would occasionally get caught up between the multi-story buildings. People rushed between them, refusing to stop to chat, or even give directions.

A few hijab-clad women scurried around in front of us, sometimes with children in tow. Not only would they not speak to us, but they also refused to look at us, at all, despite my most English, "Pardon me?" and my guide's Swedish equivalent.

"Maybe they don't know what I'm saying in Swedish," he remarked. And it would make sense that at least some of them didn't. Some estimates put the population of Herregarden's housing estates at 96 percent foreign-born or of foreign background.[2]

As of 2015, Sweden's 9.9 million population included over 1.3 million foreign-born people, with a majority coming from Syria, Iraq, Iran, Turkey, Somalia, and the former Yugoslavia. Around

150,000 people came from Sweden's neighbor, Finland, and a significant number of Poles (88,000) were also included in the figures.[3]

Even the staunchest advocates of mass migration and of Sweden's impressive track record of taking in refugees have to admit the numbers currently being allowed in are almost unprecedented. The country saw 51,000 Syrians cross its border in 2016, contributing to a total of around 100,000 new migrants and refugees since the outbreak of the Syrian Civil War.[4] This, compared with the country's own migration agency statistics on how many Yugoslavs sought refugee status during the Yugoslav wars, reveals a drastic uptick for such a small country: "In 1992, a total of 84,000 people, mainly from former Yugoslavia, sought asylum in Sweden."[5]

While the Syrian war has raged for just over half the time the Yugoslav war lasted, Syria, which is almost 2,000 miles away from Sweden, will end up attracting more migrants to one Scandinavian country than Yugoslavia, which is comparable in population to Syria and only 900 miles away from Sweden. It is fair to say that between aid agencies and non-governmental organizations (NGOs), Syrians—initially fighting age men—were encouraged to leave their country, make the journey through Turkey, breaching a number of borders of "safe" countries, and find their way to welfare paradises. Even the United Nations was forced to admit that at the peak of this migrant crisis, men between the ages of sixteen and sixty made up the largest number of "refugees." They "abandoned" their families and their country, only to send back for them later. For the NGOs and for the families of these men, there was some logic to this. Many young children would not have survived the crossings on makeshift rafts across the Mediterranean, and many women would not have been safe.

The finger of blame for this can only be pointed at the nonexistent "international community" and its cheerleaders—then President Barack Obama, German Chancellor Angela Merkel, European Union leaders, and Britain's then Prime Minister David Cameron. But that is a topic for another day.

The result of this new migration, including migrants seeking asylum from Iraq, Iran, Somalia, Turkey, Afghanistan, Eritrea, Lebanon, Somalia, and other war-torn countries, is ghettoization, mass unemployment, criminality, and—in a lot of cases—exploitation of these new arrivals. While "human rights" activists will tell you that they are in the right for supporting open border asylum policies, in reality they are playing into the hands of criminal gangs that profit from the continuation and proliferation of these policies.

In May 2016, Arbetsförmedlingen, the Swedish employment agency, reported that just 500 of the 163,000 people who applied for asylum in Sweden in 2015 found jobs.[6] That is a success rate of just 0.3 percent. To suppose that the other 99.97 percent of these immigrants are just sitting at home claiming welfare is naïve. They may very well be claiming welfare, but many are also operating in the black market, under the radar, or are involved in criminal activity, including the country's flourishing drug trade. While the harder drugs are handled by those affiliated with biker gangs, which Sweden has a lot of, the pushers and clients for softer drugs, such as hashish or marijuana, are migrants in suburbs such as Husby.

Within minutes of exiting a cab outside the town's central square, I was surrounded by four drug dealers pushing "hashish" and "marijuana." One of them asked for a cigarette. It may have been an innocuous attempt to get a nicotine fix, though I'm told bumming a smoke is also a common way criminals attempt to engage and disarm visitors in the area. It was similar in Aulnay in France.

———————

Media reporting on No Go Zones can be either alarmist or dismissive of the area's problems. *Vice News* went out of its way to promote an article that reflected the views of "locals" in Tensta, a suburb of Stockholm. Somehow, the outfit only managed to find smiling, young, well-dressed liberals who took issue with media reporting. One interviewee—Suhul—let more slip than perhaps the *Vice* reporter knew when publishing an article entitled "People in Sweden's Alleged 'No-Go Zones' Talk About What It's Like to Live There." "Even our local newspaper usually reports on Tensta in a negative way. There are a lot of immigrants here and the news reflects that segregation," Suhul revealed. [7]

Suhul's comments betray the article's narrative—that foreign media organizations observe some illegal activity in the town centers and report it unfairly—by suggesting that even local beat reporters have found it necessary to focus on the area's high crime and migration links.

Political parties, government agencies, and top-level emergency service officials have sought to deny charges about No Go Zones. But locals tell a different story, which is reflected in the newfound uptick of support enjoyed by the anti-mass migration Sweden Democrats Party.

One cab driver by the name of Jamal told me he was offered free government housing in Rinkeby, but he refused on the basis of safety. A former police officer confided that she felt safer in Sudan than in some of Sweden's suburbs. And beat cops to the tune of 80 percent claim they are considering a career change due to the increasingly dangerous nature of their jobs.[8] Police Sergeant Peter Larsson told Norway's public broadcaster NRK: "We have a major crisis. Many colleagues have chosen to leave. We will not be able [to] investigate crimes, we have no time to travel to the call-outs we are set to do. A worsened working environment means that many colleagues are now looking around for something else."[9]

Around three police officers are leaving the force every day, leaving a massive capability gap for police chiefs. They would rather take their lives into their own hands than work for 2,700 dollars a month. Unsurprising perhaps, considering the murder rate in Sweden increased by 26 percent from 2014 to 2015.

I spoke with Torsten Elofsson, a former INTERPOL officer and retired chief of the Criminal Investigation division for Sweden's police in Malmö, about the issue driving so many officers away from the force. He has commented before on how the media and politicians attempt to paint rosy pictures of Malmö, all the while ignoring basic facts on the ground as established by police officers. Elofsson doesn't like the phrase No Go Zones, mostly because, he explains, police are constantly having to go into them. But the situation, he says, has changed drastically in recent years.

"A couple of years ago when we had a case of a crime in progress, we sent a unit and that was it. But now you have to send two or three units where one of the units guard the police cars just to be on the safe side," he said, adding, "From time to time there are some riots when we have apprehended some person, it may cause some trouble with the guys living in the area because they are dissatisfied with the police work and they consider the turf their own turf and they have their own rules and regulations and it can be rather tough but it's not a no go zone in the sense that we never go there."

This matched what I saw in Husby in Stockholm, where just moments after being surrounded by drug dealers, I moved into the central square and watched as two police vans filled with officers attempted to negotiate the arrest or detention of a man from an apartment building. The building onto which the metro station backed—leaving two narrow passages leading up to its entrance—appeared to be guarded by a group of five or six non-native men. The policeman appearing to lead his colleagues, a bald-headed man around six feet tall, kept his head down as he approached the building. The officers were visibly uncomfortable, and perhaps discomforted, by the presence of onlookers too. For this reason, we stood far enough away so as not to agitate the situation. The police vans moved back and forth on the square.

"They don't want to get trapped in," my guide said.

After a few minutes passed, a young man in a hoodie appeared to voluntarily join the police in their vans. This was no ordinary arrest or detention. The police looked scarcely like authority figures and more like individuals resigned to taking actions they didn't want to. I returned to the same square the next day, to see what would happen in daylight. As I arrived, a group—possibly even the same group of young men—shouted "Po po! Po po!" in order to gauge my reaction. They wanted to see if—in fact they probably believed that—I was an undercover police officer.

I spoke with some women on a bench outside the station. Their heads were uncovered, and they were taking pictures of what appeared to be a reunion of friends. I took some snaps for them on their camera, and they obliged me in conversation, translated via my guide. They told me that while they didn't feel particularly unsafe sitting on a bench in the middle of the afternoon, they made it a point to rarely leave home after 9:00 p.m.

Pretty sad, I thought, to be a hostage in your own neighborhood. One woman had lived there for decades and had seen the area change around her. She noted that while she was familiar enough with young troublemakers and criminals so they wouldn't target her, she still wasn't comfortable leaving her house at night.

"We've had some problems with postmen, with deliveries in the areas, they have been harassed by the people living there," said Elofsson. He added, "In general terms it is criminality that drives it. Power, selling drugs, making quick money. What we see here is that you build up a parallel structure, a parallel society. Mainly dealing in trafficking in drugs, trafficking in humans, and also a black market, selling fruit, vegetables, cars, everything, without paying taxes, without any bookkeeping, that is becoming a big issue here."

It is a similar situation to Molenbeek, where shop owners can curiously and routinely charge what seems below cost price for goods and services. "The parallel society is growing intensely," he told me and continued,

> Barbers cut your hair for a couple of bucks, you can repair your car, wash your car, to everyone it's obvious this is too cheap, this cannot be a serious business. But it's a double moral in a way because people like to get things cheap, so it is a blooming business.
>
> You have a street called Norra Grängesbergsgatan. When you move there you feel like you're not in Malmö, like you're in the Middle East or whatever. I

used to work on the West Bank so I can see it is similar
to what is there. You have the shops, everything is very
cheap. The guys standing there. A mix of the black
market and crime, the night clubs without permissions.
The drugs, the prostitution…all under cover…you
have a shop that is the front of this business.

The dilemmas this illegal activity creates are multi-faceted.
Of course, criminality abounds, but there are greater implica-
tions for the country's tax policy. In a nation heavily reliant on
tax intake for its all-encompassing welfare state, thousands or
even hundreds of thousands of people never contributing to a
system from which they benefit from cradle to grave presents
major obstacles in policy making and resourcing.

"The picture of Sweden is double sided…we have a great
economy…but the main, tough situation is on the public sector
because Sweden is known as a welfare state…we take care of our
people from birth down to the day you die and we pay high taxes
for that," Elofsson opines. He adds, "Now you can see there is
strain on healthcare, on social security, on the police and so
on…retired people think they don't get the pensions they should,
rightfully, because we pay too much to the people coming in."

Solving the problem is no easier. Officials and even private
business owners face threats for attempting to implement basic
laws in these areas.

If you are trying to run a serious business you are
programmed to lose everything because you cannot
sell merchandise or services for such a low price, if
you want to pay your taxes, pay decent salaries to
staff and so on. In the long term it is a threat to society

and to serious business in Sweden because everyone will be beaten by these. It's a big challenge for the tax authorities and so on.

When you come there as an auditor from the tax authority you tend to get threatened...they scare you.

We had a real estate owner who had some houses in Rosengård and some families caused a lot of problems. Heavy criminality. Finally they were not welcome as renters anymore. They started to threaten the real estate owner, they put explosives at his office. That went on for some time. It scares the hell out of some people.

Authorities who were formerly tongue-tied are now starting to speak out on the issue, viewing the current situation as a tinderbox. Ambulance Union Chief Gordon Grattidge told journalist Paulina Neuding in February 2017, "I know it's sensitive and controversial, but for us it's really a no go because we have directives not to go into dangerous situations. We are also clear about that but sometimes you end up there anyway. In that case, it feels good if you have adequate protection. We are supposed to get personal protection from the police when we enter [no-go zones]."[10] He added, "It's too dangerous to enter [some areas]. We can be prevented from entering. We may be blocked from getting out. Vehicles can be sabotaged at the site. We can be exposed to physical violence. In seconds it can turn to attacks on our vehicles or against us personally... It can be stone throwing and even worse. Hand grenades have been thrown at police so that is a great concern."

His comments were delivered just one week after the establishment media, as well as left-leaning and centrist politicians and activists around the world, ridiculed President Donald Trump for mentioning Sweden's migration issues at his Florida rally. For weeks on end, President Trump was mocked by European, and especially Swedish, world leaders. Liberal Left Twitter users created the popular hashtags #swedenincident, #LastNightInSweden and #PrayForSweden in an attempt to deride the president's comments. Then, just one day after the media's onslaught, Rinkeby was aflame.

While defending the area, which has a foreign-born majority population, police had to retreat as dozens of thugs began to torch vehicles and pelt them with rocks. "Our officers were attacked by a number of people, some of them masked, who threw stones. They felt under so much pressure that a shot had to be fired," said police spokesperson Lars Bystrom.[11]

A journalist for the left-leaning *Dagens Nyheter* newspaper—the fourth largest media outlet in the country—reported how he was "hit with a lot of punches and kicks to the body and head, and spent the night in [the] hospital." Of course the police were powerless to help.

"I was shocked for hours afterwards. The police eventually came and I made a complaint about the assault and aggravated theft. They said that the chances of the perpetrators or the camera is found is small. Non-existent," the journalist testified to his own newspaper.[12]

Another journalist working with the state-owned outlet SVT said of the incident, "I've witnessed turmoil and civil unrest before, but this is something else. It looks like a war zone here."

As punctual as Sweden's trains, the media fell silent. No one issued an apology to Mr. Trump or to the public for unfair reporting. The tweets and Facebook posts and hot takes remain online to this day. But the mockery stopped. The media moved on to other topics as quickly as possible, probably realizing that a public apology would only tighten the noose on the establishment media's already shrinking credibility. The new tactic? Sweep it under the rug. Distract the public with something else. Hopefully, the media thought, we'll all forget.

Media bias on this subject is a recurring theme. *The Guardian* ridiculed President Trump on February 19, 2017, following his comments on Sweden. But in March 2015, the newspaper reported on the "ghettos without hope" following the death of Petar Petrovic, a Swede of Serbian descent who "died in the storm of bullets" following a gang-related shooting, which left two dead and a dozen injured.

Author David Crouch admits, "The tragedy has also shone a spotlight on a hidden aspect of Swedish society that reads like the sub-plot of a Stieg Larsson novel, in which poverty, racism and segregation are driving young men from immigrant backgrounds into gangs and gun crime." He noted that just two years before "[Police] confiscated 200 firearms, including 50 machine-guns, and 30kg of plastic explosives [during raids]."[13]

Many of these weapons found their way into the country in the 90s while the wars in Yugoslavia raged, and authorities turned a relative blind eye to who and what was coming into the country at this time.

Elofsson used the term "smuggling" to describe this phenomenon. He added,

> Up until now we didn't have any border controls. It was decided by the government to implement border controls in November or December last year...now we have police standing at the bridge. And you can see an increase in the number of crimes, they've seized

drugs and weapons and so on so that's a good thing. Up until November/December you could travel between Sweden and Denmark without, you could go through the European Union without being stopped anywhere. Once you're in Schengen [European open border zone] territory, you can go anywhere.

While all this occurs on the surface, something darker bubbles beneath No Go Zones. The covert spread of fundamentalist Islam, the first port of call on the voyage to radicalization and terrorism, is still scarcely mentioned and almost never seriously discussed.

———

How are young, foreign-born or foreign background Swedish residents supposed to find common cause with their nation of residence if they are scarcely exposed to the nation's culture, its laws, its language, or even its native people? When authorities including ambulance workers, firefighters, policemen, mailmen, and even real estate businessmen are targeted as outsiders in their native countries, what chance does integration stand? Apparently, not much of a chance at all.

In 2016, the International Centre for the Study of Radicalisation at King's College London revealed that while Belgium and Denmark were the top two countries for Islamic State recruits per capita, Sweden was the third.[14] It was a statistic that shocked many who, to this day, believe Sweden is a peaceful, liberal-left paradise. And it cut the arguments in favor of multiculturalism, mass migration, and welfarism to the quick.

Elofsson opined,

Part of it is connected to religion in the way that you have the Sharia law that some people try to implement in Swedish society...under the surface you have some sort of Sharia law, that they deal with family business...settle their own problems and disputes in accordance with the Sharia law. In that sense it has to do with religion.

It also has to do with religion when you come to talk about women coming from those countries. In Sweden we are fairly liberal, we think, about the equality between men and women. But when you come to these areas you have forces trying to push for the Islamic view on women: they should cover their hair, stay at home, and so on and so on. We've had a number of crimes related to honor, girls, women coming from the Middle East or North Africa where they have this honor culture. They try to liberate themselves here it is not accepted by the family, by the family head and so on. You can see they are honor related killings.

There have been a number of high profile, "honor" based attacks or killings over the past two decades in Sweden. A report from the left-wing, pan-European news website *The Local* stated,

More than 4,000 teenagers in Stockholm are exposed on a daily basis to cultures of honour that involve traditions which run counter to Swedish law, according to an estimate based on a new official study....

Almost a quarter of female respondents, 23 percent, said they were expected to retain their virginity until marriage and were not allowed to have a boy-friend. Sixteen percent of girls were not allowed to have male friends or decide whom they would marry.

Seven percent of girls and three percent of boys said they were exposed to serious violations in the form of threats and violence.

And ten percent of girls and four percent of boys said their lives were limited to the extent that they could not live in the same way as other people their own age.

The majority of teenagers who matched the honour culture profile have parents born outside Sweden.[15]

The report was written in 2009. Since then, Sweden's population has grown by roughly 7–8 percent. This is mostly due to migration, which may explain why a poster on a noticeboard outside Rinkeby's central square reads, "Are you afraid of your partner or family? Contact Us."

The notice from the city of Stockholm includes translations in English, Arabic, Turkish, Somali, and other eastern languages. The service, it states, is available in Asalla, Husby, Rinkeby, and Kista—all areas with high migrant if not majority migrant populations.

Perhaps the poster was also a response to several disturbing incidents that occurred in areas dominated by these populations. One such incident involved a twenty-six-year-old, Turkish-born girl named Fadime Sahindal who was shot in the head by her father after she refused to take part in an arranged marriage, and after she dated a Swedish man. Before her death, Sahindal sued her family for unlawfully threatening her to commit to the arranged marriage. She won the lawsuit and received state support to date her boyfriend, but only a month later he died in a car accident. Sahindal also shared her story and spoke about integration at seminars before her murder.[16]

Sadly, there are many other stories just like Sahindal's that have even more gruesome endings. Abbas Rezai was beaten with a baseball bat and iron pole before being scalded with hot oil and stabbed to death in an honor killing.[17] Subhi Othman stabbed his daughter fifty-three times after accusing her of leading an "indecent" life.[18] A seventeen-year-old boy of Iraqi origin was sentenced to just eight years in prison after stabbing his sister 107 times in an honor killing.[19] An Iranian professor cut off his wife's lips and ate them after suspecting she was having an affair.

These are just some of the cases that have received media attention. But as Elofsson told me, "People say the press is covering up stories, that they don't tell the truth and if you go out and talk about it you will be considered a racist or something like that. That tends to silence the discussion."

And the discussion about radical Islam is almost non-existent as well.

> It is worrisome, I read the newspaper [just] this morning there was a big article about two guys being apprehended in Turkey under suspicion of terrorist acts…planning to make terrorist actions in Europe. One was a Danish citizen with Lebanese background. The other one was a Swedish citizen from Malmö with an Iraqi background. Obviously trained with ISIS…another guy in Brussels…also involvement with the Paris attacks…Malmö is one of the cities in Sweden with the largest recruits to ISIS.

You have the cellar mosques...in the base-
ments...you have quite a lot of mosques in Malmö, I
don't know how many.

It is unsurprising that ISIS felt able to claim credit for an
arson attack involving Molotov cocktails that targeted a community center used by Shia Muslims, or "infidels," in 2016.
However, it *is* surprising that the Swedish city of Lund launched
a program to "rehabilitate former Isis fighters and other extremists with housing, employment, education and financial support."[20] This is the very definition of hoping the crocodile will
eat you last.

Different migrant communities fighting amongst themselves
is something often ignored by establishment politicians and
journalists. The migrants caught up in this violence are often as
much victims as the natives of the country who get caught in the
crossfire. Unfortunately, this violence is enabled through liberal-
left or neo-liberal mass migration policies. These policies exploit
the kindness and naivety of locals and diminish the value of the
migrants' lives. They create an underclass of people who cannot
get jobs, or who will work for nearly nothing, in exchange for
housing and reunification with their extended families from their
native countries.

To statists, liberals, and the state, these people are expend-
able. This is the same rationale employed by NGOs to justify the
hundreds of thousands of people crossing borders and seas to
reach mainland Europe. Their justification—whether they know
it or not—is bound up with corporatism and electoral politics.
In many ways they are all lay lobbyists for the major multina-
tional corporations or hedge fund managers who need cheap,
migrant labor to keep their profits high.

No greater example of how locals and migrants suffer due to immigrant violence that occurs with effective complicity from the state and media can be found than the case of Alexandra Mezher. She was an asylum center worker of Lebanese origin who was brutally murdered at the hands of those she worked tirelessly to help. On January 25, 2016, Mezher turned up to work at the asylum center in Mölndal near Gothenburg. She was the only one on duty in the center that houses supposed "minors," fourteen- to seventeen-year-old migrants. Her parents, Lebanese immigrants, and her status as a foreign-background asylum center worker seemed not to matter to her killer, who was revealed to have been an adult placed in a youth center because of a failure in policy by the Swedish government agencies concerned with identifying the ages and backgrounds of recent migrants.[21]

Similar incidents occurred in Germany from 2015 until 2016 when the country's migration agency (BAMF) admitted that it had allowed people to enter Germany who were either "paperless" and couldn't prove their ages or countries of origin, or had forged documents they used to claim more welfare from the state.[22]

Mezher appears to have been one of many victims of liberal immigration policies. Hers was a particularly high profile case presumably because of her youth, stunning looks, altruism, and immigrant background. The asylum center allowed Mezher's killer, Youssaf Khaliif Nuur, to reside in the underage migrant center despite knowing he was "at least three years older" than he claimed to be (fifteen). Authorities refused to release his identity and the details surrounding his stay for three full days after the incident. But when one of the largest newspapers in the world dispatched a reporter to Sweden and broke the news on the age of Mr. Khaliif Nuur, the authorities had to voluntarily block their own article from Sweden so as not to prejudice the investigation and trial.

While working at the asylum center, Mezher had even complained that she was supervising "big powerful men" who were clearly not suited for an underage migrant's center. It was later estimated that Khaliif Nuur was over twenty-one years old. But instead of facing jail time for murdering Mezher, he was sent to a psychiatric care unit. This is a perversion of justice for a woman who was stabbed to death by an adult.

Elofsson and other mass migration critics would agree.

Tino Sanandaji, a Kurdish-background academic with Iranian roots, engages with "both sides" of the mass migration debate in equally excoriating terms. He addressed President Trump's comments on this topic in *National Review*:

> The increase in sexual assault and violent crime is not as spectacular a development as the Fox News segment made it out to be. Even in Swedish immigrant enclaves, criminality is still fairly mild compared with U.S. crime hubs. Last year the famously multicultural Swedish city of Malmö had a homicide rate of 3 per 100,000, far lower than the 28 per 100,000 rate in Chicago.
>
> In their response to Donald Trump, the Swedish government has pointed out that the homicide rate in Sweden is lower now than in 1990. We should nevertheless note that the homicide rate has decreased in almost every Western country since 1990, owing to social reasons, changes in attitudes, and, in part, medical advances that save the lives of more crime victims.

The homicide rate in Sweden has declined less than in the United States, Western Europe, and other Nordic countries, and has increased again the last few years.

Between 1990 and 2015, the homicide rate in Sweden declined from 1.3 to 1.1 per 100,000. This drop is less than that in Western Europe as a whole, where the homicide rate declined from 1.3 to 0.6 in 2013, the latest year reported by the World Health Organization.

In Finland, the homicide rate declined from 3.2 to 1.3 during the same period, and in Norway from 1.1 to 0.4. The rate was stable at 0.8 in Denmark.

While the homicide rate inevitably varies in a small country year by year, Sweden appears to have transformed from one of the lower-crime countries in Western Europe to above average. We cannot say for certain how much immigration contributes to violent crime in Sweden. The numbers are collected by statistical agencies in Sweden, but they have not been reported since 2005 because of the informal taboo on linking immigration to crime.[23]

This taboo, he argues, is the real scandal. Elofsson agrees:

If you look at the population in Sweden, 17 percent are of foreign origin but if you look at the number of inmates in prison, you have 54 percent of the people sitting there. If you look at unemployment you have a large number of people coming from those countries. If you look at rapes and sexual harassment you have a majority of offenders from Middle East and North Africa and so on.

When asked why the government refuses to disclose hard data on the latter, Elofsson remarked, "[The establishment] is afraid of what will happen. They might put petrol on the fire. Now you have social media they can't control it…it will be an important issue for the next election, for 2018."

Currently, Sweden is accepting one of the highest numbers of refugees and migrants per 100,000 of its population in the Western world. According to Eurostat data, it was second only to Hungary in 2015 for the number of asylum applications it received.[24] However, Hungary scarcely approves asylum applications. Sweden effectively approves them by default.

At the end of 2016, the political pressure surrounding mass migration in Sweden started to become too much for the government to weather, and stricter controls were implemented. But in a lot of ways, the damage was already done.

"Refugee is a misused word," said Elofsson. He continued,

> Everyone that comes here seeking asylum is considered a refugee but if you look at the statistics from 2015, 30 percent of the people came from Syria. If you come from Syria you are allowed to get asylum in Sweden because it is a war zone, no question about that. But 70 percent of asylum seekers came from elsewhere in the world…I can understand…They see we have welfare, [we] have a good standard [of living], but it's up to the Swedish authorities to decide because we want regulated migration here. Okay, you have the right to get your case tested, suddenly you find out you're not allowed to stay, you have to go back…you're not a refugee, you have to go back.

But that isn't happening.

In 2015, thirty-three Eritreans were slated to be relocated from Italy to Sweden for a European-Union-coordinated photo opportunity. The whole production was supposed to show how the EU had everything under control, how the migrant crisis was no crisis at all, and how "responsible" European Union member states were voluntarily pulling their weight. But of the thirty-three people due to move, fourteen absconded, diverging from the process they were supposed to follow, and disappeared somewhere in Europe. In early 2016, German authorities were forced to admit that around 130,000 of the one million plus migrants they allowed in over the course of the year had done the same, failing to show up at asylum or processing centers upon arrival.[25]

By March 2017, even the European Commission—the executive arm of the EU—was forced to propose tougher processing procedures in an attempt to stem the leak, or deluge, of absconders. An EU Commission press release dated March 2, 2017, stated that member states needed to "Prevent absconding by detaining people who have received a return decision and who show signs they will not comply such as refusal to cooperate in the identification process or opposing a return operation violently or fraudulently."[26] Again, too little too late.

According to Mikael Ribbenvik, head of operations at the Swedish Migration Agency, assessing all of Sweden's asylum applications was "an enormous feat to accomplish." He explained, "A lot of people leave voluntarily and a lot of people abscond. And then we have a few people that are staying on that are impossible to remove because of identification purposes."[27]

Elofsson confirmed this for me: "First when the borders were open, we don't know how many arrived, you only have the number who registered with the migration office. But we guess there are twice as [many]...they live here without papers, illegally more or less...they just disappear, you can't actually extradite them...Morocco for instance, refused to take [people back]...Afghanistan...the authorities do not want to co-oper-ate on this matter."

How these paperless, jobless migrants will fit into Swedish soci-ety remains to be seen. It will take some time to realize the full extent of the liberal migration policy, but by 2018, the Sweden Democrats may well be topping the opinion polls. What we do know—for instance, that the Simon Wiesenthal Center issued a warning for Jewish people visiting Malmö due to a rise in anti-Semitism,[28] that public swimming pools have been used by migrants for sexual assault and public masturbation, and that the authorities launched a "don't touch me" wristband in an effort to deter sexual abuse of young girls[29]—paints a very sorry picture of the nation.

———

Sweden, with its lush greenery (when it isn't snowing) and liberal politics, has developed a reputation of being the "rape capital of the world" or "of Europe" in recent years. Yet, for the most part, the media continues to deny that this problem exists. *The Local*, for instance, insists that the recent explosion of reported rape in Sweden is merely the result of different report-ing standards: "Evidence for the claim usually comes in the form of comparative international statistics suggesting for example that Sweden has 63.5 reported rape incidents per 100,000 citi-zens, compared to 27.3 per 100,000 in the US, or 27.9 per 100,000 in Belgium, the nearest European country based on those numbers."[30]

Journalists attempting to excuse Sweden's shocking new reputation claim that Swedish women are more likely to report such crimes than people in other countries. This may very well be true. For instance, in Sub-Saharan African countries where male-dominated families and marriages pervade, there is less of a likelihood that women will report such crimes or that such crimes will be taken seriously by police.

But none of that excuses Sweden's increase in sexual harassment and rape reports. Statistics on the matter are not vague, though the liberal-left media is often seen to attempt to muddy the waters of the debate by comparing reporting methodologies between other Western nations and Sweden.

The BBC claimed in 2012: "...the major explanation is partly that people go to the police more often, but also the fact that in 2005 there has been reform in the sex crime legislation, which made the legal definition of rape much wider than before."[31]

Since 2005, the reporting methods had indeed changed, but it was only from 2012 onwards when the country began to see a drastic rise in reports of sexual assault and rape. As such, no significant correlation can be said to exist between the change in reporting methods and the rise in crime. But this doesn't stop those trying to obfuscate and confuse the facts—just like the Swedish political establishment did with rapes at music festivals.

In 2006, the country saw 12,147 reports. By 2014 this was at 20,326 reports, with nearly 60 percent of offences occurring in a public place. Since 1975, the number of reported rapes alone, leaving out molestation and sexual harassment, was up by nearly 1,500 percent.

Compare Sweden with its neighbors and the official "explanations" for the increase in crime—when they do admit it— become even less credible. According to UN-collated 2010 statistics, even before the recent spike, Sweden had 63.5 rapes per 100,000 citizens. This put the country just behind South Africa (132.4 per 100,000) and Botswana (92.9 per 100,000).[32] In third place, one can appreciate how Sweden got the moniker the "rape capital of the West" at the very least.

In stark contrast to U.S. norms, most of the assaults—69 percent—were conducted by attackers unknown to the victims.[33] According to the Rape, Abuse & Incest National Network (RAINN), the largest organization of its kind in the United States, rapists are known to the victims in 70 percent of U.S. cases.[34]

This implies something deeply disturbing about Swedish public life.

Sweden's National Council for Crime Prevention, Brottsföre-byggande rådet (Brå), also acknowledges that the rate of offence is higher in "multiple dwelling blocks," the types of which litter major city suburbs such as Rosengård, Husby, or Rinkeby: "Residents of multiple dwelling blocks are exposed to a greater extent than residents of detached or semi-detached dwellings (2.5% as compared with 1.0%). Exposure to sex offences is more common among persons living in major metropolitan regions (2.4%) as compared with those who live in other larger city (1.6%) or in small towns or in rural areas (0.9%)."[35]

Additionally, the high exposure rate for migrant communities and their children ties with theories on multiculturalism and integration. Older generations who migrated to Europe have a lesser chance of rape or sexual assault for various reasons ranging from an acceptance of marital rape, arranged marriage, or simply pre-migration marriages that continue on happily once the couple has moved countries. But when the next generation finds itself in Western society, there is a higher exposure to rape. Possible reasons for this include living in poor and dangerous neighborhoods (ghettoization) and "honor"-related crimes. The

Rinkeby poster asking, "Are you afraid of your partner or family?" takes on a darker meaning.

Brå notes, "The percentage of persons exposed to sex offences is higher among persons born in Sweden with two parents born abroad (2.6%) than persons born abroad and persons born in Sweden with at least one parent born in Sweden (1.0% and 1.8%, respectively)."[36]

Perhaps, since the Left and its establishment friends keep seeking to undercut the very statistics they rely on to make their claims over Sweden's rape crisis, it would be better to use another measure.

The Swedish Crime Survey (SCS) revealed in 2005 that 0.8 percent of 15,000 respondents considered themselves to have been a victim of sexual crime. By 2015, this figure had almost doubled. Meanwhile, other types of crimes—muggings, threats, harassment, assault, and fraud—had stayed relatively stagnant, with some rising slightly and some falling.

By the Left's logic, Swedish men over a period of ten years must have become insatiable and aggressive along with it, with no external factors explaining the leap in this single area.

Even the Swedish government's own claims undermine the idea that a rise in reporting is simply linked to a change in how the reports happen: "Of the offences against the person reported in the 2016 SCS, approximately one-fourth (26%) were reported to the police. The reporting rate increased from 24 percent in 2005 to 33 percent in 2010. It then remained at approximately the same level until 2014, when the percentage of police reported offences against the person declined and returned to the same level as when the survey was first conducted."[37]

If the reporting rate went up between 2005 and 2010, one would expect a rise in the number of incidents per report. This would vindicate the Left's position. But the fact that reporting went back down and the number of reported incidents still went up means that either every rape became a lot more complicated, very suddenly, or there were simply a higher number of incidents.

Additionally, the more recent numbers continue to rise:

> In 2015, 1.7 percent of persons stated that they had been exposed to a sexual offence. This is an increase as compared with 2014, when 1.0 percent stated that they had been exposed. Sexual offences remained at a relatively stable level for the period 2005-2012 with approximately 1 percent exposure, and an increase occurred thereafter. ... Sexual offences are most common in a public place and in most cases the perpetrator is unknown to the victim.[38]

Sweden is clearly anomalous, and any claims to the contrary must surely be regarded as politically expedient. In other words, a cover-up.

In March 2017, Sweden's minister for employment and integration, Ylva Johansson, had to apologize after she was found to be using selective statistics in order to deny Sweden's rape problem. She told the BBC that the level of rape in Sweden was "going down, and going down, and going down." She also stated, "The level of rapes is not actually high in Sweden," but she was caught out by members of the country's "Moderate Party," which sits alongside Angela Merkel's Christian Democratic Union in the European Parliament (not exactly a "far-right" source, in other words).

"We don't need more fake news," the Moderate Party's labor policy spokeswoman Elisabeth Svantesson tweeted. She added, "In what way is the number of sex crimes decreasing?"

Johansson had to apologize just a few days later. She explained, "I based my answer on information that I had at the time, that the number of reports of rapes went down in 2015. It was wrong of me to speak of a development that was only based on one year. The preliminary figures for 2016 unfortunately show that the figures are on the rise. It's important to be correct, of course." [39]

Rape numbers rose by 13 percent from 2015 to 2016.

The "foreign-born" element to criminality in the country is often quickly and intentionally overlooked by establishment media journalists.

In May 2016, Canada's *The Globe and Mail* published an article by Doug Saunders, an author known for his pro-migration books *Arrival City* and *The Myth of the Muslim Tide*.

Saunders's article, entitled "Sweden's rape crisis isn't what it seems," was a 750-word apologia on behalf of the Swedish political establishment, in which he parroted the establishment's claims about rape statistics, pausing for just over one hundred words to use "poverty" to excuse migrant criminality:

Statistics show that the foreign-born in Sweden, as in most European countries, do have a higher rate of criminal charges than the native-born, in everything from shoplifting to murder (though not enough to affect the crime rate by more than a tiny margin). The opposite is true in North America, where immigrants have lower-than-average crime rates.

Why the difference? Because people who go to Sweden are poorer, and crime rates are mostly a product not of ethnicity but of class. In a 2013 analysis of 63,000 Swedish residents, Prof. Sarnecki and his colleagues found that 75 percent of the difference in foreign-born crime is accounted for by income and neighbourhood, both indicators of poverty.[40]

It is almost a compelling argument, except for the fact that in many cases this so-called "poverty" is either self-inflicted, state-inflicted, or a personal choice. There are reasons why men sit for hours on end in cafes in Rinkeby central. They may not know the native language and are not encouraged to learn it. They may prefer to earn "fast money" through drug dealing than to earn less money through honest work. They may get "enough" benefits from welfare and see no point in rising with the sun and scarcely being at home just for an extra few Kroner a week.

The statistical difference between crimes committed by native-born Swedes and foreign-born people is staggering. It is truly unfortunate that even *Mother Jones*, one of America's most leftist news websites, can acknowledge this difference and *The Globe and Mail* cannot. Writing for *Mother Jones* in February 2017, shortly after President Trump's comments, author Kevin Drum acknowledged,

Whenever I see writing that carefully avoids providing comparative statistics, my BS detector goes off. Sure enough, Saunders didn't "rigorously" do anything. He linked to an old report that tallies crime rates for the years 1997–2001—which is all but useless in 2017[1]—and then glided quickly past his eventual acknowledgment that the foreign-born have "a higher rate of criminal charges than the native-born."[41]

The data Saunders links to shows that the non-native crime statistics for murder, rape, assault, robbery, and sexual assault dwarf the same crime statistics for Swedes by ratios ranging from 2.5–1 and 3.5–1. East Africans, Middle Easterners, and North Africans all have significantly higher rates of criminality than native Swedes.

Drum concluded, " . . . if we bring up this subject at all, we have to present the statistics fairly. In the US, immigrants seem to commit crimes at lower rates than native-born Americans. But Sweden is a different country, and the statistics suggest that foreign-born immigrants do indeed commit crimes there in much larger numbers than native Swedes."

Fortunately, none of the cover-up explanations for these statistics can fully silence the high-profile incidents—which have been widely reported—that confirm them. In 2014 and 2015, at the popular "We Are Sthlm" festival for young people in Stockholm, there were thirty-eight reported incidents of sexual assault and harassment targeted primarily at young Swedish girls, most of whom were under the age of fifteen. An internal memo emerged two years later that revealed the Swedish police had failed to disclose the details of or report on the incident. In other words, they staged a cover-up through silence.[42]

A major national newspaper, *Dagens Nyheter*, was dragged into the scandal after a competitor paper accused it of not reporting the 2015 incidents even though it had information about them. *Dagens Nyheter* claimed it was not able to cover the incidents properly because the police failed to assist it and maintain a clear line of communication on the matter.[43] Sweden's liberal-left Prime Minister Stefan Löfven called the elaborate cover-up a "double betrayal" of Sweden's girls and the nation's goodwill and trust in the political establishment.

The group responsible for the attacks— "Afghan refugee youth[s]"—had their identities suppressed so the debate surrounding migration and refugees would not be inflamed. Police spokesman Varg Gyllander noted at the time, "There are police employees that are afraid of talking about these things in the context of the immigration debate today."

The incidents led *Guardian* newspaper writer and 2009 Orwell prizewinner Andrew Brown to opine,

> The news that the Swedish authorities covered up widespread sexual assaults by immigrant gangs on teenage girls at a Stockholm music festival, and possibly other incidents too, is immensely damaging for race relations in Sweden because it conforms so precisely to two stereotypes.
>
> It has been quite clearly established that there has been an increase in violent crime, and in reported rape, over the last 40 years in Sweden. In 1995, the first year for which statistics are easily available on the Crime Agency's website, there were 179 murders in Sweden, of which 29 involved guns; in 2014 there were 317, of which 74 involved guns.
>
> Some of the violence is closely linked to the appearance of gangs of Balkan and Middle Eastern origin among refugee groupings who fight for control of the drugs trade, among other things. There were around 40 unsolved gang murders on police files at the end of last year.[44]

While his thesis—that nationalist and populist political parties seek to gain from negative news stories about migrants—is not unique, even he, writing for a left-wing news outlet, had to conclude, "So teenage girls were systematically assaulted and robbed by gangs of young foreign men because too many powerful people found their suffering was inconvenient. The result of this cover-up will be far more damaging than the truth could have been."

Arguably, the incident would have received little coverage if the story about mass migrant sexual assault in Cologne and other German cities on New Year's Eve hadn't broken just days before. My colleague Oliver Lane and I broke it on *Breitbart London*, which led even the most establishment news outlets like the *Times of London* to laud us for our coverage.[45]

Mass migrant sexual assault became a focal point in the media for a short time thereafter, with multiple news outlets reporting on "*taharrush jam*"—a phenomenon in which gangs of men intentionally prey on women in crowded areas. In fact, Google Trends reveals a massive spike in the number of times the term *taharrush* was searched during the week of January 18–24 in 2016, with almost no search activity for the term before that.

"Why are there so many satellite dishes?" I asked one of my guides as we drove around Swedish housing estates at night. I was curious to know why the estates were littered, like Molenbeek, with gargantuan receivers precariously positioned on outside walls, or taking up entire balconies.

"They don't watch Swedish television. They don't speak Swedish. They want to receive television from their home countries in their native languages," my guide explained.

This, apparently, is the well-integrated paradise CNN wants you to believe in.

As we continued our drive, it became clear to me that the problems in these areas—drugs, rape, police assaults, and more—were created in large part by state-sponsored "multiculturalism." Sweden's liberal migration policies, that is to say a failure to maintain any sort of border control over the past few decades, have led to ghettoized communities that the state props up with generous welfare payments and socialist lecturing.

Sweden's migration and integration problems are demonstrable and variegated. Just a few days before my visit, police officers in the area were punched, kicked, and attacked with glass bottles while on a routine patrol. In the following weeks, the country experienced more embarrassing incidents the media failed to report, even in the shadow of President Trump's comments: two men were shot in the Kista suburb, Malmö's population doubled due to migration, a respected war correspondent called the embattled Iraqi city of Mosul safer than Stockholm for women, police and journalists were attacked by a mob of migrant youths, reports cropped up of crime soaring in Uppsala as young people mugged pensioners for drug money.

While migration is not 100 percent responsible for the state of Sweden's No Go Zones, the trends, culprits, and prima facie evidence is undoubtedly clear: Sweden has a mass migration and integration problem, and the country's establishment is burying its head in the sand over it.

FIRST ADDENDUM:

After I finished writing this chapter, PostNord—the joint Swedish-Danish postal delivery company—stopped delivering to two hundred addresses in Hjulsta, Rinkeby. The company cited a "messy" situation in Hjulsta as the reason and expressed fear for the safety of its employees.

One local told the *Nyhter24* news outlet, "We should not have to suffer in this way...I can't afford a bus pass and have problems with my legs, so I can't get myself there [to the collection office]."

If this chapter hasn't yet proven how bad some parts of Rinkeby have become, this addendum should surely be enough to convince you of the fact.

SECOND ADDENDUM:

During the final stages of editing this book, a leaked report from within the Swedish government confirmed a rise in No Go Zones of around 50 percent.

There are now twenty-three areas in the country that the state describes as "vulnerable," including the neighborhoods I visited.

Once again, *Breitbart London* was the only major English-language outfit to re-report what had gripped Sweden's national papers.[46]

FIVE

FROM FRANCE, WITH HATE

You're back in Paris. But you're not in France.

—ONE OF MY TOUR GUIDES IN THE PARIS SUBURBS

F rance's flirtation with jihadism has been sudden and devastating. Since 2012, radical Islamic terrorists have slaughtered at least 270 people on French soil. Over two thirds of these victims lost their lives in the past two years alone. In July 2016, at least eighty-four people were killed in the Bastille Day truck massacre in Nice, and 130 were killed in the November 2015 terrorist attacks in Paris. As the British Foreign Office puts it, "There is a high threat from terrorism. Attacks could be indiscriminate."

While the perpetrators of many of these atrocities are often described as "French citizens" or "Belgian citizens," there is, arguably, nothing European about them, nor would they embrace such an identifier. From Abdelhamid Abaaoud to Mohammed Merah, the people who committed these acts of terrorism in France over the course of thirteen years hold two crucial things in common: fealty to Allah, and foreign descent.

Linking either of these commonalities to terrorist attacks is now considered "Islamophobic" or "racist" or "xenophobic." But the truth is, without investigating these common threads, you cannot square the circle of these terrorists' intent. The difference between these terrorists and the five million Muslims in France who choose not to blow themselves up or shoot up theaters is not "poverty" or "hardship" or "stigmatization"—as the liberal Left would have the world believe. It is a strict and undoubting obedience to the strictures of the Quran and the Hadiths of the Islamic prophet, Muhammad.

France is in a constant state of high alert and that is not likely to change any time soon. Security measures to mitigate this state are blunted at every turn by the liberal Left, which undermines the effectiveness of the measures by spreading lies about how they are racist. As a result, No Go Zones are slowly spreading in France and most are too blind to notice. For those who aren't, the influence of these dangerous areas is easiest to see in the Parisian suburbs, or banlieues.

Even in Barbes, which hardly qualifies as a No Go Zone, this influence is evident. Close to the city center and next to the Gare du Nord station, which connects France to London, Germany, and the Netherlands, there is a smattering of mosques, halal butchers, and Islamic bookshops. To the outside observer, they seem like harmless landmarks. But to journalists like me, they are clearly the reason I was advised to "keep your hands in your pockets" and "don't take pictures" while tiptoeing through the streets.

"Why?" I ask.

"Pickpockets. And people who hate pictures," my guide replies.

"But I want to take a picture of this halal butcher!" I exclaimed. My guide had already trotted halfway down the road. I got the picture anyway.

What is so fascinating to me about a halal butcher? The fact that *all* the butcheries I saw in the area looked like they were halal. What's the problem with halal butchers? Well, barring the obvious barbarity toward animals, many French people don't want to fund the halal certification process, which is effectively forced compliance with Sharia law. Nonetheless, halal slaughterhouses overproduce in France, and the supply bleeds (not literally) into broader French society as a result.

French fast food restaurants have even been known to drop non-halal compliant products in order to ensure their establishments remain within the confines of Sharia law. In 2010, the popular fast food chain Quick—France's equivalent to Burger King—completely dropped pork from its menu in eight of its French city suburb locations. They replaced it with turkey.[1]

"You also need to clarify the situation with the halal system," Marion Maréchal-Le Pen tells me. Marion, a strikingly beautiful twenty-seven-year-old and then Member of Parliament, who is also former Party Leader Marine Le Pen's niece, has strong feelings on this issue. "Today it has started to be all around Paris. All the meat is halal. So I pay for halal. The exception has started to be the principle. It is forbidden to have the information if the meat is halal or not. If it's not halal certification you have no right to know."

The halal debate is clearly less about meat than it is about identity. A report from Institut Montaigne, a French think tank specializing in "social cohesion," noted in a landmark report just six years after the massive, widespread riots in the Paris suburbs, "This explosion of halal is one of the most significant phenomena in the transformation and identity affirmation of Islam in France in the first decade of the 21st century."[2] Halal as a concept, the report suggests, is not simply about meat or food. It has extended, as Islam dictates, to the way people live their lives. This covers family, relationships, marriage, children, public behavior, and more.

Over time, the banlieues have experienced greater and greater "Islamification," which has led to further ghettoization and a rejection of French values in these areas. As I walked through Seine-Saint-Denis, Barbes, and Aulnay-sous-Bois, this was increasingly evident. On a Friday afternoon my guides and I witness masses pouring out of the mosque in Aulnay. Prior rioting made the journey there almost impossible.

Just a few days before my trip, a young man by the name of Theo was allegedly sodomized by police with their batons during an altercation. The protests and riots that ensued were indicative and emblematic of a dissociation between the residents of the banlieues and wider French society.

For whatever it means and for whatever it is worth, I saw just one person who looked typically French in the traditional sense as we traversed the icy cold Aulnay suburb. The young, white girl standing at the bus stop didn't look comfortable. My guide cautiously approached her and asked her how we could get to the areas where the riots occurred the night before.

She explained, "The buses are not running the same since the incident. They won't stop there."

"What incident?" we asked, feigning ignorance.

"You know what incident," she replied. She was visibly uncomfortable discussing it. I suspected she had her doubts about the veracity of Theo's claims. But to say so may have drawn a response of "Racist!" from us if we were part of the political Left. Perhaps it is "racist" of me to note that hers was the only white face we saw all night.

It was bitterly cold and raining when we got on the bus with her. As we rode along, I couldn't help but notice that Aulnay-sous-Bois seemed eerily calm. The area had just experienced the first protest that would domino across the Parisian suburbs. The same thing happened back in 2005 when up to 25,000 people joined in marches and riots across the city and the banlieues. Back then the riots lasted for about a month, and during that time an estimated 8,000 vehicles were burned across Clichy-sous-Bois—just three miles from Aulnay—and a handful of other northern Parisian suburbs. In total, nearly 3,000 people were arrested, a state of emergency was declared, three civilians died as a result of the riots, and estimates for the damage escalated to hundreds of millions of euros.

A French voice on the bus's loudspeaker declared the vehicle would not be stopping where we needed. Our new female friend advised us to get off a lot earlier than one usually would have to. As we walked down the street, my guide looked back and said, "From now on, no more smoking."

"No more smoking?" I asked. "Why on Earth not?"

Often, I confess, I use the act of smoking a cigarette to disguise myself in "dangerous" places. I've done it in Kiev (Ukraine) during anti-government protests. I've done it in Molenbeek. I've even done it in South London late at night. There's a sort of camaraderie among smokers. When someone asks me for a smoke or a light, I will often remark, "Of course. We're a dying breed, you and I. Literally."

It's a great icebreaker, and it can bond people together. I've lost count of the number of times I've stood huddled with strangers, under a leaky awning or on some windy terrace in the middle of the night, only to make friends simply over the words "Got a light?" So for me, the idea of *not* smoking in a neighborhood like Aulnay, one day after the riots, was almost like taking off a bullet proof vest in Mosul.

"It is how they start a conversation with you, to rob you, or to find out where you are from," he replied. "No more smoking from now on."

I didn't like that. But he was right. Thinking back on it, even at train stations groups of young men loitered, begging for cigarettes and hurling abuse at our female companion. Maybe they just wanted cigarettes, I thought. Either way, who was I to question a native who knew the state of the area a lot better than I did?

When we reached our destination, the area was predictably quiet as it was a Friday night. While protesters had gathered nearby to rage against police just twenty-four hours ago, tonight the largest gathering of people was pouring out of the Grande Mosquée d'Aulnay-sous-Bois. The building itself is magnificent—vast and looming with an Andalusian theme. There are windowed doors offering views inside the ground floor, and a minaret with a circular plaque proclaiming the name of Allah in Arabic dominates the skyline for many blocks.

To the modern multiculturalist, the scene I just described may seem normal. But according to the locals I spoke with, this is alien and indicative of those seeking an anti-French identity. In the parlance of the 2016 U.S. elections, these locals could be termed "deplorable" or "irredeemable." But they are not alone in their views.

In February 2017, Marine Le Pen of the anti-mass migration National Front Party rode high in the polls, often topping predictions for the first round of voting in the country. France's electoral system, however, is curiously complex. The most popular candidate is usually defeated by an establishment-left coalition by the second round of voting. How else to explain the defeat of such a popular candidate who was clearly addressing the concerns of most citizens? If such concerns were truly "overhyped," why were so many voters, who see and feel the effects of mass migration every day, backing a National Front candidate at first? I asked as many people as I could why the problems surrounding immigration and national identity had less of an influence on voters later on in the election process. I had to know what could have created such a drastic shift in the national debate surrounding the election.

"The European Union?" was one answer. And not a bad one either. But what was it about the European Union that voters disliked so much? "Open borders" was the reply. So we're back to square one.

One of the most striking things I noticed about the streets of Aulnay-sous-Bois on that night, besides them being dominated by men leaving the mosque, was the distinct lack of police cars and policing. Just days before, protesters and rioters had lined the streets and shut down roads. Wouldn't the precedent from 2005 warrant an increased police presence?

Well, for a start it was Friday. A holy day for many of the town's inhabitants, and perhaps an unlikely day for major protests. But the scarcity of police was probably rooted in politics. A heavy police presence would have been considered a provocation. Consider that statement for a moment. The taxpayer funded, state-authorized, police of France, being present in a French town, would be considered a "provocation."

This is a phenomenon I heard about all around France, and all around Europe. In the small, ancient town of Beziers—one of the eighty areas the French government considers "Priority Security Zones"—my guides and the local police were all too familiar with it.

"We feel afraid to go there at night," one long-serving police chief tells me as we drive in the daylight to the area named La Deveze. With the condition that he would remain anonymous—he had a wife and children—he agreed to tell me about how he and his colleagues have had to adapt to the problems in migrant-dominated ghettos, including a change in tactics, numbers, and equipment. The change has been relatively swift, he said, taking place over the past twenty years.

It was a holiday, and small groups of non-native youths stood on street corners, eyeing unfamiliar cars—like ours—that drove by. Some disappeared into cafes and shops when we lingered on a corner. Others became animated, as if to put on a show for us. We weren't in a marked police car, but residents didn't recognize us. For them, that seemed enough cause for suspicion.

"It's not as bad as it used to be," one of my four guides remarked.

Ever since Mayor Robert Ménard had been elected, the circumstances in the suburbs had drastically changed, they said.

"He cleaned up downtown [Beziers] and he invested in these areas. They have nicer places to live now, but they know they have to keep them clean to get more investment. That's the deal," one told me.

Ménard is an intriguing character with a fascinating history.

With his diminutive stature he cuts a resemblance to a slimmer Napoleon. He looks *very* French, even though he was actually born in Algeria.

His parents, Roman Catholics of French native descent, had moved to Algeria before moving back to France after the African country gained its independence. He was a leftist for much of his life. He grew up as a Trotskyite and served as the head of the Reporters San Frontieres (Reporters Without Borders) group, taking part in direct action and protests for traditionally left-wing human rights causes. His subsequent journey to the political Right—he was elected in 2013 on a sort of coalition ticket for the "Arise The Republic" party as well as the National Front—is a microcosmic tale of what happened with Brexit in the United Kingdom and with Donald Trump's victory in the United States in 2016.

"He is not concerned with left or right," I was told. Rather, he appears to be concerned with the identity of his nation, and the "pride"—a word everyone around him keeps using—of his town.

Ménard—who has opposed same sex marriage and even used such incendiary phrases as "I will not let Beziers become a kebab capital"—used his first few years in office to clean up the central parts of town. Since then, he has directed his attention to the problems in the outskirts. Curiously, mentioning his name in the presence of local mosque leaders doesn't elicit the gasps or scowls you might expect if you've listened to what the establishment press or centrist politicians say about his beliefs or his policies.

Under his direction, the center of town is almost immaculately clean. And Ménard appears to have done something that other towns and cities across Europe have failed to do: calm the ghettos. He has accomplished this through a variety of methods, some strong-handed, some more relaxed. In other words, he has mastered the delicate dance of compromise. That's a word that irks people like me, who see no room for compromise in national law, policing, and on issues like integration and assimilation. But

Ménard and his team consider compromise worthwhile because, for them, its primary end is regaining control.

Police in Beziers now receive firearms training when they didn't previously, and local mosques have been asked to sign a pledge of allegiance of sorts to France. Though some mosques refused, their refusal informed the local government of problem areas and mosques. Ménard set to work rebuilding problem areas with the understanding that if they weren't kept clean and if their crime rates weren't kept low, there would be no more funds or support for them. At virtually the same time, posters went up around Beziers reading, "Beziers aide les Chretiens D'Orient," which translates as "Beziers helps the Christians of the Middle East."

"This is somewhat of a provocation on our behalf," one local official tells me. "It is supposed to remind the people here what we stand for."

I know he didn't mean "provocation" in the strictest sense. He meant it was a line in the sand: while the local government was happy to help these communities build roads and mosques and gain greater security, it would not forget that it operates in a Christian nation. While this is a strong message—especially when you realize at least half the public billboards in town are dedicated to it—the initiative that created the most change in La Deveze was not the "provocation" or the "rebuilding." It was Robert Ménard's "big brother" program.

Since he was elected, Ménard has implemented what many of us would be uncomfortable with: a quasi-two-tier policing system.

When there is a problem with a local gang—usually migrant-origin youths—the first to attend the situation will often not be the municipal police. Instead, men with the words "Animation

Prevention" emblazoned on their blue windbreakers will attend the scene. They don't look like typical French police and that is because they aren't. These young men have foreign origins and are part of a group of volunteers who patrol in problem areas in unmarked cars, sorting out the problems of "their" communities. They are willing to endure the dangers of this role because they believe in Ménard's vision for these areas.

"He wants to bring peace, and pride," they tell me.

They aren't political, or partisan. But they hate seeing crimes caused by drugs and gangs plaguing their communities.

"We know their [the offenders'] parents or grandparents. We grew up here. If there is a problem, they know us too. And they don't fear us," they report.

The Animation Prevention unit's sole responsibility is to suppress and manage local disputes, local crimes, and local flare-ups as quickly as possible. In their estimation and in Ménard's, it can be incredibly detrimental for the police to intervene first in these situations. And the police seem grateful that this is the case. One former senior officer, who is now in a more political role, showed me how the teams work alongside the police—who have complete confidence in them—to address these issues. But it is hard to ignore the fact that this process has effectively created a multi-tier policing system in the city. And it is a system that not everyone believes in. During my conversations with conservative journalists and activists throughout France, all I heard in response to this policy was skepticism.

"Yes, and when things get really bad, [the Animation Prevention] will side with their own people," the argument generally went.

I saw no evidence to suggest that this would ever happen. In fact, Beziers was in a relative state of calm during my visit, unlike

Paris. But it was still an oft-repeated fear. Skeptics continued to insist that when a community polices itself, it will always be insular and aggressive to outsiders, even if they are representatives of the state. I think it is strange that these naysayers disparaged the moderately controlled Beziers.

Meanwhile, against the backdrop of the alleged sodomization of young Theo, Paris burned. These protests became violent and spread across the Parisian suburbs. Very few reporters risked their lives to get into the fray and deliver video evidence of what was happening across Aulnay, Saint-Denis, and other suburbs. Even after six weeks—though Theo's name would quickly be forgotten by the mainstream reporters—rioters clashed with police in central districts of Paris.

On March 19, several thousand protesters gathered at the Place de La Republique just south of the Gare de l'Est train station. Roughly one thousand of them clashed with police, hurling Molotov cocktails and smashing bank windows. Their battle cry was eerily familiar, as were the groups involved in fueling the discord. "No justice, no peace!" they cried as they marched with banners that translated to "There aren't too many Muslims or those without papers." Some of the material sported "New Anti-Capitalist Party" logos—a political party that achieved a humiliating 1.15 percent of the presidential vote in 2012.

Meanwhile, in 2017, Ms. Le Pen and her Front National were roughly tied in first place with Emmanuel Macron's establishment En Marche! Party. Curiously, despite this polling, the former was decried as "fringe" by establishment media outlets the world over.

In its coverage of the protests, *Al Jazeera* referenced a report by the Open Society Justice Initiative,[3] a George Soros organization that shares the goals of open borders and mass migration with dozens of "grassroots" activist groups—which receive funding from Open Society Foundations. The report, *Al Jazeera* noted, "found that a person of African or Caribbean background is six times more likely to be stopped by French police than a white person." No further information was offered.[4] No surprises as to why.

The methodology of the report is highly questionable, and it appears to serve more as a political or advocacy tool than a genuine assessment of how the police interact with minorities in the country. The authors used just 500 police interactions around major train stations, resulting in the conclusion that ethnic profiling "violates European human rights standards which prohibit distinctions on the basis of race or ethnicity when these have no objective or reasonable justification." This, even though the report suggests clothing, gender, age, and the type of bag a person was carrying all contributed to whether or not someone was stopped by the police.

The locations chosen for the report also skew the results significantly because any visitor to the five locations (yes, just five) knows there is scarcely a loitering, begging, or criminal problem involving native French people there. The locations were the Gare du Nord station, a platform at the same station, a concourse at the same station, the nearby Châtelet Station, and the plaza near the Châtelet Station. Visitors to Paris—especially those changing trains between the Gare du Nord and the Gare de l'Est stations—will immediately notice how such areas are rife with migrant youths and beggars.

Without even meaning to, I stumbled upon Les Halles, the shopping mall attached to the Châtelet Station. What I saw there surprised me; security teams were checking people walking into the mall.

"Is that normal?" I asked one of my guides.

"It is now," she said, "since the terror attacks."

France has been in a state of high alert—a state of emergency in fact—since the November 2015 attacks. The French Parliament extended the heightened police activity until at least the summer of 2017. It can hardly be considered normal for a nation to be in a state of emergency for nineteen months. And at what point will the "international community"—the media, the activists, the NGOs, and other governments around the world—recognize this? I recognized it immediately outside Les Halles, as I watched a small group of migrant youths verbally abusing heavily-armed members of the military who were patrolling just outside of the mall.

"Assholes," muttered my guide, as I reflected on how such incidents, though not completely unheard of, were not commonplace in Britain or in the United States.

"Is *that* normal?" I asked again.

"Too normal," she shot back and lamented not intervening. I was glad she didn't.

It is laughable for the Open Society Institute to claim that ethnic profiling, especially in these areas, is worthy of reproach. And while their report was authored in 2009, the 2015 terror attacks have only underscored the need for such measures, to the chagrin of European human rights standards. The contention of the report is that white people should be stopped in proportion to how many of them pass through the station, and the same should apply to Arabs, blacks, and other minorities. But this contention ignores the most basic evidence available to researchers: ethnic minorities have a massive over-representation in criminality statistics. While France doesn't officially record such statistics, studies—including those based on prison records and those conducted by foreign governments—reveal this disturbing trend.[5]

The French prison population has soared since 2000. Even establishment news outlets noted this trend, though they now seek to avoid it. In fact, between 2008 and 2015, *The Telegraph*, *The Economist*, *The Washington Post*, and *The New York Times* all acknowledged that the country's foreign-born prison population was spiking. What they wrote then—which they may regret now for reasons related to political expediency—is that Muslims in particular accounted for prison overcrowding.

According to *The Telegraph*, "of the 67,500 people currently behind bars in France, it is estimated that 70 per cent are Muslim—when they comprise only eight per cent of the French public."[6]

The Economist noted:

> Muslims make up an estimated 8-10% of France's population (the exact share is unknown because collecting religious statistics is banned). Yet they are perhaps 60% of prison inmates, according to a parliamentary report. Farhad Khosrokhavar, the author of a forthcoming book, "The Prisons of France," says a more realistic estimate is 40-50%, with 60-70% only in certain big prisons near Paris. Such skewed proportions are not unique: in England and Wales, 15% of the prison population is Muslim, compared with 5% of the population. But the French ratio appears to be particularly high.[7]

The Washington Post said:

> On a continent where immigrants and the children of immigrants are disproportionately represented in almost every prison system, the French figures are the

most marked, according to researchers, criminologists and Muslim leaders.

"The high percentage of Muslims in prisons is a direct consequence of the failure of the integration of minorities in France," said Moussa Khedimellah, a sociologist who has spent several years conducting research on Muslims in the French penal system.[8]

The New York Times reported:

Muslims account for about 7-10 percent of France's total population but around half of its prison population of 68,000. Muslims are even more numerous in facilities near large cities, particularly in maisons d'arrêt, which hold prisoners serving shorter sentences.

Precise figures are unavailable because laïcité, France's strict form of secularism, prohibits officially asking and collecting data about people's religious preferences. These estimates are based on research I conducted in French prisons in 2000-3 and again in 2011-13, when I interviewed some 160 inmates and many guards, doctors and social workers in four major facilities, some among the largest in Europe. Fifteen of those inmates had been sentenced for terrorist acts.[9]

Of course, the Open Society Justice Initiative would prefer to drive the "racist" wedge through French society rather than face these uncomfortable statistics and recognize that policing is probably based on evidence rather than on mindless discrimination. It even has to concede in its previously mentioned report,

"Although persons from all ethnic backgrounds reported police behavior to be generally polite or neutral, those who were most targeted for police stops and identity checks—Blacks and Arabs—nevertheless expressed anger and frustration at what they believed was a pattern of police singling them out for stops and searches."[10] Again, the methodology employed for the report undermines that last claim.

According to the report, the last question asked of interviewees who were stopped by police was "How do you feel after this police stop?" Well, unless they were handed a 100 Euro note, I doubt they felt particularly "good" about being delayed. But so what? Since when do people's feelings constitute good or bad security policies? A cherry-picked list of just thirteen answers to this question is held up as an example of how the French police are racist. One of these thirteen answers was "There's no justice; it's always the same people being stopped: the Blacks and the Arabs." It's not. Another answer was "It's racism, plain and simple." Again, it's not. Yet another answer was "For cops, there is a criminal under every baseball cap. I understand that they are doing their job, but most of the criminals are wearing suits. There was more dialogue when we had community police." This shows how clothing played into the situation, and how the old French socialist mindset about people in suits being criminals was noticeable even to those who were "wrongly" stopped.

Unsurprisingly, the report's conclusion is not convincing: "In establishing that Blacks and Arabs, particularly those dressed in youth clothing, are disproportionately targeted for identity checks at all five observation sites, particularly those who are dressed in youth clothing, *Profiling Minorities* provides the first quantitative evidence that police in France are engaging in ethnic profiling."[11] Equating racial profiling to these incidents in which people wearing "youth clothing" were disproportionately targeted for identity checks is both risible and racist in and of itself. But this is the France the open borders establishment seeks to create: one driven by identity politics and ludicrous charges of xenophobia.

On the streets, it becomes clear how out of touch the authors and sponsors of such reports are. Within a mile of the Basilica of St. Denis, where nearly every French king is buried, one girl brave enough to traverse the streets with me was inundated by insults and catcalls. Young ethnic-minority women are perhaps the worst victims, as Marion Le Pen told me, "No [I can't walk in these areas]." She continued, "I am very well known. But if I were a normal citizen and being a young white woman in a skirt, to be sure, I would be harassed, or physically [assaulted]. Even worse, for a French girl from North Africa, if they refuse the veil, or dress in jeans or anything like that they are in a very very bad situation. It starts with insults like 'you're a whore' and after it can get worse than that."

She wasn't kidding. Our worst encounter with intimidation tactics like this happened when we were standing outside the building that was raided on November 18, 2015, when we were actively trying *not* to draw attention to ourselves. A small plaque marking the location of the November 2015 raid reads, "In memory of victims of terrorism, wounded residents and policemen, shattered lives, property lost to protect the nation. In fraternity with all the victims of terrorist attacks." The plaque is dwarfed by the multiculturalism propaganda clipped precariously to the scaffolding that surrounds the building.

As we took a picture outside the building, a small group of men, some on bicycles, others on foot, noticed our presence. A few of them were clearly dispatched to see what we were up to.

"This is what they do," my guide said. "They want to see what we're doing but also intimidate us." They more or less succeeded, and we carried on our not-so-merry way.

The reason I wanted to see the building was simple: it was the epicenter of Islamic State adherents in the Paris suburbs. I was shocked to discover it was a rickety little building in the middle of nowhere. If indeed they live among us, they live pretty poorly, I thought.

The scale of the raid back in 2015 was absolutely breathtaking. I remembered covering it for *Breitbart* as it happened. Police fired around 5,000 rounds throughout the incident, which lasted almost seven hours. In the building they found and killed Abdelhamid Abaaoud, who was believed to be one of the masterminds behind the attacks in Paris five days earlier. Several accomplices, including at least one other participant in the attacks, were either arrested or killed.

The establishment media scratched their heads over this incident before asking themselves a series of questions. What does this mean? How did they get there? And most importantly, how do we guard against the inevitable "racism" that will emerge from this incident?

That last question is answered in a series of headlines. "The Paris Attack and My Racist Facebook 'Friends'" read an article headline on *HuffPost*, wherein author Craig Considine excoriated so-called "friends" of his for making the statistically sound assumption that the attack was perpetrated by Islamists.[12] "The Racist Backlash to the Paris Attacks Is Helping the Islamic State," bleated Manisha Krishnan at *Vice*.[13] "George Takei Releases Powerful Statement Against Racism After Paris Terror Attacks" read an article in *Time* magazine,[14] which believed that a has-been actor's opinions on international security issues and social cohesion is somehow relevant.

While these headlines were flooding newsfeeds, people were still mourning their dead or recovering from injuries, and the police and international authorities were still pursuing the perpetrators. And they say the *Right* seeks to make political capital of major tragedies.

Marion Le Pen reflected on this outburst of "anti-Islamophobia" and told me, "Extreme Muslim organisations are using our rights, our culture of freedom, our freedom of speech to turn the system against us. Especially the Muslim Brotherhood. They're using all the tricks in the book. Human rights, free speech, the fight against racism, Islamophobia, they are using everything. They rewrite the rights. Today the only religion you cannot critique is Islam. It's like blasphemy. Only for one religion. Today they use the same arguments for Islamophobia and racism."

"Islamophobia" is a funny old word. It is deployed as liberally as "racist" or "xenophobe" by the political Left. According to French philosopher Pascal Bruckner, the term was invented by theocratic fundamentalists in order to shield political Islam from criticism. They should be happy to know it has succeeded.

Bruckner noted in an essay,

> At the end of the 1970s, Iranian fundamentalists invented the term 'Islamophobia' formed in analogy to 'xenophobia.' The aim of this word was to declare Islam inviolate. Whoever crosses this border is deemed a racist. This term, which is worthy of totalitarian propaganda, is deliberately unspecific about whether it

refers to a religion, a belief system or its faithful adherents around the world.

He added,

> The term "Islamophobia" serves a number of functions: it denies the reality of an Islamic offensive in Europe all the better to justify it; it attacks secularism by equating it with fundamentalism. Above all, however, it wants to silence all those Muslims who question the Koran, who demand equality of the sexes, who claim the right to renounce religion, and who want to practice their faith freely and without submitting to the dictates of the bearded and doctrinaire. It follows that young girls are stigmatised for not wearing the veil, as are French, German or English citizens of Maghribi, Turkish, African or Algerian origin who demand the right to religious indifference, the right not to believe in God, the right not to fast during Ramadan. Fingers are pointed at these renegades, they are delivered up to the wrath of their religious communities in order to quash all hope of change among the followers of the Prophet.[15]

In 2006, former and reformist Muslims, like the ones described by Bruckner, penned a letter in the French satirical magazine *Charlie Hebdo*, declaring,

> We reject the "cultural relativism" which implies an acceptance that men and women of Muslim culture

are deprived of the right to equality, freedom and secularism in the name of the respect for certain cultures and traditions.

We refuse to renounce our critical spirit out of fear of being accused of "Islamophobia," a wretched concept that confuses criticism of Islam as a religion and stigmatisation of those who believe in it.[16]

Less than ten years after the publication of this letter, the magazine and its staff paid a dear price for taking a stand to defend their freedom to critique Islam.

On January 7, 2015, Said and Cherif Kouachi entered the magazine's offices in Paris—close to the Bataclan theater where eighty-nine people would be massacred just ten months later. Once inside, the brothers killed twelve people and injured eleven. Their motivation for the attack seems to have been the magazine's depictions of the Islamic prophet Muhammad, who was regularly featured in the magazine as a figure of mockery. Among those killed in the attack were Jean Maurice Jules Cabut ("Cabu"), a well-known seventy-six-year-old cartoonist, the famous Stéphane Charbonnier ("Charb"), the director of the publication, and Charb's personal protection officer who became the director's bodyguard after Charb had received many death threats from Islamic terrorists.

I think the Kouachi brothers were motivated by more than just provocative cartoons, though. It is likely that they were radicalized by Abu Hamza al-Masri and a well-established terrorist group, Al-Muhajiroun, at the notorious Finsbury Park Mosque in London. Al-Muhajiroun has been linked to a significant percentage—around 45 percent—of the terrorist attacks in the United Kingdom. It is truly unfortunate that international, or trans-national, networks of groups just like this one can be leveraged by jihadists. But what is more unfortunate is the fact that the establishment media continues to classify attacks like this as "lone wolf attacks," which allows these networks to flourish under the radar and underpin jihadism in the West.

The mainstream media is not the only establishment at fault for the footholds jihadism finds in the West. Academia also fails to confront or curtail Islam radicalization on university campuses. Left-wing professors and their bosses have no intention of staring down the extremists visiting their campuses to radicalize students. This shameful inertia inspired me to found the anti-extremism pressure group Student Rights in 2009.

"They use our liberty against us," one of my guides noted during my trip to Brussels. The same naivety echoes through France, Britain, and the United States—a beacon of liberty as enshrined in the country's First Amendment.

Those expressing concern over opening Europe's borders to the Middle East and North Africa offer a simple—perhaps simplistic—observation that, while accepted by the establishment media, is scarcely ever reported. They point out that a majority of the terrorists who participated in the Paris attacks used the refugee crisis and the migrant route to enter Europe. This is worth noting because those who downplay concerns about Islamic terrorism in the West often claim "homegrown" terrorism occurs regardless of what happens internationally. They use "homegrown" terrorism as a smokescreen to argue, "See! Even those who are 'British' or 'French' or 'Swedish' are susceptible to jihadism. So the problem must be in us." The difference between direct, Islamic State operatives and homegrown, Islamic State-inspired attacks is important and requires two different policy responses from government and civil society. But that is an argument for another day. Or at least for another chapter.

It may seem distasteful to an American to suggest that someone's speech should be curtailed. But abusing the freedom of
speech is a major boon to radical Islamists, and it has allowed
them to create a chink in the armor of Western civilization. We
must struggle to mend this chink without compromising our core
values. "The terrorists win if we change," goes the adage. And
it is correct.

Now, in the United Kingdom, thanks to censoring behavior
ostensibly aimed at tackling Islamist speech, one in four cases
reported to the government's Preventing Violent Extremism
(PVE) strategy involves a "far right radical." Police lauded sup-
pressing the far-right as a successful way to combat violent
extremism when a fourteen-year-old schoolboy was referred to
a deradicalization program after expressing anti-Islamic views.[17]
If this tactic continues, it will effectively criminalize or at least
delegitimize any thoughtful refutation of the Quran and its
teachings. It is the same type of tactic that led Canada's parliament to pass a controversial motion (M103) that terms criticism
of Islam as Islamophobia.

This kind of cowardice is what prompted *Charlie Hebdo*'s
critics in France to claim that the magazine was tempting fate by
parodying Muhammad. Such claims reaffirm Islamists' beliefs
that it is permissible to attack and murder those who challenge
or mock their religion and its primary figures. No clearer evidence of this can be found than in the interview Cherif Kouachi
gave to a French TV network during his standoff with security
services: "We are not killers. We are defenders of the prophet,
we don't kill women. We kill no one. We defend the prophet. If
someone offends the prophet then there is no problem, we can
kill him. We don't kill women. We are not like you. You are the
ones killing women and children in Syria, Iraq and Afghanistan.

This isn't us. We have an honor code in Islam."[18] He said this shortly after he and his brother killed twelve people, including the female columnist Elsa Cayat.

Essentially, the Western media now enables Islamists and Islamism to justify anything in the perceived "defense" of a 1,400-year-dead religious and military leader. Gilles Kepel of the aforementioned Institut Montaigne confirms this in his report *Terror in France*:

> Since 2010, alongside the establishment of under-ground jihadist networks that hardened an avantgarde of militants, there have been other warning signs that a certain kind of Salafist discourse in the public sphere and on the Web and social media was moving toward violence. The growing trend toward identity politics that appeared during that year increased the visibility of markers of Islamization in the banlieues. The object was to radicalize those on the fringes of the religion, galvanizing them by denouncing the oppression that Islam allegedly suffered in France, which was popularized under the name of "Islamophobia."[19]

Kepel's paper—available in English via the Princeton University Press—is a must read for those interested in how the terrorist networks manifested themselves over the course of several decades. But we are concerned with the areas in which they manifest rather than the complexity of networks themselves. "A very good example [of what is going on in these areas] is [illustrated in] a TV investigation. They were in Sevran, in the Paris suburbs which is near to Saint-Denis, where bars are forbidden to women," Marion Le Pen says. She's speaking about how many public areas are now devoid of female representation. In late 2016 a film crew from France 2—a publicly owned channel—set out to investigate reports of women being unwelcome in the high migrant populated suburb of Sevran, right next door to Aulnay-sous-Bois. Their report uncovered coffee shop terraces and streets that, in their words, "have one thing in common: women seem to be erased."

Recently, Sevran was revealed to have a migrant or foreign-background population of just over 50 percent, with locals saying around 80 percent of inhabitants are Muslim.[20] It is without a doubt one of the most impoverished areas of Paris, and it boasts unemployment statistics that are three times higher than the national average. Sevran's residents live mostly in government housing, and the men there spend their days frequenting cafes and coffee shops, dominating the streets with scarcely a woman in sight.

France 2, alongside women's rights activists Nadia Remadna and Aziza Sayah, revealed a highly inorganic demographic split in the area. It's not that women didn't want to go to places like cafes during the day. They weren't welcome. In one cafe, a man was recorded remarking, "We're in Sevran, not (central) Paris," while another added, "The mentalities are different, here it's like it is back in the old country."

These mentalities seem to be rooted in Islam, as *The Telegraph* discovered when it followed up on the story. Twenty-eight-year-old Mehdi, a regular at one of the cafes, told the newspaper, "Women are not banned here but this is a place for men. A practicing Muslim woman who knows her religion would not come here."

The claims that religion influences these cultural norms come from the residents themselves, not journalists, activists, or politicians who visited the area. Still, some politicians tried to play down the shocking report, the impact of which resonated not just in France but around the world. "The journalist interviewed Benoit Hamon, an [election] contender for the Parti Socialiste," Marion Le Pen told me. She added, "They asked him questions regarding the situation in Sevran. His answer was: 'Stop this…its the old machismo of the workers.'"

What Hamon effectively says is that this sort of sex segregation was scarcely different from how working men treated women a few decades ago. "As if that excuses it. Why would you want that to come back, even if it was true? It's not true by the way. This is France. Women have always been everywhere. This is the home of Jeanne d'Arc," one of my female guides protested.

But for all the condemnation the issue received, very little is being done to mitigate the male-Muslim-dominated culture in these areas. "Police receive direct orders to not pop up in those areas," Le Pen explains. She continues,

> They are very afraid that if those people see cops, they start to riot with a domino effect in all of France. They have a deal for the "social peace" with the drug dealers. The deal is: deal as you want in coke and hashish but you keep order and no riots in your neighborhoods.
>
> The deal is very bad because it is like a substitution of power. I give you the power, I leave you the power in those districts. None of the parties except the Front National accept the risk of massive riots for weeks, but to break the situation you need to have a party and political class ready to fight and ready to accept that it will be bad, maybe bloody [at first].

This is the fear that fuels the political establishment. No one wants this situation to get "bloody." No one wants to be held responsible for nationwide riots again, like those that occurred in 2005. Certainly, if the real problems in the banlieues were confronted, the ensuring riots would likely last for months if not years. I know this because the 2005 riot never actually ended.

In reality, there has been a continuation of the same kind of unrest—sometimes milder, sometimes more intense—for the past twelve years now. To think of this as a social problem, or an integration problem, is naive. France is at war with vast swathes of its own residents. And while these residents realize it, and the political Left seeks to leverage it, France as a whole has yet to accept it. After flitting around the Bobo areas in downtown Paris, I've come to doubt it ever will.

SIX

FROM THE UNITED KINGDOM, WITH SHARIA

I will break your camera...are you spies?

—CHAIRMAN OF THE AL-HIKMAH CENTRE, BATLEY, UNITED KINGDOM

Throughout my travels for this book, I scarcely expected to be most overtly threatened in Batley, a sleepy little Yorkshire town that hit the headlines in 2016 after the murder of local Member of Parliament Jo Cox.

Batley and the surrounding towns are stunningly gorgeous places. Hills and roads roll into valleys and soar above the landscape, revealing picturesque views of the old English countryside. When discussing the issue of immigration, a Londoner will often say, "There's loads of space." They then point to the English countryside which remains unspoiled in some areas, though much of it is succumbing to housing demands fueled by migration. And while northerners, at least in Yorkshire, are known for their hospitality and neighborly demeanor, there are some more recent communities that have been transplanted into these areas that are perhaps not quite as welcoming.

During my visit, the Al-Hikmah Centre—the Indian Muslim Welfare Society—struck me as a good place to "drop by" due to the center's community outreach after Mrs. Cox's murder. In the immediate aftermath of the incident, the center issued the following statement:

> It is with great sadness that we hear of the murder of our local MP Jo Cox.
>
> Our thoughts and prayers are with Jo's family and close ones at this troubling time.
>
> Ever since Jo stood as a candidate she went out of her way to engage with individuals and organisations and as such I had the privilege to meet and talk with her on many occasions. She was a personal friend too.
>
> She was inspiring and full of ambition for the constituency and was always willing to support and promote causes close to the community.[1]

Excellent, I thought. This center could provide a counterbalance to the doom and gloom I've encountered on my trip so far. This community-minded group would surely love to "weigh in" on some of the issues I had been investigating. So we stopped in.

The premises were vast. There was a school area, a space for eating, what looked like residences, and more. The gates were open—a far cry from compounds like Islamberg in New York state, which guards against visitors. One can only imagine why.

We stepped out of the car. Immediately, I was struck by the dated glory of the buildings. I began to take a few, innocuous pictures. Not in the windows, not of the cars, and not of anyone on the grounds. Respect is key on private property. But within a few minutes, we were confronted by an aggrieved and wildly gesticulating man, demanding to know who we were and why we were there.

I began to answer, "We're just doing a tour of the area…"

"What is your name!" he interjected.

"My name's Raheem…"

"Why are you snooping around?!" he demanded, following up with, "I will break your camera[phone]." Finally, he asked us if we were "spies."

I replied, jokingly, "Yes. We're spies. We work for MI5." As we walked away, my recording picked up me muttering, "You're a weird guy, man."

In that moment, I couldn't help but notice the irony of "Hikmah," meaning "wisdom" or "reason." This man had lost his mind over two people standing in his parking lot. It wasn't the welcome I expected. We tried to explain to him that Rachel—my fellow traveler and photographer—had been at the center after the murder of Jo Cox, attending a vigil that the center had held in her memory. He was having none of it and began to take pictures of us. I smiled and waved for the camera, of course, before he demanded we leave. We got in our car and started to leave when he decided to stand in front of it, raving like a madman. Then he demanded we stay, claiming he was "calling the police." In reality, he seemed to be calling friends.

It was a terribly bizarre and unfortunate experience. One that may have been avoided, you might think, by telephoning ahead. But for investigations and field research, it usually pays to not allow people time to put their talking points in order. In this case, it definitely paid off: we got to see a deeply paranoid and offensive side of the Al-Hikmah Centre that has never previously been documented. It gave me a lot to mull over.

The paranoia and hostility we encountered shocked me. I wondered why a center would have to worry about being spied on. Did people usually make trouble at the center? Certainly there was no public evidence to suggest such a thing, and the organization appears to take pride in its engagement with the local community through social services, such as day care for the elderly. That day, at least, the center fell short of this engagement. I wondered why its commitment to engaging the community could fluctuate.

Perhaps it was due to the organization's Deobandi roots. Deobandism is linked to about half the mosques in Britain and most of the Indian Muslim Welfare Society's "Area Representative Members," according to the society's 2013–14 annual report.[2] Interesting, one might think, given that this particular sect of Islam originated from a response to British rule in India. The sect's active support of local communities is laudable, but this might be a cover for something much darker. The group segregates by gender, boasts over its advocacy work and fundraising for "Palestine" and Gaza, and has held a conference for Khatme Nabuwat, an Islamist group that encourages persecution of Ahmadiyya Muslims.

In 2011, one Deobandi mosque in Stockwell (in South London) was mentioned in leaflets that were circulated in Pakistan. The documents called for the murder of Ahmadi Muslims and included the web address of the London mosque.[3] The mosque denied any links to the Pakistani group that circulated the leaflets. But it is impossible to deny the link between Deobandis in the United Kingdom and a hardline opposition to Ahmadi Muslims, which the Khatme Nabuwat is known for. Effectively, the politics of Pakistan are playing out on the streets of the United Kingdom, with activists using community work as a smoke-screen for their support of causes like fundamentalist Islam and sectarianism.

This smokescreen is so effective that when an Ahmadi Muslim, Asad Shah, was killed in the United Kingdom, the domestic political Left jumped to the conclusion that it must have been an "Islamophobic attack." It soon became apparent, however, that Shah—a shopkeeper in Glasgow, Scotland—had been murdered by a Muslim from Yorkshire, where the Deobandi movement has its most impressive stronghold outside Southeast Asia. The murderer, Tanveer Ahmed, was from the Barelvi school of Islam and issued a statement claiming that he murdered Mr. Shah because the shopkeeper "disrespected the messenger of Islam the Prophet Muhammad peace be upon him."[4]

The differences between Barelvis and Deobandis—both of the Hanafi school of Islamic jurisprudence—are often pronounced but not insurmountable. They have commonalities.

Differences between Barelvis and Deobandis versus Salafists and Wahhabists often comes down to jurisprudence and interpretations of the Quran. With Ahmadis, however, it comes down to something much more pivotal: the prominence of Muhammad in their faith. But they also have distinctions stemming from their interpretations of the Quran and the prominence of Muhammad in their faiths.

Another incident involving violence between different Muslim sects took place in Rochdale, just a short drive down the M62 motorway (highway) from Dewsbury. When seventy-one-year-old imam Jalal Uddin was bludgeoned to death in 2016, the political Left blamed "Islamophobia." One leftist activist, Sarah Wilkinson, who is affiliated with the anti-Israel "Palestine Solidarity

Campaign" and the hard-left "Unite Against Fascism" group, tweeted about the incident: "Islamophobia comes in many forms. Sometimes its [sic] just blantantly [sic] evil and deserves exposure." She punctuated her tweet with the tags #StandUpToRacism and #JalalUddin.

Mr. Uddin's killer was Mohammed Hussain Syeedy. The BBC reported that Uddin's "spiritual healing practices" were the reason Syeedy murdered him. The broadcasting company's online news article explained, "…he practised a form of Islamic healing in Rochdale's Bangladeshi community which the so-called Islamic State (IS) considers 'black magic.'"[5] But such practices are not uncommon outside the majoritarian Sunni Islam. The BBC's inability to report the sectarian elements at play in this crime—instead presenting it as bickering over some niche extremist gripe—underscores how badly Ahmadiyya Muslims are represented in the West. Yet they continue to perform charitable work and public relations efforts that help bolster the image of those who would kill them.

In 2007, the *Times of London* reported that Riyadh ul Haq, one of the leading Deobandis in the United Kingdom, "supports armed jihad and preaches contempt for Jews." But the article, written by Andrew Norfolk, was dismissed by Britain's various Sunni Muslim communities due to its heavy reliance on rudimentary information about the Deobandi sect Tablighi Jamaat.

Tablighis, missionary-style spin-offs of the Deobandi school, tend to be ultra-conservative and often demand incredible fealty from their Muslim followers. In 2005, the *New York Times* revealed that the group was expanding its dominance in France and detailed the curious demands the group placed on its adherents:

Raouf Ben Halima, 39, sleeps on his side, never on his stomach.

He enters the bathroom leading with his left foot, but puts his pants on leading with his right.

He does not use a fork when he eats; he uses his index finger, middle finger and thumb.

Halima is a member of the Tablighi Jamaat, or Preaching Party, a global army of Muslim missionaries helping to expand their religion and reinforce their faith. They believe that emulating the habits of the Prophet Muhammad is the surest way to restore Islam to its intended path.

So Halima and his associates shave their upper lips but let their beards grow. They wear their pants or robes above the ankle because the prophet said letting clothes drag on the ground is a sign of arrogance. "Halfway between the knee and the ankle is best," Halima explained, sitting amid stacks of religious tracts in his small home.

His comments during conversations about the growth of militant Islam offered a glimpse into the beliefs of a group that is unsettling to many in France. The Tablighi are one of the primary forces spreading Islamic fundamentalism in Europe, and many young men pass through the group on their way to an extreme, militant interpretation of the religion.[6]

The article goes on to explain that security services have failed to penetrate the Tablighis and that the group refuses to take political positions. Instead, it prioritizes its proselytization of a strictly enforced Islamic doctrine that instructs its followers to live their lives as close to the way Muhammad lived his as possible. While not all Deobandis are Tablighis, all Tablighis are Deobandi. And these are people who—with their isolationist and segregationist mindsets—have gained access to the largest number of mosques in Britain, earning themselves the name "the Army of Darkness" along the way. Readers can be forgiven if they have never heard of this group before. The Tablighis—unlike their Salafist "Death to America!" counterparts—scarcely make it into the news because journalists, being lazier than ever, are unable or unwilling to wrap their heads around the differences between Muslim groups.

Though this oversight is not permissible, it is understandable. The journalists who manage to understand the distinctions between these groups usually find themselves on the receiving end of opprobrium from self-appointed and semi-relevant Muslim "authorities." One such "authority" is the Muslim Council of Britain (MCB), a group that the British government has often supported in its attempts to foster "dialogue" with Britain's Muslims.

Critics of the MCB allege that the group's history and motives do not keep with British traditions or values. For example, the group has been outed for refusing to attend Holocaust Memorial Day, opposing drawings of Muhammad, and for allowing its Deputy Secretary General (yes, this is a real title they gave him), Daud Abdullah, to sign the "Istanbul Declaration" which advocated acts of violence against troops and Jewish people.[7] However, the media still calls upon this group as an authority to speak on behalf of all British Muslims. The British government severed ties with the group in 2009, but this only lasted for about a year. As recently as 2014, the group has been criticized in a government investigation for its role in the "Trojan

Horse" scandal, which involved strict religious guidelines that were imposed on schoolchildren in the United Kingdom.

Despite how involved many of these groups are in local communities, there is a horrific undercurrent of fundamentalism that they all share.

In Dewsbury, where the Markazi Masjid—one of the largest mosques in Europe and Western centerpiece of Tablighi thought—is located, the charitable aims of groups like the Indian Muslim Welfare Association is welcomed with open arms, as local government struggles to provide public services. It is perceived as refreshing to many who fail to scratch beneath the surface that in an area closely linked with Islamist extremism— the 7/7 tube bombers went to the Markazi Masjid—there are Muslim groups serving the community.

Dewsbury is also home to the Sharee Council, a Sharia or Islamic law-based mediation council, which ostensibly seeks to advise Muslims in Britain on matters pertaining to marriages, disputes, and family affairs. These have become colloquially known as the "Shariah courts," and there are believed to be around eighty-five operating in the United Kingdom.

A visit to the Sharee Council yields—for an Englishman— immediate ominous overtones. Once a pub called the White Hart Inn, the building stands on the bridge adjacent the River Calder and—as is common with such institutions—has several names associated with it. One part is the Masjid Heera—a Deobandi mosque. That, alongside the Sharee Council, is owned by the Islamic Research Institute, which got planning approval for an innocuous sounding "prayer hall, religious school and Asian women's help centre" after the pub's closure in 2002.

As early as 2006, alarm bells were ringing over what was taking place in these "courts." They still ring today.

You might be asking yourself "Why are these 'courts' allowed to exist in Britain?" The simple answer is that UK law allows them to. Sharia councils finds their legitimacy in the Arbitration Act of 1996, which allows "parties" to be "free to agree how their disputes are resolved, subject only to such safeguards as are necessary in the public interest." Those who defend Sharia councils try to insist that whatever the all-male panel of council "judges" decides, their judgments and decisions are still subject to UK law and are nothing more than "evidence" to be presented to British judges in formal proceedings. But in practice, the propensity of Sharia councils to consider the testimonies of men to be worth more than that of women—in keeping with the Islamic tradition that a female's testimony is worth half a male's—has caused deep consternation across the political spectrum in the UK.

One group which opposes Sharia—One Law for All—is run by a secularist and communist by the name of Maryam Namazie. On the other side, parties like the UK Independence Party (UKIP) have had representatives, including me, demand that the Arbitration Act be changed to ensure Sharia councils no longer have any legitimacy in Muslim communities and in Britain's courts. Author Denis MacEoin revealed in his 2009 report entitled *Shariah Law or 'One Law for All?'* that "fatwas"—decrees pertaining to Islamic jurisprudence and its practical applications—give some insight into what may be taking place inside Sharia councils:

> Among the rulings…we find some that advise illegal actions and others that transgress human rights standards as they are applied by British courts.

Here are some examples: a Muslim woman may not under any circumstances marry a non-Muslim man unless he converts to Islam; such a woman's children will be separated from her until she marries a Muslim man; polygamous marriage (i.e. two to four wives) is considered legal...a husband has conjugal rights over his wife, and she should normally answer his summons to have sex (but she cannot summon him for the same reason); a woman may not stay with her husband if he leaves Islam; non-Muslims may be deprived of their share in an inheritance...a wife has no property rights in the event of divorce...sharia law must override the judgements of British courts; rights of child custody may differ from those in UK law...taking out insurance is prohibited, even if required by law; there is no requirement to register a marriage according to the law of the country...a Muslim lawyer has to act contrary to UK law where it contradicts sharia...women are restricted in leaving their homes and driving cars...sharia law of legitimacy contradicts the Legitimacy Act 1976; a woman may not leave her home without her husband's consent (which may constitute false imprisonment); legal adoption is forbidden...a woman may not retain custody of her child after seven (for a boy) or nine (for a girl)...fighting the Americans and British is a religious duty; recommendation of severe punishments for homosexuals...a woman cannot marry without the presence (and permission) of a male guardian...an illegitimate child may not inherit from his/her father.[8]

MacEoin is not the only one putting these councils under the microscope. On behalf of the Gatestone Institute—where I am a senior distinguished fellow—Distinguished Professor Emeritus in political science at Rutgers University Michael Curtis discusses in some detail the practical problems with Sharia councils:

> The procedures of these courts present problems. The presiding judges are imams; there is no agreed-upon selection process based on experience and credentials over their appointment. Furthermore, there is little or no access to legal representation for defendants and there is no real right of appeal even when there may not be genuine consent by both parties to the arbitration. The proceedings themselves are not even recorded.
>
> Another issue is the fact that different legal systems for individuals of different religions living in the same country and under the same government promote division. Some of the rulings of the Sharia courts are both contrary to British common law, particularly those that are discriminatory against women and non-Muslims. Sharia courts and British courts hold different standards. Sharia courts have tried to ban alcohol, drugs, gambling, smoking, prostitution, pornography, homosexuality, and the mixing of sexes in public. Extremist Muslim groups, especially *Muslims against the Crusades*, have even called for the creation of a "Sharia controlled zone" in three boroughs in London (Waltham Forest, Tower Hamlets, and Newham), and in several towns including Bradford, Luton, Leicester, and Dewsbury. These would be autonomous entities

operating outside British law. Their objective is to defeat "Western decadence" in Britain. These controlled zones would be the first step in the creation of an Islamic state.[9]

Simply put, adherence to the diktats or even recommendations of imams is seen as the thin end of the wedge. Historically, this is a relatively new development in modern Britain. But it is a new reality that we must guard against, especially for the sake of women. Unfortunately, successive governments have shirked their respective responsibilities when it comes to dealing with the matter of Sharia councils. Lip service is often paid to the issue, but that is essentially it. Obviously, no change can be effected without stronger government action. The same lip service is paid to the proliferation of female genital mutilation and of Islamic radicalization in prisons, but radicalization still occurs in prisons and a case of female genital mutilation is reported *every hour* in Britain.[10]

The media also needs to start shouldering its responsibility when addressing this issue. Sadly, center-right tabloid newspapers only splash their front pages with the issue on occasion, and the liberal-leaning press, such as the *Guardian*, often allows self-appointed Islamic scholars and representatives to wax lyrical about this topic in their pages. In 2007, Inayat Bunglawala—affectionately, though disparagingly, referred to as "Bungles" by the counter-extremism community in the United Kingdom—asserted in the *Guardian*, "The fact is that under English law people are free to devise their own way to settle a dispute before an agreed third party. The Shariah courts that exist do not—at all—deal with criminal issues which are a matter for the British courts, they entirely deal with civil matters such as marriage and divorce. The arrangement is entirely voluntary and the two parties have recourse to the UK courts at any time should they wish."[11]

Bungles, surprise, surprise, was the media spokesman for the Muslim Council of Britain. He has previously claimed that the British media is "Zionist" in nature—far from the truth—and has had to row back from comments about Osama bin Laden, allegedly made just five months before the 9/11 attacks. It was reported that he referred to the Al Qaeda leader as a "freedom fighter" and circulated the terrorist's writings to many British Muslims. While he retracted the comments, he was still called upon by the editors of the *Guardian*'s opinion section to write a defense of Sharia councils.[12]

The government and the media need to stop neglecting and exacerbating this issue because both are enabling elements of Islam extremism to grow and take root in the UK. The people responsible for creating footholds for these elements are becoming institutionalized in Britain because their power and authority remain unchecked. For instance, the Dewsbury Sharee Council is headed by the famous Sheikh Yaqub Munshi of the local and incredibly powerful Munshi family. You cannot whisper the name Munshi in Dewsbury without raising eyebrows or pricking up ears. And it's no wonder why. Sheikh Munshi is the grandfather of one of Britain's youngest terrorists, Hammaad Munshi. At sixteen, Hammaad Munshi was arrested and later found guilty of using "the Internet to circulate material including technical documents on how to make napalm and homemade explosives, and [discussing] how to smuggle a sword through airport security."[13]

In 2015, it was reported that another one of the Sheikh's grandchildren, Hassan Munshi, travelled from Dewsbury to

Syria with his friend Talha Asmal, who is believed to have taken part in a suicide bombing in the Iraqi city of Baiji.[14]

Sheikh Munshi is also one of the leading figures at the Markazi Masjid, which sits at the corner of Pentland Road and South Street. Five times a day, men in long, Islamic robes shuffle their way—usually late and in a hurried manner—down these streets to the vast building. The mosque includes a boarding school and a seminary. The nearest businesses sell Islamic garbs for men and women, including the oft-seen and much debated hijab. A Muslim girls school is just a few roads away. And at least four other mosques are within spitting distance. Welcome to Savile Town.

The depressing little area of row houses (or terraces) has experienced serious deprivation since local manufacturing tanked between the mid-80s and early 1990s. Now, the place is almost exclusively Muslim to the point where "outsiders" like my camerawoman are seen not as a threat but almost as a novelty. There were palpable double takes as residents and business owners saw the pair of us bounding down the roads.

We didn't feel overtly threatened in the area. Massively out of place? Yes. Unwelcome? On occasion. But for the most part residents seemed to operate under the unspoken rule that if we didn't bother them, they wouldn't bother us. Perhaps this rule was in effect because within the last few years they have attracted significant and unwelcome attention from both the media and security services due to their proximity—literally and ideologically—to people who have committed Sharia-related atrocities across the world.

The *Daily Mail* wrote a feature on the town in 2016. The piece cited the 2011 census in Britain that revealed just forty-eight of the 4,033 people in the town identified as white British.[15]

And, just like the residents in Belgium and Swedish No Go Zones, residents in Savile Town scarcely watch British television. What's worse is that women in the town are routinely kept indoors and behind robes. These revelations reinforce the theory that such areas are total Islamic enclaves. But Dewsbury is different still.

"[It] is a complex," says Philip Haney, a former Department of Homeland Security official who has investigated Tablighi Jamaat during his time with the U.S. government. He continued to opine about the situation in Dewsbury:

> That's very common in the Indian subcontinent. In other parts of the Muslim world. To have a series of Madrassahs and complexes. The one in Dewsbury is just a typical example of the structure that is all over the Tablighi world, which is 75-125 million people. They're called the Army of Darkness outside of the United States because of their stealthy abilities. They're also able, like water, to take the shape of any group they come into contact with. They're pro-Jihad. They're encouraging brethren to go back to the way of prophet Muhammed. They're essentially accepted by virtually every branch of Islam all over the world. Especially Sunni.

In light of what Haney says, it is surprising that there is not much gang violence in these areas, on the surface at least. Of course, old rivalries run deep, but—perhaps due to strictly enforced local power structures—these scarcely attract national attention. Yet there is definitely unrest in these areas. Local resident and author Danny Lockwood revealed in his forebodingly entitled book *The Islamic Republic of Dewsbury* that non-Deobandi populations find it difficult to get a foothold:

> Pakistani and Iraqi Kurd gangs are involved in running street battles in Savile Town with baseball bats and metal bars on the night of Sunday July 23rd. One Kurd underwent brain surgery in Leeds, after 12 police cars and riot officers brought the situation under control. Only two men were arrested.
>
> The asylum seekers were living in Savile Manor, a building used as a hostel by Kirklees Council. Four more men were arrested after more clashes on the next night, Monday, and the violence spread to Ravensthorpe on the Wednesday night when a gang of Pakistanis surrounded a car with three Iraqis inside.
>
> Police said there were unconfirmed reports of shots being fired. Two of the Iraqis escaped but the third, Sirkot Mahmoud, 22, was hit by an iron bar before he fled to his home.[16]

Apparently, the existing community that has been there since the 1960s will be damned before it gives up its turf to some Johnny-come-lately asylum seekers.

Lockwood seemed to echo this sentiment in the interview I had with him for this book. He told me all about his experiences in Dewsbury, Savile Town, and the surrounding areas. "The takeover is complete," he began, reflecting upon the changes between the first edition of his book and the second, the latter of which portrays a far more up-to-date picture of the locality. "I must have done five tours with TV, news channels. France, Singapore, Russian TV, BBC, *Daily Mail*," he says, citing media

interest in the situation. Interestingly, he was far less complimen-
tary about the BBC and local government than he was about his
Muslim neighbors. "We went round Savile Town. We talked
about this entire concept of No Go. My view on it has evolved,"
he said.

When I asked him how his view has evolved, he explained,
"I'm more informed now. I am more embedded in parts of the
Muslim community and understanding of its culture than I was."
Like any lifelong journalist, Lockwood has taken it upon himself
to ingratiate himself with the relative newcomers to his hometown. Despite the stark truths embedded in his reporting, Lockwood claims that he's scarcely heard a peep of criticism from his
muses: "I have not had one word of criticism out of Dewsbury
or Batley's Muslim community about that book. Not one. People
find that quite stunning because they think you must have had
death threats, this, that, and the other. Not a minute of that."

Here is how Lockwood explained his fascination with this
community:

> I'm a journalist. I started as a trainee news journalist
> at the *Dewsbury Reporter* in 1978. Back then I had
> just come out of college and there were two Muslim
> students in my entire college year. Both good friends
> of mine. Both still are. One went to be a police officer
> in Bradford. [The other] is still a restaurateur locally.
> Dewsbury market was the biggest, most thriving mar-
> ket in Yorkshire if not England. At that time I lived in
> Thornhill, Leeds. Where I lived has now been com-
> pletely subsumed. I lived on the same road where
> Mohammed Siddique Khan lived at that time. He
> lived around the corner. Now there are maybe three

white families out of maybe 120 on that street. But I knew no Asian or Muslim families at that time in 1978.

He voluntarily discussed the subject of No Go Zones, having familiarized himself with Molenbeek in Brussels in 2016:

I used to do a nighttime job driving a van for John Menzies delivering newspapers. And I'd walk from home right up until about '81, I'd walk from home through Savile Town to go to work at 2 o'clock in the morning. And it was still safe. And now no one, no one would make that journey. And no one does anymore. Now does that constitute a No Go Zone?

One would argue that it probably does. Lockwood details incidents of violence and criminality in *The Islamic Republic of Dewsbury*. These incidents, in addition to the fact that non-Muslims basically have no reason to visit the area, reveal that Savile Town is a No Go Zone, just of another kind. "People just don't [go there]," he explained, and I could hear the frustration in his voice as he explained to me—someone who is relatively educated on the subject—the finer points of how his neighborhood has changed.

"You would not walk through Savile Town at two in the morning because there have been [attacks]. And you get good Samaritans of the Muslim community who will pick up a bloody white lad who's had the shit kicked out of him on the side of the road," he said. Violence, he explains, has been commonplace in the area, though now it mostly occurs between different migrant communities rather than the displaced native families who have long fled the area. From assaults and robberies in April 2002 to drug crimes and money laundering in 2008, Lockwood details a rich and surprisingly vast history of local criminality for what many consider a small and "sleepy" area.

"I have friends and members of my family who have suffered assault and the police do not even recognise it, report it or acknowledge it. They suppress it. On a daily and weekly basis. My reality around here is not the reality the BBC or all the sweethearts in West London live with," he said. Lockwood then explained that in addition to not wanting to risk going there, especially at certain times of the night, there is scarcely cause to go to Savile Town anymore. He still tends to stop by for the sake of his reporting, though. As a result, he is one of the few people in the world who has any serious expertise on how religion affects places like Savile Town and on Indian/Pakistani Muslim power politics and culture. As far as I'm concerned, this is a massive indictment of local and national government as well as the media and police. I have scarcely spoken to anyone besides Lockwood who has such an impressive knowledge of the area.

"The are no pubs left. There's a pub down by the canal," he explains, and he adds, "but that's kind of on the periphery in a semi-industrial area anyway. You'd never walk there. You'd get a taxi or you'd drive. You'd not walk. But with all the rest of the shops gone, the only store there is [an Asian] grocers which I still go to...if I'm driving up Thornhill, which I do frequently, I stop off at Mullacos and pick up some king prawns and fresh fruit and veg because it's half the price that I can get anywhere else."

Lockwood isn't a bitter or angry man. He's cheerful, upbeat, and laughed a lot during our interview about the characters he's seen come and go in the area. Still, he admits, there's no getting Savile Town back. He explains,

Sue Reid [from the *Daily Mail*] came round over a year ago looking for these nominal forty-odd white people remaining in the population of 5,000.

I said "they aren't here." That was the 2011 census. The old lady we did find, Jean Wood, Jean actually is officially [in] Thornhill, Leeds. She's one of the few left. So [people are] not going to visit anybody in Savile Town. All the sports teams were driven off all of the sports fields. That area of conflict—and it was physical conflict—does not exist anymore because all of those facilities have been literally gifted...to the community, by the Tories when they were trying to do a bit of gerrymandering.

So Savile Town, the old working men's club, the bowling club, they've all gone. There is no longer the conflicts we used to have because actually, the take-over is complete. There's no reason for anyone to go there.

These words would echo through my mind later on in my travels as I passed through areas of America that looked like South Asian suburbs.

"When the drugs gangs kick off...or when the council puts some Shia refugees in there," he says of recent violence, "...all of a sudden you have bloody running battles between the local youths." He then described a recent local shooting, which is somewhat of a rarity in the United Kingdom—especially compared to the United States. He recalled the incident was a shooting and a hijacking, and he also remembered how local authorities addressed the issue: "Again the police did not acknowledge that. With a case in the autumn, it took a Facebook post picked up by the *Daily Mail* before the police would acknowledge there had been a public order incident. Daylight. Muslim gangs fighting on the streets of Ravensthorpe which is the Sufi-Barelvi community. The Pakistani community. It's a lot poorer than Savile Town."

Sadly, the poorer areas are in fact more prone to criminality as locals resort to theft, drugs, and violence. With large families crammed into small row houses, young people are more likely to be on the streets in the evenings. For them, it is a form of freedom. "And that is where the criminal activity is centered," Lockwood explains of the very same part of town he was born in. "A mob of 150 local youths pursued this one guy and he locked himself in the toilet in Gregg's [a chain bakers] until the police arrived. The police came and rescued him. They were going at it in the middle of the street with baseball bats," he said.

That sounds a bit like a war zone to me. But when I visited, it was relatively quiet in the area. It is just like the suburbs of Paris, Molenbeek, and Sweden: there are "flare ups" in these places rather than a continuous state of anarchy. Still, these flares have led some to predict that there will eventually be constant states of turmoil in such neighborhoods, as French author Michel Houllebecq details in his 2015 novel, *Submission*.

Lockwood could be Britain's "wizard" on these issues if the establishment actually listened to him. Instead he is stuck reporting actual facts and chastising the mainstream press for failing to tell the story of places like Dewsbury: "Look at the BBC…they don't have anyone I'd employ. They're all soft. Anything that actually requires work or investigation, and if it smacks of controversy…which all races by default do, because you get banged over the head by the [anti-fascists]…they've had public meetings, descended on the police station to have me [arrested]."

What he said about controversy made me wonder if he had encountered resistance after his book was published despite never receiving criticism from the area's local Muslims. Surely, he must be rubbing *someone* the wrong way if everything he says is true. Lockwood admitted, "I have an ongoing thing with the local Muslim mafia godfather, a guy called Tahir 'Terry' Zaman. Terry was [Member of Parliament] Shahid Malik's landlord...he got Shahid in the shit over his MP's expenses because he had a little number going." This was covered by the national newspapers, probably because it involved a Member of Parliament. In 2009, *The Telegraph* reported,

> ...Malik has claimed the maximum amount allowable for a second home, amounting to £66,827 over three years. Last year, he claimed £23,083 from the taxpayer for his London town house, equivalent to £443 per week. The Telegraph can disclose that the "main home" for which Mr. Malik pays out of his own pocket—a three-bedroom house in his constituency of Dewsbury, West Yorks—has been secured at a discounted rent of less than £100 per week from a local landlord who was fined for letting an "uninhabitable" house.
>
> Mr. Malik also rents a constituency office from the same businessman, Tahir Zaman.[17]

It is no surprise that the paper described Zaman as a "slum landlord" in its headline. "Terry's a gangster. Terry's a bona fide gangster," said Lockwood. He added, "I embarrass, humiliate, and disrupt his activities frequently." Lockwood claims that Zaman was behind a hit piece written about him that appeared on the front page of a local paper called the *Urban Echo*. Lockwood has printed his allegations in his own paper, the *Press News*, and they remain online to this day. Mr. Zaman did not return my request for comment on the matter or the other allegations made by Lockwood.

Urban Echo has also run front page headlines such as "Is the West at War with Islam?" and "Trump: Full of Hate, Contempt, and Intolerance."[18] It seems unlikely that the paper's editorial position would be sympathetic toward Lockwood in any instance. According to Lockwood, the paper's piece about him "[It was posted] To everyone that was in my village in York." He said,

> You know what? He sent it to every one of our customers. Advertisers, saying the "community" would boycott [businesses] supporting us. I had one guy call up and say "I'm cancelling my quarter page ad, Danny. I'm taking a full page this week. Because no one tells me [what to do]."
>
> A lot of the [people now here] are full of contradictions…this papering over the image issue they've got. And I get it. As much as people accuse me, I don't broad brushstroke everything. I'm aware of the differences. I'm not saying everybody is [like this].

In light of this, I started to wonder what the people there thought about the issues stemming from areas like this. We often hear the argument that all Muslims shouldn't be lumped in with a minority of extremists—a fair point if the evidence bore out the claim. But a lot of survey and polling data suggests that even within a minority, support for Sharia, extremism, and other

Islamic customs and cultures in the West is not exactly limited to a small minority. "There's a perception that there's this 90 percent against fundamental Islam and 10 percent for," said Lockwood of his local communities. He continued, "And actually it is the other way around. The uncomfortable truth that shall not be spoken."

Perhaps this "uncomfortable" truth explains the solidarity that is sometimes exhibited by vast swaths of the Muslim communities in these areas. When one of the local Muslim community leaders died, Lockwood found himself at the leader's massive funeral. Here is his account of the event:

> I went to the funeral of Hafiz Patel who founded the Markazi Masjid. They brought him over in the '60s from Gujarat to be their spiritual leader. It was mostly Saudi money that built that mega mosque. When he died [in 2016] we were actually burying my mum's ashes in Dewsbury cemetery and I saw them preparing this big funeral area and they said "It's Mr. Patel's funeral this afternoon in Savile Town" on those big playing fields. So I went up. There were a couple of [police] and me with my camera.
>
> There were about 8,000 at his funeral, and I got some inquisitive remarks, and some hostile ones. I said "Why have you got a problem with me paying my respects to Mr. Patel?" It put them on the defensive.

Considering certain aspects of Muslim burial rites—the body must be in the ground within twenty-four hours of a person's death—this was an incredible turnout for a funeral on some playing fields in a small town in West Yorkshire. Some news outlets reported the size of the funeral to be up to 30,000 people strong. Such is the pull of a local Muslim leader in the area.

Links between the town's Muslim population and Britain's political establishment stretch deep too. Lockwood explained,

> We have a businessman. Solly Adam. He's a real part of the Dewsbury community. He got invited to the Queen's garden party. I went down to Savile Town and saw Solly and his wife, took his picture and every-thing. I said, "Which mosque do you go to?" He said, "It depends who I want to do business with."
>
> The Deobandis—that [Markazi] mosque itself is Tablighi Jamaat—they are actually, that's the one Mohammed Siddique Khan [one of the London 7/7 bombers] and two or three of them [terrorists] went there and worshipped at some point.
>
> That is not the mosque that runs Savile Town. The people who come there come from all over the coun-try. The Islamic seminary they have, students from around the world. And if you want the mosque that actually runs Savile Town? That'd be the Zakaria mosque.

I had noted the importance of the Zakaria mosque before. I wondered why its name was familiar to me. Then I remembered the Zakaria mosque was the subject of an article *Breitbart London* published in 2016, after we revealed that British Army soldiers had visited and even prayed there. These soldiers of the Fourth Infantry Brigade of Catterick, North Yorkshire, also visited the Institute of Islamic Education at the Markazi Masjid as part of some bizarre community relations strategy.

"It is vital that the Army reflects the society from which it is drawn," an army spokesman told me at the time. He added, "To do that we need to engage with all our communities and break down the myths about what the Army does and who we are. The visit to Dewsbury did exactly that and was part of a wider strategy of demonstrating that service with the British Army is entirely consistent with Islam."[19] This is curious, especially when you see the photos of UK army officers praying like Muslims and performing the pre-prayer ablutions. The fact that this took place in an area known for its links to terrorists and extremists—and at an "Army of Darkness" mosque—is chilling.

"Those guys are basically the Labour Party grandees as well," Lockwood says of the Zakaria mosque's attendees. "The Muslims run the Labour Party in that part of Dewsbury as well," he added.

I asked Lockwood what he thought of the Sharee Council. He replied, "Sheikh Yaqub Munshi," a local Muslim grandee, "founded the Sharia court...the ex White Hart pub. It was the poshest pub in town once upon a time. And so the Munshis are still big there. And he is royalty. Sheikh Yaqub was part of that inner circle—they've been here throughout. They're embedded, they've got the roots. The Munshis, the Patels...They're the beating heart of the big mosques."

He went on to tell a fascinating story about the inclusion of Sharia proceedings in the case of a non-Muslim local who was wrongly accused of taking part in robberies:

> We're not chopping off hands here. But they're settling community disputes.
>
> If you work in building, joinery, plumbing, roofing, heating round here...you are working...90 percent of your customers are Muslim because that's

where the business is. So you don't wanna upset the community.

There were a lot of robberies on Muslim properties last summer [2016]. Eastern Europeans were going in, kicking in the door, taking their money. We knew it was all being directed by a member of the Muslim community. It had to be. Tensions were high.

This one guy was working on a roof in Savile Town and all of a sudden there's a howling mob because they think it is his van that's been used in these robberies. And so there's a mob and luckily he's on the roof. All of a sudden the guy who owns the house comes up— he's a very respect[ed] man—he stands them down and vouches for this guy.

Next day the guy gets a phone call: "You're required at a meeting in Savile Town at the Community Center."

He said "What have I done wrong? I've done nothing wrong."

They said, "No no no, you've been wronged. A member of our community has wronged you. We'd like you to turn up and you'll have the option to accept the apology and then the [Sharia] council will pass judgment. Or if you don't, they will ruminate on it and come to their own conclusion."

It was a Sharia court and he was going along to accept an apology—a white roofer. He went in that room. There were two police officers [who] sat bearing witness.

We got told it was a community dispute resolution meeting. That's one way of describing it. I call it a Sharia court.

Local police have never admitted that they oversaw the Sharee Council. And referring to it as a "dispute resolution" meeting seems to be a cover-up for the disturbing fact that this community is basically policing itself with the tacit approval of the state. I started to wonder, "If non-Muslims are already being dragged into internal Muslim proceedings, what else could be going on in this community?" I didn't have to wonder for long.

The Labour Party is known for its postal vote machine all across the United Kingdom, and there have been allegations of voter fraud across the country. Lockwood seemed to think postal votes were being used for voter fraud in Dewsbury: "[People were] going door to door taking people's postal votes off them. We reported it. It was criminal fraud. Kirklees Council bottled it. They had to call in the police but it was just a few police cautions, so they don't have to name who the culprits are. But we knew who they were. There's a Muslim mosque committee...since 1987...owed over 50,000 in rent that Kirklees Council had never pursued because of 'sensitivities.'"

The more I learned about this community, the more it seemed to subsist separately from the state. Lockwood even revealed that it had its own way of "managing" funerals and burying the dead: "They didn't have a burial register. People didn't know who was in the ground. The council gave them six months to tidy it up. They were charging Pakistani families nearly twice as much as Indian, Gujarati families. So that's the Masonic element of it if you like...where the favours are. A lot of the criminality around here stems from the poorer community, which is not to say it doesn't go [deeper] it certainly does."

Lockwood also pointed out that the community has a local drug problem—similar to many No Go Zones in Europe:

Back in 1996/97, the director of Lifeline [a UK drug addict charity] said Dewsbury's heroin problem was worse than London, Liverpool, or Glasgow. Our addicts were, on average, five years younger. I lost my best mate to an overdose. I can name ten friends who have lost children or grandchildren to heroin.

Mostly it comes from Afghanistan/Pakistan. In terms of how it gets here—East Africa and then back round. [Sometimes] through Turkey. [Sometimes] through mainland Europe. [They're] massive on cocaine now. A bed manufacturing family—three directors were caught on the Paraguay, Colombia, Brazil border they were caught with a kilogram of cocaine and £100,000 which they said was to provide timber bed frames.

Are they selling to themselves? Their own community? Their own kids?

They have a problem, but mostly [they sell to] the white community.

After learning about the many changes this area has experienced, I started to wonder if it would ever return to the way it was. Lockwood is not optimistic about getting his hometown back from its new inhabitants. He explains,

The retail profile of the town has radically altered. It's gone. We can't even sustain a McDonald's in this town anymore.

No, there's nothing to get back. I'm not warning that. It's just reflecting on it. Because Kirklees Council has plans to build 4,000 homes on greenbelt land…there's two things you never see when you go around Savile Town: a dog or a for sale sign. They're building those 4,000 homes, not for me, my family. They're building it for the people who need it who are right there.

Both [people coming in and having so many kids]. And again you talk about the unacknowledged issues...It's a perfect storm.

Dewsbury may be an extreme example of what can happen when such a dramatic shift occurs in an area's demographics. But it is not a unique instance of what can happen when migration is left unchecked. Britain's population is drastically changing across the board. The white British population was 86.8 percent across England in 2001. In 2011, it stood at 79.8 percent. In Birmingham in 2001, it was 65.6 percent. Now it is less than 53.1 percent. Luton has gone from 64.9 percent to 44.6 percent, and Newham, a borough in East London, has gone from 33.6 percent to 16.7 percent in just ten years.

East London was the scene of the aforementioned Tower Hamlets scandal involving the now deposed Mayor Lutfur Rahman. Walking on the streets outside the Saudi-funded East London mosque is like being transplanted to some Bangladeshi or Pakistani city center. Even the street signs are in Urdu—a language associated with Muslims in India, Pakistan, and Bangladesh. The mosque itself has hosted the usual, unsavory types, and it has been investigated for terrorist links and leaflets that were allegedly handed out in its vicinity promoting death for those who insult Islam.

It is jarring to see the words "BRICK LANE"—one of the area's only remaining tourist attractions, ironically due to its South Asian cuisine—emblazoned in a foreign language beneath an English sign. Even the staunchest proponents of multiculturalism would surely agree that a native culture should always maintain its identity when it is introduced to other cultures. Sadly, the surrounding areas of the Commercial Road—which is just moments away from Britain's financial center (Canary Wharf)—are basically unicultural, and the predominant culture is not British.

The same translated signs appear on almost every street nearby. Even local landmarks have been renamed in honor of the area's newest residents. Altab Ali Park, just a few steps from the mosque, was renamed in 1998 in honor of a Bangladeshi man who was murdered nearby in a racially motivated attack in 1978. Before that, it was known as St. Mary's Park, after the fourteenth century church that stood next to it. The church was bombed during the World War II London Blitz. Dilapidated graves of historical British figures still sit in the center of the park. Their epitaphs are barely legible, and a modernist, metallic memorial overshadows them from the other side of the park.

The son of King Charles I's hangman is buried there, as is Sir John Cass who helped build many churches around the capital. In a sense, it is a fitting epitaph in itself that besides the East London Mosque, he is buried where his legacy has been most trodden upon.

The supplantation of Britain's churches by mosques came up recently when the Gatestone Institute reported 500 churches have closed in Britain's capital since 2001 and the number of mosques in the city is now above 420. The institute noted,

The Hyatt United Church was bought by the Egyptian community to be converted to a mosque. St Peter's Church has been converted into the Madina Mosque. The Brick Lane Mosque was built on a former Methodist church. Not only buildings are converted, but also people. The number of converts to Islam has doubled; often they embrace radical Islam, as with Khalid Masood, the terrorist who struck Westminster.

The *Daily Mail* published photographs of a church and a mosque a few meters from each other in the heart of London. At the Church of San Giorgio, designed to accommodate 1,230 worshipers, only 12 people gathered to celebrate Mass. At the Church of Santa Maria, there were 20.

The nearby Brune Street Estate mosque has a different problem: overcrowding. It's [a] small room and can contain only 100. On Friday, the faithful must pour into the street to pray. Given the current trends, Christianity in England is becoming a relic, while Islam will be the religion of the future.[20]

Houses of worship are not the only buildings in the area that are being influenced by these new residents. The restaurants in the area are all halal, and almost all the clothing stores sell hijabs, niqabs, and traditional Islamic menswear.

Even graffiti is influenced by the shifting demographics in the area. "No Borders" is scrawled across walls as well as stenciled signs declaring, "Liberation not Deportation," and urging locals to "Resist Immigration Raids."

The long-standing street market that runs the one-third mile stretch between Vallance Road and the Blind Beggar pub is now an almost entirely South Asian affair. While the city's crony capitalistic excess looms in the backdrop—exemplified by London's newborn, modernist, glass and steel skyscrapers—men and women of Pakistani, Bengali, Indian, and other Asian descent shuffle up and down the street picking up ingredients for dinner, stopping to chat, and bagging some bargains from the street stalls selling jewelry and clothing for unbelievably low prices.

On the surface, this area seems perfectly pleasant. But behind the scenes, local Islamic bookshops sell books making the Quranic case for polygamy and encouraging women to wear the niqab. In fact, if you pay attention to the political material in the area, you will notice a pattern tying into other Muslim-dominated areas in Europe. "How can we fight for socialism?" reads a poster wrapped around a lamppost. "Gaza Needs Our Voices Now," reads a t-shirt hanging in the window of a local clothing store, with a web link to an anti-Israel page promoting links to anti-Semitic authors, websites, and other resources.

The marker-pen-scrawled graffiti on the outside of Booth House, which was named for the Salvation Army founder William Booth, reveals something about the local mindset. For whatever reason, a local rumor pervades that Booth was a gay drug taker. Scribbled on some outdoor signage are the following sentences: "F**k Booth House," "0207 123 C**T," "William Booth was an opium addicted homosexual." What I found particularly upsetting about these sentences wasn't that they lacked a typical dry, British wit, but that they conveyed an irrational anger typical of those who flirt with radicalism.

While reporting the recent influx of mosques in Britain, the Gatestone Institute also pointed out an interesting development in Birmingham: "In Birmingham, the second-largest British city, where many jihadists live and orchestrate their attacks, an Islamic minaret dominates the sky. There are petitions to allow British mosques to call the Islamic faithful to prayer on loudspeakers three times a day." Though the minaret and petition are unsettling, what is most disturbing about Birmingham is the fact that Sparkbrook, an inner-city area in Southeast Birmingham, is quickly becoming known as Britain's jihadist capital.

Freelance journalist Patrick Christys—whose reporting was featured in the *Daily Mirror* newspaper shortly after the Westminster Bridge attack—provided an exclusive report for the purposes of this book after visiting Sparkbrook:

> Before he became Prime Minister, David Cameron went to visit Balsall Heath, a deprived, Muslim-dominated area just south of Birmingham City Centre. During that 2007 trip he stayed with a man called Abdullah Rehman for three days, developing his flagship concept "The Big Society" which he fashioned as defining the tenure as Prime Minister.
>
> Now, the region where Mr. Cameron formed his vision for Britain is a hotbed of Islamic extremism and one of the most segregated, divided communities in the country.
>
> There is a strange paradox about Balsall Heath, which lies within Birmingham's "Balti Triangle"—an area famed for its Indian and South Asian foods. The

Muslim community is often given credit for drasti-cally improving Balsall Heath and then, in the eyes of some locals at least, ruining it again.

The inner city ward was arguably Europe's largest open air brothel until 1995, when a group of vigilan-tes, many Muslims, took a stand and engaged in street patrols in order to stop such behaviors.

Amazingly, the well armed gangsters and pimps backed off—a major success for local campaigners.

But what sprung up in its place was a section of Britain's second largest city where English is a second language and white faces are stared at when they walk down the street.

Down the road in Sparkbrook, Reverend Becky Allan told me she was "the exception" because she was the only white woman living on her road, and her children were the only youths with blonde hair.

A Henry Jackson Society report into the terrorism connections in the United Kingdom noted 39 people had been imprisoned for terror offences in Balsall Heath, Sparkbrook, Springfield and a handful of other surrounding towns.

The chief councillor at anti-terror and substance abuse clinic "KIKIT" told me that 370 people had been referred to him in the last year alone, 70 of which required intensive de-radicalization. Two had already bought flights to Syria.

Local elected councillors are adamant that the figures are distorted because of the 39 currently in prison, who were all part of just two jihadi gangs. They are keen to stress there were not 39 separate, completely unique terrorists, rather just two terror cells.

But when asked if this means one can expect the number of terrorists from Sparkbrook and neighboring towns to drastically diminish, the answer is no.

Councillor Mohammad Azim said: "We can't say the problem has completely gone. There will be others, other actors, other groups.

"But the community strength is building and with that, we can protect against extremism.

"This isn't a great place for extremists, you are more likely to get caught here than other places."

The notion that more terrorists are being caught in the West Midlands because the anti-terror police here are better than anywhere else in the country is folly. The police are better at catching terrorists in Birmingham because there are more would-be terrorists in Birmingham.

You only have to walk down Haguely Road, where Westminster attacker Khalid Masood once called home, and Alum Rock Road, where armed police routinely arrest terror suspects on the street, to take in the pungent smell of cannabis and see needles lining the streets.

Radicalism across the continent is closely correlated to drugs, crime, and poverty. But it is also important to stress that while the political Left would stop here in terms of motivating factors, the tipping point, or core issue, always comes back down to one book and those interpreting it for the people unable to interpret it themselves: the Quran.

Even in the Middle East, in its original Arabic, the Quran is said to be incredibly difficult to interpret. A handful of translations are attributed to just one phrase, or sentence. In English, it is even harder and it is also considered no longer the true word of Allah by the most fundamental of Islamic scholars.

Patrick continues,

> Still, KIKIT's leader Mohammed Ashfaq says the root cause of terror in the region is youth unemployment, poverty, and perhaps the most anti-Islamic of things—drugs.
>
> Ashfaq said: "I had a young lad come to me once saying he was having extremist thoughts. He was smoking skunk and crack every night in the park.
>
> "What happened was a hate preacher had started tagging along with their group and filling their minds with shit while they were high, showing them videos of dead Muslims killed by U.S. airstrikes.
>
> "I told him to listen to this preacher when he wasn't high. He did and came back the next day and said he'd never listen to him again."
>
> Drugs also offer another way into jihadism. Mind altering substances are forbidden under Islam and any users are de facto sinners. But jihad offers "a fast-track to redemption."
>
> Mr Ashfaq said: "Vulnerable people are turning to religion and they're being manipulated. They're lied to about the Quran and they're told jihad will absolve them of the crimes of their past."

But the Quran does indeed offer absolution for "martyrs," and the Quran, as evidenced earlier, is at its core a violent tract filled with aggression towards Jews, Christians, unbelievers (kuffar), apostates, and those committing Fitna (a term I'll get into later in this book).

Hate preachers are not so much telling lies about the Quran as they are telling the blood-curdling, honest truth about it. And young, malleable minds on drugs are empty vessels to be filled with this hate.

The fact they have this vacuum in their minds is of course linked to national identity and a void of British values that has been brought about since the 1960s. The Left's long march through Britain's institutions—stripping away conservatism and Christian morals—has left these people with nothing to guide them. No flag to rally around. In many cases, quite literally. It is extremely rare to come across a British flag, even on government buildings. As opposed to the monopoly Old Glory has in many towns and cities in the United States. When they come for your flag, they're coming for your identity. When they kill your identity, evil flourishes.

Patrick continues,

In an area like Sparkbrook, where unemployment, boredom, and poverty breed petty crime and drug abuse, there is often a lot that needs absolving through faith–it's fertile ground.

The term "Muslim area" can mean several things, but in Sparkbrook it means it belongs to the Muslims, that much is obvious.

As I walked down Alum Rock Road one man shouted: "Welcome to Alum Rock, white boy!"

One worker at the Mushtaq sweet shop said: "This is the most dangerous road in Britain, you don't go out here at night."

One local man, Paul Venn, added: "You should be teaching your kids to be a part of British society and life. But I had a terrorist living opposite me before he was sentenced to lifetime imprisonment.

"It's a closed off society. It's upsets community cohesion. There's a closed off, segregated mentality and they're not doing enough to tackle extremism."

But if you ask the leading figures from Sparkbrook Masjid and Islamic Centre about whether the area is a No Go Zone, they will tell you it is actually incredibly welcoming and they are doing everything within their powers to combat extremism.

The imam is adamant radicalization is taking place on laptops at home and not in the mosque. Indeed, the mosque is running anti-extremism programmes. He added: "Extremists cannot come here. They will be hounded out and reported to the police."

He admitted there are extremists in the area, but said they never come to the mosque and they do not make their true feelings known to the wider community.

He showed me a video [of] a West Indian man who arrived at the mosque the day after the Westminster terror attack demanding to convert to Islam.

They were concerned about his motives and recorded him consenting to become a Muslim of his own free will and with the best of intentions, just to be sure.

The mosque is currently serving the *Daily Mail* with a legal notice because the paper printed a picture of the mosque alongside a group of jihadis who had never visited it.

But they let me inside and, when the tour was over, the curator said, jokingly: "Look, now you can see, there are no AK-47s and bombs hidden anywhere!"

Another man who had assisted, Mohammed Ramzan, pointed at a board showing what times prayer would be. He quipped: "I'll even go to the extra sixth prayer, but I'll see you in the pub afterwards!"

The imam then added: "We cannot understand what the government and police are doing. These terrorists always seem to have been monitored for several years, so why are they still allowed on the streets? We call on the government and MI5 to do more to combat these terrorists."

The Muslims at the mosque were some of the most welcoming, kind-hearted and open people you could ever meet, but one wonders whether they just don't quite get it on two fronts:

a) Are these middle aged men out of touch with the firebrand Islamic youth of the day to the point where they, completely accidentally, miss the warning signs or,

b) When this area is described as 'no go', it's not to say every Muslim is unwelcoming of the kuffar. No, it's just that it is undeniably an area with no white faces, little in the way of the English language, and the constant impending threat of drug and gang related crime mixed in with, in places, utter squalor.

Khalid Masood's apartment was above a Persian restaurant called Shiraz. The landlord has flown back to Iran since Masood's attack and has already sub-letted it to six other people.

It backs onto a rat-infested, needle-ridden alley-way with piles of human excrement on the floor.

The owner of a corner shop next door, whose landlord is the cousin, said he served Masood regularly and he usually smelled of alcohol. He would buy scratch-cards, Red Bull, and cashew nuts. That was it. [The owner] never saw him at any of the local mosques and did not deem him to be religious.

A letter from Her Majesty's Revenue and Customs—Britain's IRS—shows he had not paid his taxes and was clearly in debt.

Neighbours say they woke up to police pointing guns at them in their own bedrooms, and only found out Masood's address because when he was shot dead he had a letter in his back pocket with his flat number and postcode on it.

The defining characteristic of Sparkbrook is perhaps one of the prime examples of how we use the word "Muslim" too liberally and without further delineation. Too often, the "Muslim community" is presented to the world as one, singular, and indistinguishable group despite its vast differences and violent rivalries. For instance, Britain's Ahmadiyya community is very different from other Muslim communities. It is often on the front lines of the fight against extremism in Islam, and it also does public relations for the same people who would see its community slaughtered as apostates.

Ahmadis, originating from northern India, are a reformist Islamic movement that is believed to be unrepresentative of Islam, especially by doctrinaire Sunnis. They have been persecuted the world over. And they are often held up by the establishment press as examples of "good Muslims" who oppose terrorism without any mention of the differences that set them apart from other Muslims.

No better example of this exists than in the reporting that immediately followed the terrorist attack on Britain's Parliament in March 2017. After Khalid Masood mowed down people on the Westminster Bridge, killing four and injuring dozens, Britain's media leapt to the defense of the country's three million Muslims. Stories about a group of Muslim women linking hands on Westminster Bridge and condemning terrorism spread across the media. The *Metro* newspaper mentioned Ahmadi activism in the eleventh of fourteen paragraphs on the matter, but it refused to dedicate any space to an explanation of who the Ahmadiyya are. The same explanation was lacking in the coverage from the *Independent*, the *Telegraph*, and the *Mirror*. CNN, *HuffPost*, and the *Sun* made no mention at all of Ahmadis or how they make up less than 1 percent of Britain's Muslim population and are regarded as unbelievers by the majority. This means that when reformist Ahmadis stand up to terrorism, they are presented as public relations buffers for a large number of Muslims in the United Kingdom who do not reject terrorism, Sharia, or other negative elements of Islam.

Before you ask, there is plenty of evidence to support the claim that a large number of Muslims in the United Kingdom have abhorrent, murderous, and criminal views. Twenty-seven percent of those polled in the United Kingdom said they sympathized with the attacks on the French magazine *Charlie Hebdo*, with a staggering 78 percent supporting punishment for the publication of cartoons featuring Muhammad. Sixty-eight percent of those polled said they support the arrest and prosecution of British people who "insult Islam."[21] Public polling from ICM in 2006 revealed that 20 percent of British Muslims sympathize with the 7/7 bombers who brought terror to the streets of the British capital, killing fifty-two and injuring hundreds.[22] This number rose to one in four British Muslims, according to the NOP Research Group's findings for Britain's Channel 4 television station. Today, with a British Muslim population of over three million, "one in four" Muslims translates to roughly 750,000 terror-sympathizing, or at least terror-excusing, people in the United Kingdom.

As I noted in an article[23] exactly one year to the day before the Westminster Attack, this number rises for younger British Muslims—a sure sign that radicalization in schools, mosques, and prisons (often via Saudi-funded groups) is creating a long-term problem in Europe. Thirty-one percent of younger British Muslims endorsed or excused the 7/7 bombings of 2005, and 18 percent have said they would not report a planned terrorist attack if they knew of a plot. Such statistics are echoed throughout the Western world. In 2007, the Pew Research Center found that 26 percent of young Muslims in America believed suicide bombings are justified. Thirty-five percent in Britain, 42 percent in France, 22 percent in Germany, and 29 percent in Spain agreed.[24]

Devout Muslims are reportedly three times more likely to believe that suicide bombings are justified. This is deeply concerning, especially when you consider that 86 percent of Muslims in Britain "feel that religion is the most important thing in their life."[25] In 2015, it was revealed that 45 percent of British Muslims think that hate preachers who advocate violence against the West represent "mainstream Islam."

The devastating facts continue:

- Forty percent of British Muslims say they want Sharia law in the West, while 41 percent oppose it
- One in five prisoners in the United Kingdom's top security jails is now Muslim, a rise of 23 percent from just six years ago
- In total, a 20 percent increase in the jail population in Britain has been outstripped by the rise in Muslim inmates—up 122 percent over thirteen years
- Thirty-six percent of sixteen- to twenty-four-year-old Muslims believe that if a Muslim converts to another religion, they should be punished by death
- Thirty-five percent of Muslims say they would prefer to send their children to an Islamic school, and 37 percent of sixteen- to twenty-four-year-olds say they want government-funded Islamic schools to send their kids to
- Seventy-four percent of sixteen- to twenty-four-year-olds prefer Muslim women to wear the veil, compared with only 28 percent for those over the age of fifty-five[26]

In light of these statistics, it is not surprising that Britain's security services have, at a minimum, three thousand people under surveillance in the United Kingdom at any given time. But there is simply no way that an MI5 with four thousand employees can effectively monitor everyone harboring jihadist sympathies, whether overtly or covertly. This was evident in the aftermath of Khalid Masood's terrorist attack when Prime Minister Theresa May said that Masood was "not part of the current intelligence picture." She stated this at the same time an Al Qaeda terrorist manual was downloaded at least 55,000 times from British-based IP addresses in a three-month period.[27]

Britain's struggle with radical Islam is incredibly complex. Though it is the subject of many reports, books, documentaries, and investigations, even the British government finds it difficult to fully expose and investigate the matter, which is not the least due to foreign interference. Britain's government has had an "Arabist leaning" for centuries, and the current government is no different. It still encourages and attracts vast investments and trade deals with Arab nations. But these relationships come at a hefty price diplomatically and domestically.

Qatar, for instance, is said to own more London real estate than the Queen, commanding a whopping twenty-four million square feet of space. And the British government has almost obsessively looked to the Saudis for a source of military equipment sales revenue. The contracts—most famously underscored by Margaret Thatcher's billion-pound Al-Yamamah deal in the 1980s—appear to have come with strings attached and serious consequences: the British government is expected to turn a blind eye to Saudi mosque funding in the United Kingdom, and Britain must give fealty to whatever the capricious Saudi stance on the Muslim Brotherhood may be.

Most recently, the Muslim Brotherhood—an early twentieth-century Islamist movement led by Mohamed Badie—found itself at the nexus of UK-Saudi relations. In 2014, the British government commissioned a report on the Brotherhood's activities led by then Ambassador to Saudi Arabia Sir John Jenkins. Those who had any background on this issue or any inclination to investigate it knew it was a conflict of interest. For their usual convoluted, internecine reasons, the Saudis and the Brotherhood were "on a break." They weren't getting along, to put it mildly.

The chairman of the House of Commons Foreign Affairs Committee put his finger on the issue in the parliamentary report on political Islam. The report stated that Sir John Jenkins's appointment to lead the review, while he served as UK ambassador to Saudi Arabia, was misguided. It created the perception that Saudi Arabia, an interested party that had designated the Brotherhood as a terrorist organization the month before the review was announced, might have undue influence on the review's report. The Saudis, it seemed, were attempting to leverage British government pressure against the Brotherhood for their own domestic and regional aims. Once this had been achieved, the government's report was massively watered down and its scope was reduced.

"The main findings of the review support the conclusion that membership of, association with, or influence by the Muslim Brotherhood should be considered as a possible indicator of extremism," said former Prime Minister of the United Kingdom David Cameron. This statement was a far cry from the terror-affiliation rationale that the British government had first proffered.

Saudi Arabia's influence, while significant, is not a dominating factor in British Islam. As Innes Bowen at the *Spectator* noted in 2014, Saudi Arabia supports fewer than 10 percent of Britain's mosques.[28] While the Saudis are undoubtedly responsible for supporting extremist-leaning mosques and schools—the source of Wahhabism and Salafism across the West—we have learned that a predominant number of mosques in the United Kingdom are supported by or follow the shadowy Deobandi sect of Islam. The reach of this sect has stretched from Northern England to San Bernardino, California. We will learn more about this terrifying reach in the next chapter.

SEVEN

FROM SAN BERNARDINO, WITH LIES

We cannot turn against one another by letting this fight be defined as a war between America and Islam. That, too, is what groups like ISIL want. ISIL does not speak for Islam.

—FORMER PRESIDENT BARACK OBAMA,
FOLLOWING THE SAN BERNARDINO TERRORIST ATTACK

"I t's that one. It's definitely that mosque," I told my colleague Michelle as I swiped across Google Maps on my iPhone, looking for mosques and masjids in the San Bernardino area, just hours after Syed Farook and his radical bride Tashfeen Malik slaughtered fourteen people at a holiday work party in the Californian city.

The attack on Wednesday, December 2, 2015, had sent us hurtling up highways 15 and 215 from San Diego, equipped only with my laptop, Michelle's ageing SLR camera, and the knowledge that we would go to places and ask questions that "mainstream" journalists wouldn't dare.

Once we arrived on scene, police tape was easily circumvented. We should always be grateful for our first responders and those who keep us safe, but it was evident to me in those early hours after the attack that the local police were not trained, equipped, or ready to deal with a situation like this. Whole blocks had to be shut down and reopened minute-by-minute, and the entire international press corps had descended and were, as we always do, demanding answers to questions that hadn't even been asked yet.

At one point the barricades blocking the road that led to the scene of the attack extended just beyond a church parking lot. We easily drove through the parking lot and exited on the other side, right in the middle of the crime scene. If we had wanted to, we could have tampered with the crime scene, planted evidence, or destroyed some. It was all a bit embarrassing, really. We snapped a few photos down the road and left before anyone saw us.

At the same time, journalists from CBS, NBC, and almost every other news network stood penned in half a mile away, tweeting "live shots" from a press conference that would take place four hours later. But I wanted more than that. And I don't particularly like standing for hours on end in hot weather, on concrete. The journalists were holding press conferences in the middle of a road. And constantly pushing them back by minutes and hours. I simply didn't have the patience for that.

That need for real news and interesting information brought us face-to-face with bomb disposal robots, as concerned residents looked on and police wondered how two pesky journalists had stumbled upon their follow-up operations. Drive. Literally and psychologically, a drive had brought us there. We refused to be confined to the persistently delayed press conference where all we'd be treated to was a confirmation of a chain of events established hours ago. If we were lucky, perhaps a good communications staffer would toss out a piece of color for headline writers.

During those first few days, we found our own color, whether it was bullet holes peppering the pavement or the wailing mother desperate to reach her child, who was left home alone for hours as a result of the area's lockdown. I was half-tempted to tell her, "You know we can probably find a way around that roadblock." But in situations like this, you rely on luck as much as you rely on intuition. Push too much and you'll end up on the "shit list," and that would have made Michelle's job as our liaison with the police and FBI much more difficult.

In a way it is a balancing act. But when everyone else is happy to sit in the middle of the seesaw, it seems especially interesting to me to try to tilt it back and forth, even just a little. And that is precisely what we did: rock it just enough to expose something that eventually led to much larger questions. Questions like, "Why did the U.S. government stop monitoring a hardline Islamist group?" and "How did Tashfeen Malik pass her background checks to get into the country?" and "What are they teaching people in these mosques, and why is no one willing to ask even the most rudimentary questions about it?"

Allegedly, the cause of Farook and Malik's December attack was the Christmas party they were required to attend. However, anyone familiar with terror and its ideologies will tell you Christmas is scarcely a radicalizing factor. No one sees a strip of tinsel and decides to start assembling pipe bombs as a result. I was determined to get to the root of their hatred for the country they had made their home. This same hatred had caused them to abandon their children, their families, and commit one of the most shocking acts of terror in America since 9/11.

It wasn't the scale or even the method of the attack that made it shocking. It was the fact that these two people in their late twenties slaughtered people they knew—coworkers, people they presumably exchanged pleasantries with every week. What causes a person—and even more gruesome, two married parents—to be so callous that familial and community bonds are so easily severed?

"Yeah it's definitely that one," I said again to Michelle as we sped towards the Dar Al Uloom Al Islamiyah mosque in the northern part of the city.

My instincts were correct, as counter-terrorism analyst Phil Haney later confirmed to the media and also to me in an interview for this book. Was he surprised San Bernardino was the site of a terrorist attack? I asked him in April 2017, and he replied, "No. I recognized [San Bernardino]…the people who transited through that Masjid were already in our case. Surprise is not the right word. I knew, infuriating? Yes. Surprising? No."

Haney claimed the U.S. government under the Obama administration had shut down his investigations into Tablighi Jamaat. To this day, at the time of this book's publication, Haney is still fighting the U.S. government even after the change in administration. He wants the government to admit that it had an open investigation about this movement and lied about closing it. So far, he hasn't had any luck in this endeavor. But Haney and others still maintain documents and files that confirm what the government refuses to admit.

Customs and Border Protection, which is part of the Department for Homeland Security, commented on the matter with a predictably unintelligible garble of newspeak:

On September 16, 2003, in alignment with the Homeland Security Presidential Directive-6 the Terrorist Screening Center (TSC) was established to maintain the

United States Government's Consolidated Terrorist Watchlist and to support all Federal, state, local, territorial, and tribal law enforcement agencies that conduct terrorist related screening. With the inception of the TSC, the United States Government established a streamlined process for creation and tracking of lookouts or watchlist records for those individuals who are known to be or suspected of involvement in terrorist related activities. CBP personnel are not permitted to independently create terrorist related lookouts for known or suspected terrorists in any CBP database. CBP personnel must provide that information through the established processes and procedures within the agency to nominate individuals into the federal government's terrorist watchlist.

The Office for Civil Rights and Civil Liberties is an important part of DHS's internal oversight. CRCL was established by Congress, in part, to ensure that all DHS employees are following proper policy and procedure, including upholding basic constitutional principles, while performing the DHS mission. CRCL reviews allegations of civil rights violations and makes policy recommendations to ensure that the Department upholds the Constitution and our laws as it carries out its operations. Any implication that CRCL does not share the important overall mission of DHS to protect the homeland is misplaced.

Basically, the organization told me that Haney had initiated and maintained the "investigation" himself, and that he shouldn't have been working on it. Thank God he was.

Even though he is clearly an expert on Islam, Haney's slightly eccentric demeanor may make it easy for authorities to dismiss him. He speaks incredibly softly but with an unexpectedly high pitch. And he reels off information like an Islam-obsessed Rain Man. "If you're a gardener you recognize weeds in your garden," he says of San Bernardino. He continues,

> If you're a counter-terrorism specialist you recognize emerging trends within the world you live. And so it wasn't surprising at all. If you have a masjid called Dar Al Uloom Al Islamiyah, if you're even adequately familiar with that name you know it's part of the Deobandi, Tablighi Jamaat movement because that's what they call their mosques. It's a brand name like Burger King or McDonalds. You know if it's a Dar Al Uloom Al Islamiyah it's gonna be a Deobandi masjid and they will probably speak Pashtun or Urdu. And they will be pro-Sharia. And they will probably be hosting people from other parts of the world to come and visit which is exactly what they do.

It all checks out. If what Haney says is true, and the Obama administration really was responsible for shutting down his investigation, then the former president should be hauled in front of a congressional committee to explain his actions, which continue to endanger U.S. citizens.

In the immediate aftermath of the San Bernardino attack, then President Barack Obama addressed the nation, stating, among other things,

> The FBI is still gathering the facts about what happened in San Bernardino, but here is what we know.

The victims were brutally murdered and injured by one of their coworkers and his wife. So far, we have no evidence that the killers were directed by a terrorist organization overseas, or that they were part of a broader conspiracy here at home. But it is clear that the two of them had gone down the dark path of radicalization, embracing a perverted interpretation of Islam that calls for war against America and the West. They had stockpiled assault weapons, ammunition, and pipe bombs. So this was an act of terrorism, designed to kill innocent people.[1]

The language of the statement is intentionally precise. The claim that Syed Farook and Tashfeen Malik were not instructed by a foreign organization—namely the Islamic State—was both premature and a means to an end. The purpose of this claim was to underscore the long-standing "lone wolf" narrative that has little bearing or relevance on the style of modern, asymmetric warfare that Islamic fundamentalists seek to encourage their followers and sympathizers to undertake. Most of these undertakings may not be directly instructed by jihadist leaders, but they are not "copycats" of "real" acts of extremist terrorism. Not when they occur so frequently in so many different parts of the world—from Berlin to San Bernardino. They should be recognized for what they are: iterations of the same prevailing, bloodthirsty, and chaos-inducing jihadist ideology. If we fail to acknowledge this, we will also fail to see the threads that tie these "copy cats" to their sources.

Before immigrating to America, Tashfeen Malik studied at the Al Huda School in Pakistan. A perfunctory intelligence check should have revealed her link to this fundamentalist, Wahhabist,

Islamic seminary for women. Instead, she was permitted to enter the United States "under the radar" on a fiancée visa that U.S. authorities now admit was not subject to the appropriate levels of scrutiny at the application level. The application was "sloppily" processed, in the words of U.S. officials speaking months after the atrocity. And it ended up costing innocent citizens their lives.

Between Tashfeen's study at Al Huda and Syed's attendance at the Darul Al Uloom Al Islamiyah, it should have been obvious that the pair showed signs of radicalism or at least a propensity for radicalization. But the West has become lazy when dealing with Islam. This is mostly thanks to social democrats, liberals, and their media colleagues who jump to the defense of fundamentally un-Western cultural characteristics, such as support for Sharia law and the hijab.

Haney often speaks of "indicators," like the ones Tashfeen and Syed displayed, that the Left is responsible for keeping off the radar. He oozes frustration when he sees his former colleagues being forced—by their politically motivated bosses—to ignore signs that are evident to even a graduate-level Islam buff. "I saw it with the madrassa boys," he said, speaking of young men identified as future leaders within Muslim communities around America. He continued,

> They've been chosen by the imam of their local masjid....they were all ordinary except for one thing...their ability to memorize the Quran. They started to become Hafiz [people who memorized the Quran]. They started memorizing the Quran since they were four, five, six years old. They go into the Madrassas here in the United States not overseas,

here. All they did was focus on memorization of the Quran.

So by the time they get to be 16, 17, 18 years old—graduation time from high school—they never even got through GED. But they were then qualified because of the fact that they're Hafiz and have been recognized by their community to attend an Alim program in South Africa where they speak in English. It only costs about $1,200 a year. Nobody's looking over their shoulder. I saw these kids go out year after year and I would interview them literally face to face during Ramadan when they would come back to spend time with their families. And they would go home and they would lead prayer. We both knew very well.

The first two or three years they didn't necessarily catch on that there was an emerging pattern.

They became a lot more assertive in our interviews. I suppose they thought that because they had mastered a subject they would leave me behind. That I wouldn't be able to keep up with them in terms of the abstract concepts. They found out that that wasn't the case.

The last year I worked on the case they all diverted, went to a different port but Atlanta. It meant they were all talking. Detroit, New York ...

What I also learned is my own colleagues at the other ports did not interview them. Which told me there's the hole. My own colleagues didn't have the most basic, fundamental capacity to look through the flights and realize there were individuals coming that were going to literally stand in front of them that had cases that were four and five years old.

Not everything can be depended on by machine. As Janet Napolitano said, "we didn't get a ping." She made us look like we were addicted to technology. The only way we would possibly recognize a terrorist is if the machine said he was one, when he's actually standing right in front of you.

And that's the corrosive effect of the policies of the last administration that we basically just handcuffed every officer on the line who should essentially be an intelligence officer that can basically recognize what I call the indicators.

There's no substitute for human intelligence. And here you have an agency with 20,000 plus people stationed at 350 airports and seaports around the country who, if all they had was the most basic, fundamental observational skills could have probably stopped most of the terrorist attacks that we've seen happen, which has been my operating premise all along. Because when you see indicators right in front of you, you need to have the authority to follow up on them. That's what the CBP was created for.

Michigan, Minnesota, New York, Atlanta—those states are among... that's also where a very large Tablighi, Deobandi community is.

Hopefully, members of Trump's administration will follow Haney's "operating premise" so other terrorist attacks that probably could be stopped are thwarted at the onset.

San Bernardino was, as you can imagine, somewhat of a ghost town during the first few days that followed the attack. Residents were in shock. It was palpable as they shuffled along the pavements outside the location of the attack—the Inland Regional Center—to light candles at the crossroads and place wreaths, flowers, teddy bears, and flags nearby.

As we arrived at the mosque, we saw a few journalists who had sussed out the location before us. It was remarkable to me that out of the several hundred journalists dispatched to the Inland Empire, there were barely over a dozen willing to question Farook's religious leaders. Or at least, I hoped they were willing to. I could sense their discomfort and unwillingness to be even mildly probing as we dawdled outside the mosque.

I've agonized over their behavior for some time. Perhaps it came down to a difference between American and British reporting. Part of the difference may also have stemmed from the fact that many of these journalists were simply local stringers who probably couldn't finger a jihadist if he or she were screaming "Allahu Akbar" in their faces.

Some of the "locals" leaned into car windows and asked basic questions that wouldn't exactly excite their editors but also wouldn't upset anyone: "Did you know Syed Farook and Tashfeen Malik? Did you ever see them at the mosque? Did they ever say anything out of place?"

Frankly, "out of place" would have been a good thing. Considering the supremacist attitude of those leading Deobandi mosques—something they impart upon their followers by encouraging them to live their lives in the way of Muhammed—an "out of place" attitude or comment in a place like the Darul Uloom Islamiyah would probably be more pro-Western.

It was a Friday afternoon, and prayers had just let out at the mosque. Cars streamed down the palm-tree-lined path from the mosque towards the road. We, like other members of the press, flagged down drivers. Most of the people leaving the Dar Al Uloom Al Islamiyah didn't want to speak to us. Understandably so, perhaps. I lost interest in the chase pretty quickly, as main-stream news reporters continued to ask softball questions, inter-rupting anything of substance that might be said.

"What are your thoughts on the attack?" I heard someone ask.

With questions like that, what did they expect? Someone to jump out of a Toyota Prius with an ISIS flag yelling, "Alhamdul-lilah! Magnificent attack! I support it 100 percent!"?

Essentially, the journalists became public relations operatives for Islamism, asking easily answered, leading questions in order to write reports like the one published by the Canadian state broadcaster CBC. Just three days after the attack, the CBC wrote,

> He prayed at their mosque here in Riverside, Calif., performed cleansing ablutions alongside them, sought counsel about how the philosophies of Islam could apply to his life. Once or twice, one worshipper said, he even led Quranic recitations when an imam was absent. "He had a beautiful voice," the former mosque board member said.
>
> And yet, Syed Rizwan Farook, the San Bernardino gunman, was by no means a true Muslim. Of this, Hussam Ayloush was unequivocal.
>
> "This crime was not committed by a Muslim," Ayloush told a congregation of the faithful, his preaching

echoing through the Mosque of Riverside during Jumu'ah, the Friday prayer service.

"It was committed by a criminal. By someone who has no value for life.... No one should feel [Farook] represents us. No one should feel we need to apologize. No one in America needs to apologize."[2]

Author Matt Kwong reported from another local mosque we visited, in Riverside, but he made the same contribution to the "Islamism PR effort" as the CBC. What he didn't realize, however, is that some of his reportage exposed the "Islam First" attitude of mosque-goers:

> As it emerged Friday that the FBI was now investigating the massacre as a "terrorist attack"—and that Malik had declared her allegiance to ISIS on Facebook—Salma Mahmoud braced for the anti-Islam blowback she has become all too familiar with.
>
> "When we heard about the shooting, the first thing we thought: 'Let it not be a Muslim. Let it not be someone Middle Eastern,'" the 18-year-old said following Friday prayers in Riverside.[3]

It's incredible that a person's first thoughts after a terrorist attack could effectively be "Oh goodness I hope this doesn't affect me or my religion" rather than "Oh goodness I hope everyone's okay." It reveals how many in these communities think. They come first. Not human life. Not the United States of America. Not human decency. Sadly, such a mindset is not so surprising when one remembers that the Quran teaches its followers to "Fight those who do not believe in Allah or in the Last

Day and who do not consider unlawful what Allah and His Messenger have made unlawful and who do not adopt the religion of truth from those who were given the Scripture—[fight] until they give the jizyah [tax on non-Muslims] willingly while they are humbled."

The same PR efforts employed by Kwong and the CBC can be seen in almost any Deobandi mosque-adjacent organization or community-facing project. What these organizations and projects do is not simply provide help and services to communities, they do these things to proselytize in the name of Islam. From Dewsbury, England, to Queens, New York, I witnessed this proselytizing first hand. And it is present in San Bernardino too.

Outside the Dar Al Uloom Al Islamiyah was a sign for the "Al-Shifa [Healing] Clinic," which provides medical services like mammograms, weight loss assistance, dental care, and much more. The first line of text on the clinic's website? "Al-Shifa Clinic is a shining example of how the teachings of Islam and compassion towards the sick and selfless service to those in need are molded into everyday practice."[4] Again, the supremacy and importance of Islam takes precedence over anything else. Whether they know it or not—and I suspect they do—they are adhering to religious instructions.

Al-Fadi, a former Muslim living in the West, identified such behavior in the book *The Quran Dilemma*, first published in 2011. "When I lived in Saudi Arabia, not only did I look at non-Muslims as second class, you would look at non-devout Muslims as second class citizens," Fadi told CBN News in an interview in 2012. "If Islam has to prosper, be the superior religion, then certain steps must be taken by its followers, including spreading Islam at any cost, including the sword and killing any opposition," he added.

He also identified where Western journalists, activists, and political leaders are going wrong:

> It is basically a proscriptive demand found in the Koran when it comes to jihad—killing the infidels, spreading Islam until there is no other religion on earth except the religion of Allah.
>
> The West does not know many, if not all, of these things because they're basically oblivious to what the Koran teaches as a whole. They're only fed portions of the Koran.[5]

That such views, whether indirectly adhered to, or intentionally directed upon, can be prevalent in de facto Los Angeles suburbs—an hour's drive away from glitzy Hollywood cocktail parties—must give us pause.

Often, the media is (wrongly) portrayed as being hostile toward Islam because, allegedly, it fixates on Muslim terrorist attacks in the West. In reality, Islam's "public relations officials" often try to distract the public from this topic by redirecting the narrative to gun-related crime or white nationalism. Indeed, Roshan Abbassi, one of the mosque leaders tasked with speaking to the press that day, used this exact tactic. "This past year we've had over 300 shootings," Abbassi claimed during the press conference held later that day. "How many of them were Muslims?" he asked.

Some leaving the mosque before we entered grinned with a childlike fascination at seeing so many cameras and journalists— a feeling of self-importance combined with awe and awkwardness. I got it. It was like the first time I walked into a television studio. I was excited and perplexed. "Who are all these people?

Are they all here for me? For us? This is strange." It's a completely natural reaction, even in the face of such carnage and tragedy. One has to reel adrenaline and bemusement in and remind oneself why this is all going on. As such, understandably, many simply drove away.

We were badgered by police and mosque leaders to stop asking the mosque congregants or "Jamaat" questions. Perhaps this wasn't their finest public relations moment. Why express so much anxiety about the congregants answering our basic questions about what goes on in a mosque just eight miles north of a terrorist attack? Finally, the levees broke. Mosque leaders could see we weren't going anywhere any time soon. What also became clear was that someone had coached the leaders on how to answer questions from the media. That coach appeared to be the Council on American-Islamic Relations (CAIR).

We trudged up the path towards the mosque, leaving the spike-topped gates, police, and palm trees behind us. Some of us just had our phones and our notepads. Others had small cameras and microphones. Some poor schmucks had been lugging around full-sized broadcasting equipment for days. One of the perils, though less of a workplace hazard than some, of being a news cameraman.

Upon entering the mosque, we removed our shoes, tucked them into shoe racks, and proceeded into an anteroom that led to the prayer hall. Men were ushered straight through, down the middle of the hallway, and into the masjid proper. Women, as you would expect, were shown through a passage to the left. It seemed like a completely arbitrary, though obviously symbolic, delineation, given we all ended up in the same room.

I was unsettled to see gender segregation in 2015 in a major U.S. city for a press conference involving some of the nation's largest news outlets. "I wonder how they treat women when there aren't cameras around," I thought. This regressive behavior has always made me very uneasy. It varies drastically depending on the location of a mosque in the world, its size, the sect of Islam the congregants adhere to, and so forth. In Queens, the Masjid Al-Falah—another leading Deobandi mosque affiliated with Tablighi activity in the United States—has a separate entrance gate on the street for women. In order to pray, the female congregants of that mosque must take a short walk down a slim, dark alley until they see a sign that reads, "Women [sic] Prayer Area."

I was lucky enough to have been raised in a relatively liberal sect of Islam. This sect is considered apostate by most Sunnis. But it allows women to wear whatever they like to the mosque—they often took full, fashionable advantage of this—and its small amounts of gender segregation are really only for show. When the mosque was full, men and women would sit alongside one another and usually socialize inside and outside of the prayer hall, before and after services.

As we waited for the conference to begin in the masjid, a few members of the mosque scurried around looking for chairs, picking them up from around the hall and setting up a row halfway toward the back of the room. "This is for your women," we were told.

Like hell it was.

Perhaps out of politeness or naive courtesy, a few women from the press gravitated toward that area. "Private property, show deference" I suppose was their logic. But just minutes after the presser began, the whole row had crept forward, leaving the confines of the chairs behind. It was heartening to see some resistance from them, but what I learned about the American press as a whole during the next thirty minutes was disappointing and terrifying.

A man in dark glasses with a shawl over his head and a chest-length, wiry, white beard identified himself as "Dr. Nadvi," the president and founder of the Dar Al Uloom Al Islamiyah congregation. He opened with a prayer:

> Bismillah, ar-Rahman, ar-Rahim. In the name of Allah, the most merciful…the Dar al Uloom Islami-yah and the Muslim community of California is deeply saddened and shocked by the recent shooting in San Bernardino, California. We pray for the victims and our deepest condolences to those affected by this tragedy. We stand with our fellow Americans in this difficult time. Please pray for the families and the victims of shootings in San Bernardino.

Odd, perhaps, that a Deobandi mosque president should think he could speak on behalf of all Muslims in California. But this is a pretty standard conflation that seeks to unite all Muslims under one banner, the Ummah. Broadly speaking, the conference was off to a good start. But just two minutes in (he was a slow speaker), the misdirection began.

"Our creator, Allah Subhanahu Wa Ta'ala [glory be to him] says," he announced, before reading in Arabic from Surah Five, Ayat Thirty-Two of the Quran, "Whoever kills a person, except as a punishment for murder or mischief in the land, [it is] as if he had killed all the human beings. And whoever will save a life shall be rewarded as if he saved all the human beings. This is the teachings of Islam." Alarm bells started ringing in my head.

Surah Five, Ayat Thirty-Two is often cited as a way to disassociate acts of terror from the teachings of the Quran. It's simply not an Islamic act, the spin doctors insist. But sadly, it isn't just the Muslim PR types who have bought into this claim. Just two months after the San Bernardino attack, then President Barack Obama sang from the same hymn sheet as the president of a Deobandi mosque. If that wasn't something to be mortified about, I don't know what is.

On the now archived Obama White House website, you can find the transcript of the president's February 2016 speech to an audience at the Islamic Society of Baltimore [emphasis added]:

> To use a little Christian expression—let your light shine. Because when you do you'll make clear that this is not a clash of civilizations between the West and Islam. This is a struggle between the peace-loving, overwhelming majority of Muslims around the world and a radical, tiny minority. And ultimately, I'm confident that the overwhelming majority will win that battle. Muslims will decide the future of your faith. And I'm confident in the direction that it will go.
>
> But across the Islamic world, influential voices should consistently speak out with an affirmative vision of their faith. And it's happening. These are the voices of Muslim clerics who teach that Islam prohibits terrorism, for **the Koran says whoever kills an innocent, it is as if he has killed all mankind.**
>
> These are the voices of Muslim scholars, some of whom join us today, who know **Islam has a tradition of respect for other faiths;** and Muslim teachers who point out that the first word revealed in the

> Koran—igra—means "read"—to seek knowledge,
> to question assumptions.[6]

Such statements are at best deeply unfortunate and at worst symbolic of a completely denialist and willful misrepresentation of the Quran itself. The fact that the president of the United States and the president of the Dar Al Uloom Al Islamiyah are both willing to revise the Quran implies that there is something deeply embarrassing about the reality of the Muslim holy book.

Throughout the press conference, the same verse was repeated in various way. By the end, it simply became "Whoever takes someone's life takes the life of all mankind." But again, this is a willful misrepresentation. Without paraphrasing, this is how Surah Five, Ayat Thirty-Two actually reads: "We ordained for the Children of Israel that if anyone slew a person—unless it be in retaliation for murder or for spreading mischief in the land—it would be as if he slew all mankind: and if anyone saved a life, it would be as if he saved the life of all humanity."

It's a subtle difference, but that caveat—"spreading mischief in the land"—reveals the actual intent of the Quran: to warn unbelievers and those who stymie the progress of Islam. In Islamic jurisprudence (fiqh) a fasadin is a person who causes "mischief." The president of the Dar Al Uloom uttered the word during his reading of the passage in Arabic.

"The nerve," I thought. Still, I understood how the mosque could probably get away with it in front of this audience of rookies and stringers.

The definition of the word fasadin extends to anyone who acts against Allah, causing disorder to the Ummah and its expansion. Disobedience and those who are disobedient toward Allah are considered "fasad," according to Islamic scholars. In Pakistan—a crucially relevant country in the context of the Hanafi school of jurisprudence which applies to Deobandis—there are legal grounds in the country's penal code for the crime of fasad-fil-arz or "causing mischief on earth."

What President Nadvi, President Obama, and the likes of the Council on American-Islamic Relations all have in common is an omission. They all fail to continue reading from the Quran when Surah Five, Ayat Thirty-Two ends. On the next line, the Islamic holy book declares, "Indeed, the penalty for those who wage war against Allah and His Messenger and strive upon earth [to cause] corruption is none but that they be killed or crucified or that their hands and feet be cut off from opposite sides or that they be exiled from the land. That is for them a disgrace in this world; and for them in the Hereafter is a great punishment…"

The chapters that follow this passage encourage repentance in the face of Islam, demand fear of Allah, and state that disbelievers will face enduring "fire" no matter what they do to try and save themselves. For instance, chapter thirty-eight states,

> [As for] the thief, the male and the female, amputate their hands in recompense for what they committed as a deterrent [punishment] from Allah. And Allah is Exalted in Might and Wise.

A passage in 5:51 reads,

> O you who have believed, do not take the Jews and the Christians as allies. They are [in fact] allies of one another. And whoever is an ally to them among you— then indeed, he is [one] of them. Indeed, Allah guides not the wrongdoing people.

These aren't cherry-picked chapters from the Quran. These are the verses that follow immediately after the few lines President Obama chose to recite just a few months after people were murdered in their name. So why didn't he feel the need to continue reading? To continue speaking the words of the Muslim holy book? Surely one line has as much validity as the next.

I kept thinking about the use of that one specific Ayat throughout the press conference and throughout the days, weeks, and months to come. It kept jumping out at me from all over the news. It was quoted in blogs, articles, debates, on television, and of course at press conferences again and again.

I also thought about my professional balancing act. How do I ask a tough question without being turfed out? We were the only ones there I could be sure would record the whole conference and upload it unedited for the world to see. We couldn't afford to be shut down or ejected from the premises for being too "hostile" (i.e. asking real questions).

Dr. Nadvi's portion of the conference didn't last long. He was an old man who clearly hadn't mastered the English language. The podium was soon turned over to one of the younger men at the pulpit, one of whom was the head of the Al-Shifa center.

The first softball question came: "What is the mosque's reaction to the FBI calling this an act of terrorism?" Dr. Nadvi's son Mahmood attempted to exculpate the mosque in his answer. He also, without authority, spoke on behalf of Muslims across the world. Mahmood claimed to know Syed Farook as well as the reporter who had asked the question and claimed not to know Tashfeen Malik in the slightest. What I perceived as palpably disingenuous speech continued for another twelve minutes before I chimed in with a question about the rules for apostasy in Islam (i.e. that leaving the faith requires the punishment of death).

No direct answer was given. Instead, I received the same paraphrasing of Surah Five, Ayat Thirty-Two, the same dancing around the question. Then the podium was handed over to a man called Roshan Abbassi.

Abbassi was clearly a hot head posing (badly) as a learned man. You could see in his swaggering and smirking that he wasn't distraught over the terrorist attack. It also quickly became evident that he was not particularly intelligent or in control of his emotions. When questions were fielded to him that he didn't like, he snapped, "So...you guys are OUR guests, and if we have no comment, you cannot force us to comment, thank you very much."

This marked a clear shift from when Nadvi and son, who both sought to come across as open-hearted and helpful as possible, were at the podium. Abbasi represented the secretly hostile underbelly of Deobandism. He was quick to anger, quick to judge, and quick to lose his patience.

There is an arrogance that only a young Hafiz [one who knows the Quran] has. It is indicative of someone who thinks he is more intelligent—as the Quran tells him—than non-Muslims. As I listened to Abbassi speak, Haney's words sprang to mind: "They became a lot more assertive in our [border] interviews. I suppose they thought that because they had mastered a subject they would leave me behind."

Abbassi snapped in response to being pressed on whether the FBI had recently interviewed him and other congregants. He simply didn't care that residents in San Bernardino were afraid another attack might be launched by another attendee of the Dar Al Uloom. It was unclear to all of us in the room why someone with nothing to hide would take this approach. Journalists began to express their frustrations as Abbassi ducked and weaved away from their questions, raising nonsensical issues like abortion, shootings, and again Surah Five, Ayat Thirty-Two.

Only after the press conference did we discover that Mr. Abbassi had exchanged numerous text messages with Mr. Malik in the months before the shooting, and that the mosque had hosted a wedding party for the couple despite claiming to not know Tashfeen Malik in the slightest. Mr. Abbassi insisted the texts were just about food; Syed had messaged Abbassi that he was bringing biryiani—a delicious, traditional South Asian dish—to the mosque. This revelation still undermined the mosque's entire narrative—that Farook was barely known to its leaders and that he was no longer an attendee there. Why would you lie about that if you didn't need to? Surely responding, "Yeah, he came. He brought food. We hosted his wedding party, we're all as shocked as you," would have been more compelling than a rapidly unraveling story.

"There's proof that it was workplace anger. Proof," Abbassi said. He probably forgot that a full FBI investigation into Syed and his wife Tashfeen's Internet history would reveal there was, as former Director James Comey said, "radicalization by the killers and the potential inspiration by foreign terrorist organizations."

In the footage of the conference, I believe you can hear the frustration in my voice when I asked my next question. "What do you teach your students about the Khilafah [Islamic caliphate]?"

"I don't teach them anything about it," Abbassi responded.

I replied, "So you don't believe in it?"

Abbassi awkwardly moved away from the microphone, stating, "I just teach how to read Arabic."

Why wouldn't he answer my question directly? Why would the mosque elders all cite the same, easily debunked Quranic verse? Why did Syed Farook and Tashfeen Malik attack their co-workers after attending a mosque run by a shady, fundamentalist sect that encourages segregation and reliance on the mosque? And why did members of the mosque lie so brazenly about how well they knew them? The answers, to me, are evident.

────────

I'm sure you're asking yourself, "Why is San Bernardino, with its predominantly white, black, and Latino population, featured in this book? What does it have to do with No Go Zones?" More than you'd think.

No Go Zones are not just physical localities in the suburbs of major European cities. They're also a mindset. A mindset of ghettoization and, curiously, a mindset of both supremacy and victimhood that occurs concurrently in minority and majority populations.

What Syed Farook and Tashfeen Malik did was cut themselves off from the outside world. They were perhaps encouraged to do so by the Internet, or by the Islamic State itself, which we know Tashfeen pledged allegiance to. That way of living is bad enough when it is restricted to one family. When it is part of the culture of entire "communities," the effects on civilization are devastating.

Senator Chris Murphy (D-CT) identified this problem in a speech to the Council on Foreign Relations in 2016. He said,

> …I want to first take you to northwest Pakistan, and ask you to imagine for a moment you are a parent of

a ten-year-old boy. You are illiterate, poor, and getting poorer by the day. Unemployment in your village in sky high, inflation is making everything unaffordable, crop yields have been miserable.

But one day, you get a visit that changes your perspective. A cleric from a nearby conservative mosque offers you a different path. He tells you that your poverty is not your fault, but simply a punishment handed down to you because of your unintentional deviation from the true path of Islam. Luckily, there's a way to get right with God—to devote the life of your only son to Islam.

And it gets even better. The cleric will offer to educate your son at his own school—we call them madrassas—and not only will you not have to pay for the education, he will actually pay you—maybe as much as $6,000. And when he finishes school, he will find employment for your son in the service of Islam. Your ten-year-old, previously destined to live a life even more hopeless than your own, will get free housing and meals, religious instruction, and the promise of a job when he is older, while you get money and improved favor with God.

For thousands of poor families in destitute places like northwest Pakistan, it's often an easy choice.

But as the years go on, you lose contact with your son. Gradually, the school cuts off your access to him. But when you do get to see him, every now and again, you see him changing.

And then one day, it's over. He's not the little boy you once knew. He's a teenager, announcing to you that the only way to show true faith to Islam is to fight for it—against the kafirs, the infidels who are trying to pollute the Muslim faith or those Westerners who are trying to destroy it. He tells you he is going to Afghanistan, or Syria, or Iraq, with some fellow students, and that you shouldn't worry about him, because God is on his side.

You start asking questions to find out what happened in that school. And you start to learn. You discover the textbooks he read that taught a brand of Islam greatly influenced by Wahhabism—a strain of Islam based on the earliest form of the religion practiced under the first four caliphs. It holds that any deviation from Islamic originalism is heresy.

In school, your son was therefore taught an ideology of hate toward the "unbeliever"—defined as Christians, Jews, and Hindus, but also Shiites, Sufis, and Sunni Muslims who do not follow Wahhabi doctrine. He is told that the Crusades never ended—that aid organizations, schools, government offices are modern weapons of the West's continuing Crusade against his faith—and that it is a religious obligation to do "battle" against the infidels.

I tell you this story because every day, some version of it plays out hundreds of times in far-flung places, from Pakistan to Kosovo, Nigeria to Indonesia. The teaching of an intolerant version of Islam to hundreds to millions of young people. In 1956 there were 244 madrassas in Pakistan. Today, there are 24,000. These schools are multiplying all over the globe. And don't get me wrong—these schools, by and large, don't teach violence. They aren't the minor leagues for Al Qaeda or ISIS. But they do teach a version of Islam that leads, very nicely, into an anti-Shia, anti-Western militancy. And I also don't mean to suggest that Wahhabism is the only sect of Islam that can be perverted into violence. Iran's Shia clerics also use religion in order to export violence into Syria and Iraq and Lebanon. But it is important to note the vicious terrorist groups that Americans knows by name are Sunni in derivation, and greatly influenced by Wahhabi, Salafist teachings.

And of course the real rub is—we've known this. We've known it for a long, long time. Secretaries of State, ambassadors, diplomats, four star generals, have all complained, over and over again about it, and yet we do very little to stop this long, slow spread of intolerance.

We don't address it because to do so would cause us to confront two very difficult issues.

The first is how we talk, sensibly, about Islam. Right now, we are caught torn between two extremes. Leading Republicans want to begin and end this discussion with a debate over what we call terrorists, and, of course, their party's leading candidate for President—Donald Trump—equates the entire religion with violence. The debate over nomenclature is overwrought, but I certainly understand the problem of labeling something "radical Islamic terrorism," giving purchase to Trump's unforgiveable argument that all Muslims are radicals or terrorists. Republicans don't seem to want to go any deeper into the conversation than a simple labeling of the threat.

But Democrats aren't that much better. The leaders of my party do backflips to avoid using these kind terms, but that forestalls any conversation about the fight within Islam for the soul of the religion. It's a disservice to this debate for Republicans to simply brand every Muslim as a threat to the West. But it's also a disservice for Democrats to refuse to acknowledge that though ISIS has perverted Islam to a degree that it is unrecognizable—the seeds of this perversion are rooted in a much more mainstream version of the faith that derives, in substantial part, from the teachings of Wahhabism.[7]

It's undeniably strong stuff. And leaving out the bluster about President Trump, his comments apply just as much to Islam in the West as it does to Pakistan, Kosovo, Nigeria, and Indonesia. It applies to the madrassas and masjids in Dewsbury, England. It applies to the communities and ghettoes in Brussels. And it applies to the hearts and minds of Muslims across the United States who are taken in and radicalized by the sects the U.S. government is unwilling or unable to stare down and eject from its constitutional republic.

No Go Zones are not just physical places, as I explained at the beginning of this book. And if they are ignored by the government, or if information about them is suppressed or censored, they can put a nation—one that would otherwise be able to take preemptive measures to protect itself from such a threat—in peril. As recently as mid-April 2017, a *New York Post* article written by Paul Sperry claimed the NYPD had "censored an anti-terror handbook to appease offended Muslims, even though it has accurately predicted radicalization patterns in recent 'homegrown' terror cases."[8] "The report was extremely accurate on how the radicalization process works and what indicators to look for," said Patrick Dunleavy, a former deputy inspector general of the New York state prisons' criminal-intelligence division. Dunleavy also worked with the NYPD's intelligence division for several years.

Perry notes that in 2007, the Council on American-Islamic Relations began to protest the document on the basis of "Islamophobia." Leftist Mayor Bill de Blasio prostrated before them, caving to their demands to withdraw the guidance for cops even though, as Perry points out,

> The authors of the report, led by Mitch Silber, former NYPD director of intelligence analysis, examined hundreds of "homegrown" terrorism cases and found that suspects followed the same "radicalization" path. Key indicators include: alienating themselves from their former lives and friends; giving up cigarettes, drinking and partying; wearing traditional Islamic clothing; growing a beard; becoming obsessed with Mideast politics and jihad; and regularly attending a hardline mosque. In other words, the more they immersed themselves in their faith, the more radical they grew.
>
> "You can take all the terrorist cases since that report and compare the information on the subject and the case and see stark similarities to what Mitch laid out," Dunleavy noted.
>
> The terrorists who carried out recent attacks in Boston; Fort Hood, Texas; Little Rock, Ark.; Chattanooga, Tenn.; San Bernardino, Ca.; Orlando, Florida;

Philadelphia and at Ohio State University, among others, followed a similar pattern of radicalization. In each case, the Muslim attacker was influenced through "incubators of extremism" within the Muslim community, including Islamic student associations, schools, bookstores and mosques. Jihadi websites also played a role, but what unifies them all is Islamic doctrine. As the NYPD study found, "The ultimate objective for any attack is always the same—to punish the West, overthrow the democratic order, re-establish the caliphate, and institute Sharia," or Islamic law.

Sharia is often the best indicator that a community has become isolated and inward-looking with the potential to radicalize its young—usually the most susceptible to jihadist ideas. San Bernardino is therefore emblematic of a wider problem regarding No Go Zones in the United States. A No Go Zone of the mind, established by liberal-left political correctness, the threat and guilt of "Islamophobia"—which we will deal with in another chapter—and the sheer lack of understanding that the Muslim Brotherhood, and the Wahhabists, are not the only threats emanating from the Muslim communities in the United States. San Bernardino may not have Muslim ghettos, but some parts of America definitely do. In these places, the radicals have already moved in and broken ground. They are establishing a momentum which, if not disrupted, will transform America into Europe in the next twenty years.

EIGHT

FROM DETROIT, WITH THE CALL TO PRAYER

My friends are all too scared to say anything [now], even to the
Mayor...I don't feel comfortable in my neighborhood anymore.

—LOCAL RESIDENT, "RUTH," RESPONDING TO AUTHORITIES WHO ARE
DISMISSING CONCERNS ABOUT THE GROWING MUSLIM POPULATION

Detroit is hell. Well, significant parts of it anyway.
While business and investment have returned to the
city and to the state of Michigan, vast No Go Zones of
another kind are spawning in the Detroit-adjacent cities and
suburbs of Dearborn and Hamtramck. Since November 2015,
the latter has boasted the first Muslim-majority controlled
city council in the United States. For anyone concerned about
the issues stemming from Islam in America—so probably
every one of you who bought this book—a closer look into
the state of Hamtramck is essential. Perhaps that is the best
reason to visit Hamtramck nowadays. Well, that, and the
food.

The city is practically a historic landmark for immigration in America. Just after the turn of the twentieth century,
Polish-Americans dominated Hamtramck for nearly one

hundred years, taking great pride in the area just outside Motor City. Now, a whole new wave of immigrants has repeated this trend. According to some reports, the Detroit-Hamtramck border is one of the only places in America where you can get ballot papers in Bengali, so large is the local Bangladeshi community.[1]

At first glance, the city might not look like it's changed much. It's still bustling with culture. I could scarcely find—between the diminishing Polish restaurants and the Middle Eastern fare—a bad place to eat. For a Londoner like me who is highly accustomed to foreign foods and cultures, Hamtramck also felt a little bit like home. The chicken gallaba and masala tea at the welcoming Yemen cafe—in the same building as a store selling Middle Eastern affects like shisha pipes and hijabs—on Joseph Campau street was to die for. The pierogis at the Polonia restaurant were equally delectable, though I was warned by one of my interviewees that the eatery was "one of the worst Polish restaurants in town." I couldn't tell, as I wolfed down the grub and guzzled down some Tyskie beer.

But upon further inspection, you can see the telltale signs of a No Go Zone in the making. In Hamtramck, I noticed the indicators—the first indicators—which were lack of integration and assimilation, that I encountered elsewhere on my travels.

Again, I saw a dominance of satellite dishes on houses. While this phenomenon could certainly have been a peculiar, local television access issue, I somehow doubted the residents were struggling to receive ESPN via cable. I investigated this a little bit, and locals seemed to agree. You rarely see satellite dishes attached to households consuming television in English. A discussion on this topic can even be found on a local Detroit message board dating back to 2006. In this discussion, Board Administrator "Lowell" says, "I have noticed a greater preponderance of satellite dishes in new immigrant neighbor-hoods such as in SW Detroit, Detroit E of Hamtramck and areas of Dearborn. I am guessing that choices for receiving program-ming in Spanish, Arabic and other languages is better provided via satellite vs. cable. Right or Wrong?"[2]

Lowell provided evidence of this trend, a picture of the Bar-bara Apartments in the then-Latino dominated community near Detroit's city center.

User "1953" replied, "I second your assertion." Another user,"Polaar," claimed, "Using these dishes is the same thing as the immigrants in the earlier part of the 20th century (like my great grandparents) who bought shortwave radios to hear news and music from their countries of origin."

For the record, the discussion was not xenophobic. Nor were any of the conversations I had with locals about the topic. People were just intrigued by the trend.

I would like to dissect Polaar's claim that immigrants in the early twentieth century would have used satellite dishes for the same reason immigrants in Hamtramck now use them. If that is true, why should locals be more concerned about their new Middle Eastern or South Asian neighbors than they were about the Polish migrant wave that effectively built the town up? The true answer is—though the political Left would never let you think so—that different immigrant groups are *shockingly* dif-ferent. That was sarcasm, in case you missed it.

Leftists tend to think immigrant communities are homoge-neous. They assume "Muslim Americans" can be shuffled into any random grouping that can be represented by any Muslim voice at any given time. Think about it. How often do you hear phrases like, "we are all immigrants" or "we are a nation of immigrants" or "America was built on immigration!" By hiding behind these phrases, open-borders and pro-mass-migration lobbyists seek to destroy the self-evident, naturally existing difference amongst immigrant groups. It allows them to perpetuate a false narrative that somehow Christian communities from Europe or Latin America are inseparable from Arab or South Asian migrants, or the various other groups that exist in the United States.

This narrative is dangerous because not all immigrants are interested in integrating into American society. To recognize the difference between immigrants who integrate and those who do not, let's first look at the example provided by the Chaldeans. Though they are a minority, the Left scarcely speaks on their behalf because they've actually assimilated and integrated into society, and they are proud of being first and second generation Americans.

Chaldeans trace their roots back to Mesopotamia, modern day Iraq. Over the past few decades, religious and ethnic persecution has driven them out of this region, in no small part thanks to the U.S. invasion of Iraq, which destabilized the country and handed it over to Islamic extremists, often sponsored by Iran. Though Chaldeans are from the Arab world, "we do not identify as Arabs," explained Sharon Hannawa of the Chaldean Community Foundation. She added that her mother arrived in the United States at the age of just eight years old, and her father arrived at the age of thirty.

Outside of Michigan and San Diego, where there are large populations of these immigrants, you would scarcely hear the word "Chaldeans." But Hannawa was keen to stress the contributions of the Chaldean community in the United States when I spoke to her. "Chaldeans have a very entrepreneurial spirit," she explained, perhaps providing some insight as to why—in a country partly distinguished from the rest of the Western world by its prevailing preference for free market capitalism—Chaldeans thrive.

"They're able to afford what they have," she said, adding, "In Southeastern Michigan we own an estimated 15,000 business." That's no small feat. And when asked about these immigrants, locals often note how successful the Chaldeans are. Some seem slightly bitter about this and even envious of the Chaldeans for their fast-paced success. Many Chaldeans drive fancy sports cars and own supermarkets, gas stations, corner stores, and other local businesses. The Chaldean Household Survey, commissioned by the Chaldean American Chamber of Commerce and administered by United Way and Walsh College, found that approximately 61 percent of Chaldean households own their own businesses, and that the median household income of a Chaldean family was $96,100, which is well above the local average of around $52,000. And many of them have lovely houses with statues of the Virgin Mary in their front yards.[3]

Chaldeans truly are living the American dream. Hannawa attributes this to strong family units and traditional values, of which education plays a big role. No wonder the Left isn't keen to ally with them or sing their praises.

"Our parents sacrificed and didn't want the same for their kids," she said. When pressed on this, she explained, "I barely saw my father growing up. [He would] leave before I went to school...I was asleep by the time [he came home]." Her story reminded me a lot of my upbringing, with parents intent on giving their children a better life. When I was growing up, my family had a four-bedroom detached house with a pool in the back yard, and our grandmother lived with us for many months of the year. We were the epitome of the upper middle class, and from what? A village called Moshi in Tanzania.

So what was the difference between Muslim migrants, my family, and Chaldeans? My discussions with Hannawa and other Chaldeans started to piece together this puzzle.

"Chaldeans are Eastern Rite Catholics," she explained. "Christians since 45 AD. We were converted by St. Thomas the Apostle," she said.

"Wow!" I replied. This was some heritage! It reminded me of what her colleague Wally told me when I visited the Chaldean community center in Sterling Heights, Michigan.

He pointed to a replica of a piece of Mesopotamian artwork on the wall and proudly declared, "That's who we are. We have been around since the beginning of time [human history]. We invented the wheel. We ARE history," he said.

Such a proud history and such wonderful traditions, I thought, are exactly what Western conservatives appreciate. It actually sent goose bumps scuttling up my right arm. But I couldn't keep the jealousy of the non-Chaldean locals out of my mind, so I asked Hannawa if Chaldeans ever experience any local hostility.

"I wouldn't say hostility," she said, adding, "[But] we have to do educating… [especially because of the] current refugee crisis." What a shame, I thought. But I knew that local experiences of migrant populations have been, perhaps, less than ideal. Native suspicions were understandable.

"People had all these stereotypes," she said, "thought we did not pay taxes."

I could find no evidence to support nor discredit this assumption. But I did note the same assumption is usually made about Muslim migrants in Europe. While local officials in places like

Molenbeek were able to point to some Arab-background migrants who were clearly not paying their taxes, I could find no evidence of extraordinarily cheap prices in Chaldean-run stores that could indicate tax evasion. Perhaps this suspicion surrounding Chaldeans comes from Michigan tax incentives that apply to particularly small and new businesses. I certainly couldn't corroborate that Chaldeans didn't pay their fair share or their own way.

Having established the locals' perception of Chaldeans, I asked Hannawa what the dynamic was between the state's Chaldeans and the current Muslim migrants. "The city was having some issues [between Muslims and Chaldeans]," she explained, careful to point out that this was not necessarily a dominant position or opinion within the community. But, apparently, there have been complaints and concerns.

"Some were protesting because there's going to be a mosque in Sterling Heights," she said. That wasn't a surprise to me. During my research into the matter, I found many people—Chaldeans and others—who were concerned about the issue. Those who had fled the Middle East were concerned about the Islamization of their newfound homes. The experiences they thought they had left behind—the oppression, the discrimination, the supremacism of Islam—loomed larger in the minds of the first generation of migrants who had made it to the Land of the Free.

"There's a lot of Chaldean refugees that have resettled," said Hannawa. She continued, "When you're here as a refugee and you were driven out of your native country because of your religion—it's a form of PTSD [post traumatic stress disorder]."

The comparison to mental health problems and those who have faced war-like or life-threatening experiences is striking to me. A February 2017 report from one local council meeting quoted a human rights activist named Nahren Anweya, who commented on the mosque protests: "The Christians from Iraq they feel they've lost everything, so when there's a mosque placed right in the heart of their community, it's not gonna stop." Anweya's family fled Iraq in 1989.

"There's gonna be a lot of hostility. The city is creating a tension there," Hannawa said. She added, "It's already starting off that way, so I didn't see it being good on any terms possible what happened last night. They know how we feel about it and how we protested it. Everyone should know the Christians of Iraq are the most warm and friendly people, and everyone has taken advantage of that—the Sunni Muslims, the Shiite Muslims and the Kurdish Muslims—and we ended up in the middle of a genocide." She went on to say, "When you're in your native country and a mosque is being built, you think you have to move out. The city has been having—people have voiced, expressed concerns and so it's a process of acculturating. A lot of it is PTSD."

In Hannawa's mind, the protests weren't simply a case of rejecting new mosques or new populations. When she says, "acculturating," she means acclimatizing, accepting, and adjusting. To many members of the Chaldean community and the community at large in a place like Sterling Heights, this is unthinkable. For those of a more liberal persuasion however, adopting a more "tolerant" approach is the only way to ensure good interfaith and community relations.

Whatever the solution to these tensions may be, it's clear one needs to be enacted soon. The Muslim immigrants in this area are not going to move away, stop having children, or stop welcoming more of their persuasion into the country.

Their presence is met with mixed feelings, even by those in their own community. Many Muslim immigrants want to live their lives, thrive, and build better lives for their children. For some, however, immigrating to areas like Hamtramck is an ideal opportunity to put down roots and preach a version of Islam that is entirely at odds with the West. It's an opportunity to conquer.

When I visited the Islamic Organization of North America mosque, a large signpost outside the Warren-based (south of Sterling Heights) masjid advertised an event discussing what Sharia law means. The mosque's website provides some answers in online articles written by the mosque's leaders. In an essay written by Dr. Ahmed Afzaal, an assistant professor of comparative religion at Concordia College, the topic of Islam and peace is addressed:

> Is Islam a religion of peace? Whenever I hear this, I want to ask a counter-question: Who wants to know? It so happens that the overwhelming majority of people who ask this question do not care about getting an informed or accurate answer. They do not raise this question because they believe they are lacking in the knowledge of the Islamic tradition, and that the response will help them overcome their ignorance by giving them new insights. The question is typically raised by those who are already sure of being in possession of the right answer.
>
> In the majority of these cases, the speaker is an Islamophobe who asks the question only to create an illusion of having carried out an objective inquiry; he/she is then able to present the right answer as an emphatic "no." Occasionally, this question is raised by an uncritical Islamophile whose response, as expected,

is an equally emphatic "yes." Unfortunately, what this well-meaning friend of Islam does not recognize is that the problem represented by the negative response to the question cannot be solved by simply giving a positive response.[4]

Afzaal's initial answer to his opening question seems odd. Later in the essay, he frames the debate surrounding Islam and peace in terms of a relativistic debate around the definitions of the words "peace" and "religion." He concludes, "In light of the above discussion, the best response I can offer to the question, 'Is Islam a religion of peace?' is no response at all." Totally bizarre.

Other articles on the website include "Modesty and Hijab," written by hijab advocate Melanie Elturk who hectors,

Allah (SWT) commands the Prophet (PBUH) to tell the believing women to take a series of steps: 1) to lower their gaze, which is mandated for both women and men alike; 2) to guard their chastity or sexuality; and 3) to conceal their natural beauty, which scholars have interpreted to mean the whole body except for the face and hands.

The word "headcovering" or "*khimar*" more familiar in our times as *hijab,* refers to the cloth that covers the head. Women at the time of the revelation wore their headcovers tied back behind their necks, leaving the front of the neck and opening at the top of the dress exposed. The revelation *confirmed* the practice of covering the head, and directed women to tie the headcover in front and let it drape down to conceal the throat and dress opening at the top.

In addition to the headcovering, modest dress includes opaque, loose fitting clothing that does not reveal a woman's shape. Make-up and perfume would defeat the purpose of dressing modestly as it attracts negative attention from the opposite sex and exploits one's sexuality.[5]

These pieces do not lead us to believe that the IONA mosque is extremely radical, but they do prompt the following question: how does the mosque's teachings fit into American culture and its local community? Local politicians, community leaders, and activists must demand an answer that doesn't involve 1,000 words of relativizing and dodging simple questions.

In its library, the mosque promotes missives pondering whether Jesus was a Muslim and books on the Tablighi movement, the comparisons between jihad and terrorism, the martyrdom of Husain, and purity within Islam. Most Islamic scholars would agree these concepts are inseparable from Islam. But if brought to their extreme end, as some sects of Islam encourage, these tracts are scarcely separable from a more puritanical, indoctrinated, and segregated way of life.

Regarding Sharia, an essay on the mosque's website states,

Shariah abhors extremism and excessiveness. Excesses in spending, eating—even worship—are prohibited in Islam. Shariah promotes following the middle path. True Muslims are moderate in all of their endeavors—religious and secular. God described them in the Quran as "the Middle Nation."

Shariah aims at facilitating life and removing hardships. Shariah beautifies life and provides comfort. It approves of good and forbids evil. It is considerate in case of necessity and hardship.

A general principle in Shariah holds that necessity makes the unlawful lawful. A Muslim is obliged to satisfy his hunger with lawful food and not to eat what has been declared forbidden. One may, however, in case of necessity—when permissible food is not available—eat unlawful foods such as pork to sustain life. Shariah comes from a kind and compassionate God.[6]

They even quote Sura Five, Ayat Thirty-Two, again, without reference to Ayat Thirty-Three.

But this is Islam in the West. And perhaps we should be thankful for the fact that these mosques are not promoting the more violent chapters of the Quran. But, what seems like moderation in effect may be nothing less than a lure. Without extreme undercover investigation, it is impossible to know how these teachings are cemented in Arabic-language lessons, or in daily sermons by imams. Perhaps we should give them the benefit of the doubt. But given the proclivity of many to carry out such teachings to violent ends, maybe we should demand the fullest and utmost transparency instead.

Forbidding foreign funding of mosques in America may also be a good idea. Many mosques in the West would not exist if their foreign funding dried up. This may point to an unaddressed problem: they are not popular with locals and there may be cause for that.

Instead of responding to an existing demand in an area, mosques can act as lures for immigrant Muslims who are looking for areas that locals can be driven away from.

This issue has reared its head many times in Detroit and its neighboring towns. Battles continue to rage over the building of mosques in, or directly adjacent to, residential areas. When I visited some of the proposed sites for mosques in Sterling Heights, it was clear that those drafting the planning applications had little to no concern for local residents. A small plot of land—barely big enough for a house—is currently being mooted for the locale of a new mosque in the area. The American Islamic Community Center (AICC) sued the local government after concerns about zoning were raised. If the AICC wins the lawsuit, taxpayers will effectively be paying for the mosque's construction. And people wonder why there are "tensions" surrounding such projects.

Regardless of these tensions, new mosques are popping up all over Michigan to cater to the different denominations of Islam. It may be a sign of poor internal relations between different Muslim denominations that they cannot share spaces effectively, but the same applies to different Christian denominations too. When some locals express to me the idea "they already have a mosque here," I have to explain that Baptists don't necessarily want to go to an Eastern Orthodox Church, or wouldn't. Similarly, a Barelvi might not want to attend a Deobandi mosque, and so forth.

Some of these new mosques provide services seven days a week, some only provide services on Fridays, some have schools and seminaries attached, and some are disguised as "community centers," which simply expand their remits over time. This practice frustrates locals. One in particular—I am going to call her Ruth—lives right next to a new Deobandi mosque, which is a few streets away from the IONA mosque. Ruth spoke with trepidation about this topic. I could hear her voice tremble as she recalled events that had occurred over the past three years in her home of Warren County, Michigan.

"What started me getting involved in this neighborhood dispute with this IONA [mosque] was that the neighbors on the side street that I know, their back yard borders a commercial property that the imam bought to make it a mosque," she began. "Now they want to make it a school," she added.

It's a familiar story, one that I've heard all over the world. First a community center. Then a school. Then a mosque. Keep adding. Keep building. In whatever order best combats local planning regulations and community resistance.

Ruth continued,

> They bought a lot on a side street, and what got all of us together meeting weekly was that they made a hole in the retainer wall that divides commercial property from residential. They didn't ask…they just did it.
>
> People start[ed] complaining about them being able to walk through [to the mosque]. They didn't want them to start parking [in the residential area] and going to the mosque for their services because they crowd their whole neighborhood with their cars. The city said they were going to give out $1000 a day fines…they broke the wall wide enough for a garden gate and they were coming through. The city never gave them ordnance violations and we tracked it. We fought with them for two and a half years and every time [residents] called the planning commission and started complaining about them not giving an ordinance violation, they came out and gave the neighbors that called violations.

One guy had five pieces of firewood by the driveway. He got one... another was a downspout that came onto the lawn, they didn't like that. And another one had brought his boat home to clean it out and they got him on that. And they predated the violations so he would be getting to where he had to pay. But he had a camera on his house but with his lawyer they proved they had written it predated.

So what happened was we started doing GoFundMe [crowdsourcing money online] for a court case. But when the city found out they filed a court case. They took the imam to court. But they never made it get rebricked up. They just left it. They really rolled over. So now they got to make a playground there. They've got a gate in the back and a gate in the front so they can just walk right through now and just park on the side street.

Ruth speaks with an alarm that an academic or journalist would perhaps be chastised for. I needed to remind myself I was speaking to residents. Residents who are watching their neighborhoods change before their eyes. For many, their towns and counties mean everything to them. I imagine it would be incredibly frustrating for them to witness *any* group of people breaching laws without reproach and getting special treatment. In fact, the locals I spoke with who opposed such moves in the area told me local journalists weren't willing to represent their perspective on this topic. For the most part, newspapers and television stations didn't want to listen to them. No one wanted to rock the boat.

There's scarcely any information available online about this local dispute, which carried on for years. This is very odd considering it is quite easy to find local reports of the mosque leader slamming President Donald Trump for his comments on refugees. In 2015—right in the middle of this local dispute—the *Oakland Press* reported the IONA imam's comments: "The Muslim community has had enough of his rhetoric."

Imam Mustapha El-Turk, a Troy resident, also said that Trump was "very Islamophobic."[7]

Ruth gave me an overview of the changes she's noticed in the area.

"It started in 2014 and it just finished up last year [2016]," Ruth explained. She continued, "Everybody just rolled over. The neighborhood on the commercial side is extremely busy...there's a lot of cars, an extreme amount of cars, they just park anywhere. One of the strip malls across the street went completely empty. Everybody moved out."

She's not far off. Nearly everybody moved out of that area a long time ago. What stands there now is the Hera Halal Food Mart, and a bunch of empty store fronts. While the food mart is broadly reviewed as a great place to pick up halal food, one Google reviewer by the name of Hasna Begum said in 2016:

> Nothing is labeled. Ever. It's like walking through a maze.
>
> The employees don't know English. They just expect everyone to know Bangla. And there are always a bunch of random dudes standing there. Just watching your every move.
>
> Oh and you can only use a credit card if your total is over $10? And the veggies are never fresh. They just sit there wilting away.[8]

Ruth again mentioned the exodus from the area. "Everybody's moving out, they're just vacating," she said, adding, "From 9 ½ Mile to 12 Mile we've got all these mosques, they just come in any building that's empty. I don't know if they're going to get a big mosque eventually but they just seem to annoy with the congestion in the neighborhood." Ruth makes the mistake of assuming all these mosques are a similar denomination of Islam. They're not.

She continued, "We took a petition—there were about 250 of us in the neighborhood—we took a petition out. One week we took our petition up the street…the neighbors were telling us that behind us came the Welcoming Michigan/America group. They had a petition asking 'were we against the Muslims coming, the refugees coming?'" She probably didn't realize how deep the rabbit hole goes in terms of the globalist lobbying that was funding the groups operating on her small street in Warren County, Michigan.

Welcoming Michigan is a chapter of Welcoming America Inc. Welcoming America is a pro-open-borders group that lists Unbound Philanthropy among its financial supporters. Unbound Philanthropy is a hedge-fund chief's charitable group, and it has donated globally to organizations affiliated with groups such as Black Lives Matter and Hope Not Hate.[9] The latter is a campaign organization in the United Kingdom that has repeatedly targeted anti-mass migration entities like the UK Independence Party, its former leader Nigel Farage MEP, and even Breitbart. com. Once, the organization went so far as to call practicing Muslims who opposed Sharia law "Islamophobes." Another group listed on Welcoming America's 990 forms is the Four Freedoms Fund, which has received large donations from groups like Ford Foundation, the Carnegie Corporation of New York, and George Soros's Open Society Foundations.

Ruth added, "It's like follow up on what we were trying to do to protest this playground area in the middle of our neighborhood. We were trying to tell them, this is our neighborhood. We have a playground up the street they could walk to. But they wanted their own. So they may make that a school and the kids will come into the neighborhood. And there'd be houses looking down onto the playground."

This was unsettling but perhaps not as unsettling as learning that Deobandism had reared its head again. "We have Dar Uloom just moved in up the street from us. That's the one I'm very afraid of," she said. She continued,

> What happened was last year I watched cable and they made a proposition. They wanted it as a boy's youth center. They said it would be very small, just for youth. Then this year, at the end of 2016, I was watching cable—we have to keep track of planning to see what they're turning into a religious organization facility now—the imam for that location, the youth center, the Dar Uloom, came on and said that he wanted to make it a mosque.
>
> The very first words out of the head of the planning commission, she said [Ruth paraphrased], "You're not being a very good neighbor, when you established this as a youth center we told you this lot is real tiny and there's not enough parking for a mosque and you can't have it as a mosque." So he comes back five months later and wants it [as] a mosque. They turned him down. She said they all

voted ahead of the meeting and zero want this to happen. So then someone got up—the man who owns that property and was leasing it to this imam—said we talked to the Catholic church next door and because they use this property to park on all the time for their festival, they would be glad to share the church parking with them anytime there's overflow they can come on to church property. Well there's just lawn and a fence between. It took just six minutes for the city to say that zero voted for it to everybody unanimously let[ting] him have it as a mosque. And if you go by there—maybe twenty cars at the mosque can park there. So they're just crowding out everyone. Now no one will join me—they're just disgusted.

My friends are all too scared to say anything [now], even to the mayor... I don't feel comfortable in my neighborhood anymore.

After digesting this, I wondered if Ruth and her friends who met with me behaved like "Islamophobes." I suppose in the strictest sense of the word they did. They are fearful. But phobias tend to be irrational, or based on unfounded fears. These fears were clearly not unfounded, and they were probably exacerbated when no one paid attention to the concerns Ruth and her friends voiced.

Islamophobia is usually attributed to anyone who expresses concern about issues stemming from Muslim immigrant communities. But Ruth never uttered a single word that I regarded as prejudiced. Instead, her concerns focused on the community and the law. But the brand of Islamophobia seemed blind to this, as is evidenced by her account of a past council meeting:

...at the council meetings, my friend was annoyed because the city makes you go up to the podium and give your name and address and who you are. And then when the imam and his son, who's a lawyer, went up there...My friend, she was going to write an article about this so she went up to the son and she said "you have to say where you live and what your name is because we have to at council. You're not behaving [according] to our rules in Warren." And he went, "Get away from me, you're scaring me." He went in a corner and hid. He was yelling and his dad stood up at [another] meeting and...got up and said "I'm afraid of these people." After, he gets out in public with one of the men and he was using F-words. He was an engineer at Chrysler for 26 years, you can't tell me he's that primitive, that he can't behave in society. You don't work at a corporation like Chrysler if you don't know how to behave with Americans. He just puts on this act and puts it on for the mayor. Then when he's with the neighbors he acts like a bully. He hasn't done it to me but he's done it to my friend.

A councilwoman called all the neighbors in Warren prejudiced, [said they were] biased, had Islamophobia. She had three ministers who got up and yelled at them. People got so rowdy they called the police to come and get rid of them.

All people said was "we want to know what's going on, why are we unheard?"

Her concerns were echoed as I traveled around the area. I even heard it in Hamtramck, which is broadly unrecognizable as an

American town. Liberals and multiculturalists claim there's no such thing as an American town and that the country was built on different migrant waves. This is mostly accurate, but America was also never shy about confronting the undesirable aspects of migration. Even President Theodore Roosevelt, an original "progressive," had the following to say on integration and assimilation:

> In the first place, we should insist that if the immigrant who comes here in good faith becomes an American and assimilates himself to us, he shall be treated on an exact equality with everyone else, for it is an outrage to discriminate against any such man because of creed, or birthplace, or origin. But this is predicated upon the person's becoming in every facet an American, and nothing but an American...There can be no divided allegiance here. Any man who says he is an American, but something else also, isn't an American at all. We have room for but one flag, the American flag...We have room for but one language here, and that is the English language...and we have room for but one sole loyalty and that is a loyalty to the American people.[10]

This 1907 quote was not his sole proclamation on the matter. In February 1916, he declared,

> I feel that by insistence upon proper housing conditions we shall indirectly approach this. I want to see the immigrant know that he has got to spend a certain amount of his money in decent housing; that he will not be allowed to live on $2.50 per month board basis.

Let us say to the immigrant not that we hope he will learn English, but that he has got to learn it. Let the immigrant who does not learn it go back. He has got to consider the interest of the United States or he should not stay here. He must be made to see that his opportunities in this country depend upon his knowing English and observing American standards. The employer cannot be permitted to regard him only as an industrial asset.

We must in every way possible encourage the immigrant to rise, help him up, give him a chance to help himself. If we try to carry him he may well prove not well worth carrying. We must in turn insist upon his showing the same standard of fealty to this country and to join with us in raising the level of our common American citizenship.[11]

In light of this declaration, it's no surprise that Roosevelt is quoted on material handed out by the ProEnglish organization. It is even less surprising that the organization has been dubbed a "hate group" by ultra-leftists like the Southern Poverty Law Center.

Roosevelt is not alone in his views. Both historical and contemporary leading figures have placed great stress on integration issues. The blanket argument for immigration—that the United States should just admit whomever, whenever, and in whatever numbers—is a relatively new theory and demonstrable nonsense. This is especially evident in Hamtramck.

Thaddeus C. Radzilowski, the president of the Hamtramck-based Piast Institute—a national center of study for Polish-American affairs—discussed the changing face of the city with me. He speaks with immense pride about Hamtramck, its history, and its modern diversity. He shows me census data and explains, "Arabs, as you know, are an ancestry group…along with the Poles and others. The Bangladeshis and Pakistanis are racial groups so they come into an entirely different category. So they're counted in different ways. The data has different accuracies [across sources]."

It makes sense that a place like Hamtramck may not be able to effectively keep track of how many people—and of what origin—are living within the city's borders. It reminds me of home, where the British government relies on a laughably imprecise system called the International Passenger Survey (IPS) to track people's movements in and out of the country. IPS data effectively relies on people walking through the airport, seaport, and Channel Tunnel entrances and exits who consent to be interviewed for five minutes—in English—by someone who looks like a supermarket's product testing intern with a clipboard. I've taken part in one of these surveys myself, and the man interviewing me admitted it was total nonsense. Essentially, Britain has no real way of knowing who is in the country, or who might have left.

———

The retail profile of Hamtramck is so bizarre nowadays. On your way into the Yemeni café, there is a full-wall mural—maybe ninety feet wide and thirty feet tall—of hijab-clad women. It's pure, oppressive propaganda. And, irony of ironies, it stands opposite to an American Eagle, which has the word "PRIDE" emblazoned underneath its sign. This is an extreme juxtaposition of two clashing cultures.

The hijabi mural, revealed in 2013, was reported in the local press as being reflective of "the future." Ismael Duran, who runs the Garage Cultural organization in Detroit, commented on the artwork: "No matter how far you go from your homeland, you have to bring your homeland with you...They are transporting themselves." Curiously, despite inter-community tensions, local Chaldean groups donated money for the commission of the mural—a sort of sop to the Arab-American community, in effect saying, "Yes, we can all get along."

So far, that seems to mostly be the case. There are no running street battles like in Europe or the United Kingdom. There aren't countless reports of Chaldeans being persecuted like the Ahmadi communities across Britain. But these things might not be far off for communities at risk of being overrun. Am I suggesting that these things are inevitable or that the Arab-American communities are hardwired to cause these things? Absolutely not. Am I worried about the hubris and supremacy that comes with population dominance? Absolutely.

When I asked him about the fully niqabed women on the streets of the city—a common sight—Dr. Radzilowski replied,

> That upsets some people. I don't get upset. [They walk] past this window. A lot of these people are going to school in the local high school, they have friends, when they take that stuff off they're wearing jeans. They go to parties. Prom. [They listen to the same] music. But publicly they have to maintain this image. The younger people are kind of aware they share a great deal [in common with each other]. The Arab students are playing football, they're playing cricket, a lot of soccer...
>
> I think it's uncomfortable for them. I don't know that anyone's going to do anything. Some people

grumble, especially women. But I don't know that there's any sharp reaction. People do pride themselves in this city on its eccentric diversity. People always say, anybody can walk down the street and nobody will pay attention to you, you could have two heads…well, probably not. So there's a kind of perverse pride in Hamtramck that anything goes.

The one thing that clearly and manifestly delineates the latest wave of migrants in Hamtramck from their predecessors is Islam. I asked Radzilowski if the "perverse pride" he mentions could lead to complacency, especially regarding the rights of women in the community.

"I think so, I think so," he said.

It was no surprise to me that just a few weeks after my visit, a major national news story, created by the complacency I feared, emanated out of Michigan. Police arrested several doctors in Livonia, which is close to Hamtramck, in the first attempt to convict for the barbaric process of female genital mutilation in the history of the United States. The victims came from the Bohra community. Bohras are actually Shias, even Ismailis—the same branch of Islam I was raised in. To make things more complicated, we were "Nizaris" whereas they are "Dawoodis." Most of them are Indian, but some are Pakistani and some are Yemeni. And, for whatever reason, they don't mind hacking their children's genitals to bits. For the record, this wasn't an occurrence, not in the slightest, in Nizari Ismailism. I never once even heard about it growing up. But then again, maybe that's half the problem.

Detroit, Michigan, and the United States are now faced with what is quite evidently an epidemic. The Centers for Disease Control has estimated that half a million young women in the

United States are vulnerable to female genital mutilation.[12] I'd say that number was on the conservative side. But, let's get back to Hamtramck.

Dr. Radzilowski speaks with such great pride about his city. I thought he was romanticizing it. Certainly, I couldn't see the Hamtramck of great Polish and Ukrainian institutions he alluded to for a large portion of our interview. Then he revealed, "I had an interview with a young woman working for the *Muslim Observer*. She asked me 'When did the Polish people leave Hamtramck?' I said, 'They didn't. They died here.'"

Ouch. Realism. He added,

> It was a good run. A hundred years [Poles] controlled this city.
>
> What you had is these people moved in. Very young immigrant families. Hamtramck became a city in 1921, and actually this area was not only heavily Polish but also Ukrainian. It also was African-American. Hamtramck, per capita, was the largest African-American population in Michigan until 1930. Detroit didn't pass it until 1930. It was largely a middle class black population. First policemen, first city doctors, first city nurse. The dentists....There's still a dentist practice here that is going into its fourth generation.
>
> They built the city from scratch. This was all farmland...created out of farmland by these new immigrants.

There was the romance. He continued,

> They had these huge families. Hamtramck sent more people to World War II than any other area because

they're all just kids. I looked at one of the Catholic parishes here. The height of the marriages was 1917–19. Height of the baptisms was 1923–26. The school, first to the eighth grade had 3,000 kids in 1930.

After WWII all these guys, you have a whole generation of young men whose formative years were spent outside of the neighborhood. They came back, they had the G.I. Bill, they could buy houses. And you know, you just landed at Normandy, fought your way across Europe, are you going to come back and live upstairs over your old man who's going to tell you what to do? No way!

The older people stayed. My family came here in 1915 and we're still here. They stayed but the younger people moved out. They didn't want to live in those crowded conditions. Roosevelt promised the American standard of living. All that new housing was going up. The population aged. Now Detroit is one of the largest metropolitan areas [in America] for Poles. It's around half a million. So they're still here but they're out in the suburbs, except for Hamtramck.

The population dropped to about 18,000 and started going up again with the first Albanians, then Bangladeshi and Yemeni populations started coming in. So yeah, they've revitalized the city. They're keeping it alive because they do represent the same kind of work ethic and family ethic that the older immigrants [had]. They're family people, they want to buy houses. They want good schools for their kids. They want safe streets. They're basically continuing on what the earlier immigrants had established here.

Dr. Radzilowski is a very fair and balanced interviewee. He's not afraid to say uncomfortable things, but he wants to give people the benefit of the doubt. This was most evident to me when we discussed the matter of the call to prayer emanating from local mosque speakers. Before we dive into that discussion, let's learn a little more about the local government in Hamtramck. Radzilowski explained,

> [Muslims] began coming into this area as early as the 1970s, mainly out of New York. We had some people move here in the 1990s. I have a friend who's running for Mayor of Hamtramck—Kamal Rahman—he came here as a teenager, he went to high school here, all his friends are Polish. Speaks excellent English. He has a very responsible position. He got a Master's Degree in finance, he runs the water system for Detroit—the billing, anyway. So he's running for Mayor of the city. But as early as 2000 we already had a Bangladeshi councilman, within 10 years [when it was] still a relatively small population.
>
> I later met Kamal, and joked with him about the fate of his fellow countryman of origin, Lutfur Rahman in Tower Hamlets.

"We're a little different here," Kamal laughed when I (jokingly) asked him if he intended to misappropriate money like his "name-fellow" Lutfur.

Many in the area, Radzilowski tells me, were concerned about the neighborhood after Hamtramck elected its first Muslim-majority city council. "We had a meeting after the last election—the [Piast]

Institute is known for non-partisanship—city officials, leaders of Polish societies, leaders of the Muslim groups and we sat around and said 'Ok, what does this mean now that you have majority in the council?' The biggest concern of the older residents was, 'You're not going to shut down the bars, are you?'" He laughed, and added, "And they said 'No.'"

He then revealed that, demographically speaking, the area is already lost to the Middle Eastern and Asian cultures. "In fact I've always told people the future of politics [in Hamtramck] is going to be Yemenis versus Bangladeshis, not Christians against Muslims," he said. I remember my eyelids widening. Then he transitioned to the call to prayer I mentioned previously: "But the issue of call to prayer came up in 2004. I detail what happened [in an article]."

He certainly did, as did the *New York Times*.

"My main objection is simple," local resident and born again Christian Joanne Golen told the paper in 2004. She continued, "I don't want to be told that Allah is the true and only God five times a day, 365 days a year."

"Everyone talks about their rights," added local Chuck Schultz, reminding the paper "The rights of Christians have been stripped from them. Last week there were Muslims praying downstairs, in a public building. If Christians tried to do that, the ACLU would shut us down."

Cindy, whom I spoke with in a local coffee store, said the same of other mosques nearby that are often billed as "community centers" which transition into mosques without the requisite permissions. Once that happens, the schools start popping up. Then the locals' houses start getting bought up. Then men in robes start knocking on doors, asking what it would take to buy them out of the neighborhood.

Of course, those who oppose the call to prayer are branded as Islamophobes. But who can blame them for being afraid when they hear "Allahu Akbar"—the clarion call of terrorists across the Western world—blasted across their senior citizens' center at five o'clock in the morning? Often we hear that people who object to cultural shifts should learn to be "tolerant." But who is demonstrating tolerance or consideration for the elderly residents who happen to live across from a "community center" that turned itself into a mosque without local approval?

The issue, according to locals, remains mostly unsettled. Sometimes the call to prayer can be heard. Sometimes not. Sometimes it is loud. Sometimes it is tolerable. But for a town with a majority-Muslim city council—and maybe a state that will have the first Muslim governor in the history of the United States—perhaps residents feel they have no recourse.

It may not be all bad, however. At least from an existential perspective. Without the wave of new migrants, Hamtramck's economy would be a basket case. I mean a bigger basket case than it currently is given Detroit's financial and economic woes, post-2008 recession. The new Americans—or Arab-Americans—are responsible for keeping the place ticking over. It is evident just by driving around town. Formerly Polish restaurants are now Middle Eastern. Old Polski Skleps (Polish shops) now sell hijabs, niqabs, and hookah pipes. And what is most striking for the motor city itself is an old car lot with signage that used to read, "CARS," but now reads, "ISLAM," in massive, green lettering hoisted high above Joseph Campau Street.

Just imagine for a second, especially if you're on the political Left and reading this, that you're not making a judgment on the matter, that you're not seeking to defend a philosophy or ideology. Just imagine how stark that image—"ISLAM"—is for a formerly Polish-dominated, manufacturing city in middle America.

Dr. Radzilowski, however, claims that the call to prayer matter "was settled relatively easily." The Piast Institute—also an official Census Information Center—was directly involved in bringing about the settlement. However residents still express concern about the settlement and some still complain about the call to prayer. Apparently, local community groups agreed to a city ordinance that allows the local government to regulate the noise if need be, and a $500 donation to a local park. The idea that a local, majority-Muslim city council would regulate the call to prayer into silence is naive. Dr. Radzilowski recounted the story of how the settlement was brought about:

> We brought the Polish council and the head of all Muslim societies in Detroit in, here, ostensibly to kick off a fundraising campaign to improve the park and statue. People were coming from all over. The Army of David—this bunch of guys from Tennessee—showed up. They'd been protesting the removal of the Ten Commandments in Alabama and they drove up here. All sorts of people, Muslims, radical Christians, also some leftists. Except the people of the city. The *New York Times* was here covering it.
>
> We had this press conference. We had six imams, a large number of Catholic clergy and including a Polish national church here, half of whose parishioners are Hispanics because it seems like a more traditional Catholic church.

We had some Protestant local clergy. We had South African Lutheran clergy. We had a Nigerian chief.

We had this big press conference, speeches, out in the street. We assembled at the statue. We had prayer service. Everybody talked about brotherhood and all that sort of this. Then by arrangement, Abdul's mosque presented a check for $500 to the committee to improve the park. Then we all went and had a meal at a Polish restaurant. Half the menu was provided by a halal restaurant. Then it died. For the next two months, before the election.

No one appeared before City Council, nobody wrote letters to the editor. All the community leaders came together and said, "Hey, you know, we just have to live together." The ordinance was passed—it was challenged—it went to a vote, the vote [was] won very handily. Although as I told Abdul, it's one of those things where you should not ask permission. The previous law permitted it. He went to city council—ridiculous—he wanted to make sure that he got permission. So they passed another ordinance which permits the city to regulate [the call to prayer]. They can even stop it if it's a public nuisance.

When I asked him where the call to prayer is being broadcasted from, he replied, "It's all [mosques]. There are seventeen, I think, in the city." That's in a city that covers about 2.1 square miles and has a population of around twenty-two thousand people. In fact, estimates for the number of mosques in Hamtramck range from twelve to seventeen. This means there's either one mosque for every 0.18 square miles or one for every 0.13

square miles. That's a lot of mosques. In comparison, the ChurchFinder website lists fourteen churches in Hamtramck.

Radzilowski had this to say about the aftermath of the settlement:

> [Complaints] were coming from all over the city…the new building, two blocks down on the corner. The original mosque is directly behind it.
>
> Some of the original complaints were about discrimination in voting, before 2004. The woman who was the city clerk…she was married to an Arab, but she was one of those who was accused of challenging—obviously Muslim or Arabic—voters.
>
> What makes this a majority Muslim city, if it is, it's pretty close, there's about 22/23 percent [who] are Yemini. About 20 percent are Bangladeshi, the remainder are Bosnians. But the Bosnians don't identify with either group and if you go to the Bosnian Islamic Center on Caniff, you'll see right across the street is the Bosnia-Herzogovina bar.

He concluded by laughing, "My Muslim friends say, 'These guys are yours.'"

The question of whether or not Hamtramck has a "majority Muslim" population came to national attention in 2015, right after its election of a majority-Muslim city council. Then Mayor Karen Majewski appeared on CNN to discuss the topic. The leftist organization Media Matters for America held up a clip of her interview as some kind of anti-Islam faux pas on anchor Carol Costello's behalf. Majewski was asked, "You govern a majority-Muslim-American city. Are you afraid?"

Majewski responded, "No, I'm not afraid."

During her interview, she said, "We have, as of our last election, which was a couple weeks ago, we elected a Muslim-majority council. Whether the demographics of the city would say we're a Muslim majority city, I don't think that we're there **yet**. I think we're probably somewhere in the 40 percent Muslim for the city overall. But our city council that will take office in January will be a majority Muslim council."[13]

In the quote above, I added emphasis on the word "yet." It proves—to me at least—that Majewski's intervention was little more than a technicality.

Once you watch the clip, it is clear that even the city's mayor isn't fully in touch with Hamtramck's shifting demographics. She seems to think that the city isn't on the cusp of becoming predominately Muslim. But if the Muslim demographic continues to grow at the rate it has been, it won't be long before Hamtramck is a majority Muslim city. It seems odd that Media Matters for America would draw attention to the leading question "Are you afraid?" Was the organization hoping to imply that it won't be long before local governments start answering "Yes" to that question? For some reason, I don't think Majewski would have changed her answer if an extra 11 percent of Muslims had tipped the city's demographic scales.

According to the city's demographic trends, those scales may be tipped very soon. Muslims are moving to Hamtramck for a variety of reasons. Some of those reasons are the same reasons people like me want to leave London, or Washington, DC, or dread having to move somewhere like New York City.

"I asked Abdul why he moved here from Queens [New York]," Dr. Radzilowski tells me. "He said, 'Well we lived opposite the bus garage. There's lots of drugs, sex in the alley, I didn't

want my kids to grow up there. We came to Hamtramck because
we liked it. One of the things Hamtramck has [is] nice, easily
affordable housing, good housing stock. It's its own separate
entity, which was very important. And it has always been an
immigrant area. So you can find...these people tend to be home-
owners, around 65 percent already, the Bangladeshis, are buying
their own homes."

Other local minority groups, he says, are being squeezed out
by the newcomers. His comments were echoed by local black
residents I spoke with. Here is what Radzilowski said on the
topic:

> In a letter I wrote to the *Review*, the local newspaper,
> [it] indicates one of the things that is happening...that
> the black population of this area is dropping very
> dramatically and they're being essentially squeezed
> out, more by the Bangladeshis than the Yemenis.
> Yemenis I believe, about 50 percent are buying their
> own houses.
>
> The Bangladeshis are also a slightly smaller group
> in Hamtramck but in the zip code that surrounds
> Hamtramck they're the dominant group. The whole
> area to the north, which was Polish and became
> increasingly black, the Bangladeshis are basically forc-
> ing them out. Bangladeshi kids are getting the sh*t
> kicked out of them at school, but they're [still] moving
> in. Because the blacks are renters.

He tells me the area's newcomers are creating a second-
generation population of Muslims. New immigrants are still
coming from all around the Arab world, South Asia, and so

forth. But the communities that are already in the city seem to be having children faster than the freshest waves of immigrants arrive. He hopes these children will grow up to become just as American as him.

I asked him if this community of first and second generation Muslims had problems with extremism. He replied,

> You always get some guy who wants to [say], "Yeah we're setting up Sharia law here!" but in fact I was at Kamal's announcement of his candidacy and one of the most respected imams got up and said, "remember, the press is going to be here now we might have a Muslim mayor and if they ask you, you say 'Sharia law? No! Sharia law? No! Sharia law? No!' We're governed by the statutes of the city of Hamtramck and by the laws of the United States. So we're not establishing Sharia law. That belongs to another place and another time. We can observe it whenever we want in our own families, but Shariah law? No!"

I was a little taken aback by the respected imam's words. As you can imagine, it was hard not to immediately picture the No Go Zones in Europe that have elements of Sharia law woven into the communities and locales they have overrun. In those places, Sharia probably started out as something residents observed in their "own families" too. This is how areas in the West become compliant with Sharia: slowly on a small scale, not all at once on a broad scale.

Perhaps I am jumping to conclusions. But the whole scenario seems too familiar to me. On the lead up to the general election in the United Kingdom in June 2017, the issues in the East

London Tower Hamlets were again placed in the forefront of my mind. Local Member of Parliament Jim Fitzpatrick, who was on the sharp end of the stick for criticizing the infiltration of the local Labour Party by Sharia-compliant Muslims, tweeted his support for Labour figures like Sadiq Khan. Khan once worked as a lawyer in defense of the Nation of Islam's Louis Farrakhan, and he once said that terrorism in the West is "part and parcel" of everyday life.

In other words, even the most well-meaning, local do-gooders can be naïve. Radzilowski is obviously a highly intelligent man who takes great pride in his area. But I fear he doesn't know what may be coming. His friendships with local imams may even cloud his judgment. I have to keep reminding myself that he knows the locals, he knows the area, and he knows the players.

Still, it is hard to forget that Michigan is vulnerable to the schemes of terrorism that probably started out as extremism. In 2006, the *Chicago Tribune* reported the case of Talal Khalil Chahine, the owner of the local Middle Eastern food chain La Shish:

> Using a double set of books, the owner of La Shish chain of 15 restaurants evaded taxes while funneling some $20 million to the Lebanese militant force Hezbollah in recent years, according to an indictment returned in May, the paper reported.
>
> The restaurateur, Talal Chahine, has fled to Lebanon but denies wrongdoing. The case is one of several across the U.S. that link Americans with smuggling operations of illicit drugs, cigarettes and even baby formula and Viagra to profit Hezbollah—designated by the State Department as a terrorist organization.[14]

222 NO GO ZONES

It would have been bad enough if the criminality surrounding Chahine had been limited to this scam. Unfortunately, it is likely he also encouraged his "sister-in-law," Nada Nadim Prouty, to follow in his footsteps. In 2007, Prouty pled guilty to fraudulently obtaining United States citizenship, gaining employment in the Federal Bureau of Investigation (FBI) and Central Intelligence Agency (CIA), and using her employment to query information about her relatives and Hezbollah. The full Department of Justice press release on her case bears careful reading:

> DETROIT—Nada Nadim Prouty, a 37-year-old Lebanese national and resident of Vienna, Va., pleaded guilty today in the Eastern District of Michigan to charges of fraudulently obtaining U.S. citizenship, which she later used to gain employment at the FBI and CIA; accessing a federal computer system to unlawfully query information about her relatives and the terrorist organization Hizballah; and conspiracy to defraud the United States.
>
> The announcement was made today by Stephen J. Murphy, U.S. Attorney for the Eastern District of Michigan; Kenneth L. Wainstein, Assistant Attorney General for National Security; Willie T. Hulon, Executive Assistant Director of the FBI's National Security Branch; Brian M. Moskowitz, Special Agent in Charge of the Detroit Office of U.S. Immigration and Customs Enforcement (ICE); and Kurt Rice, Chicago Field Office Special Agent in Charge for the U.S. State Department's Diplomatic Security Service.
>
> At a hearing in Detroit before the U.S. District Court Judge Avern Cohn, Prouty entered a plea of

guilty to counts one, two and three of a second super-seding information. Count one of the information charges conspiracy, for which the maximum penalty is five years imprisonment and a $250,000 fine. Count two charges unauthorized computer access, for which the maximum penalty is one year imprisonment and a $100,000 fine. Count three charges naturalization fraud, for which the maximum penalty is 10 years imprisonment and a $250,000 fine, and requires the court to de-naturalize the defendant.

"This case highlights the importance of conduct-ing stringent and thorough background investiga-tions," said U.S. Attorney Stephen J. Murphy. "It's hard to imagine a greater threat than the situation where a foreign national uses fraud to attain citizen-ship and then, based on that fraud insinuates herself into a sensitive position in the U.S. government. I applaud the excellent investigative work of the FBI, ICE and DHS, which led to the successful prosecution today."

"It is a sad day when one of our public servants breaches our security and trust," said Assistant Attor-ney General Kenneth L. Wainstein. "This defendant engaged in a pattern of deceit to secure U.S. citizen-ship, to gain employment in the intelligence commu-nity, and to obtain and exploit her access to sensitive counterterrorism intelligence. It is fitting that she now stands to lose both her citizenship and her liberty."

"We became aware of this compromise in Decem-ber 2005 and moved to address any further damage," said Willie T. Hulon, Executive Assistant Director of the FBI's National Security Branch. "The FBI worked closely with other agencies to investigate this matter. We continue to evaluate our security practices and will make any necessary changes."

"Nada Prouty's guilty plea should serve as a solemn warning to those who say they've pledged their allegiance to the United States and then make the conscious decision to place America's interests at risk," said Brian M. Moskowitz, Special Agent in Charge of the ICE Office of Investigations in Detroit. "Becoming a naturalized U.S. citizen is an honor and a privilege. ICE will do everything in its power to see that those who achieve this honor by fraud and deception are brought to justice."

Naturalization Fraud

According to documents filed in court by the government, Prouty first entered the United States from Lebanon on June 24, 1989, on a one-year, non-immigrant student visa. After her visa expired, she remained in the country, residing in Taylor, Mich., with her sister, Elfat El Aouar, and an individual named Samar Khalil Nabbouth. In order to remain in the United States and evade U.S. immigration laws, Prouty later offered money to an unemployed U.S. citizen to marry her. On August 9, 1990, Prouty married the U.S. citizen. As planned, Prouty never lived with her fraudulent "husband," but continued to live with her sister and Nabbouth.

Prouty later submitted a series of false, fraudulent and forged documents and letters to federal immigration officials to verify the validity of the fraudulent marriage in order to obtain permanent residency status, and, later, U.S. citizenship, thereby committing naturalization fraud. On Aug. 5, 1994, the former Immigration and Naturalization Service granted Prouty U.S. citizenship under the name "Nada Nadim Deladurantaye." The following year, she filed for a divorce from her fraudulent husband, and later obtained a U.S. passport, which she used to travel overseas.

Talal Khalil Chahine

According to court documents, from May 1992 through April 1993, and again, from August through November 1994, Prouty was employed as a waitress and hostess at La Shish Inc., a chain of Middle Eastern restaurants in Detroit that was owned by Talal Khalil Chahine. During this time, Chahine wrote a letter for submission into Prouty's immigration file attesting to the validity of Prouty's false marriage.

Chahine is currently a fugitive believed to be in Lebanon. He, along with Prouty's sister, Elfat El Aouar, and others were charged in 2006 in the Eastern District of Michigan with tax evasion in connection with a scheme to conceal more than $20 million in cash received by La Shish restaurants and to route funds to persons in Lebanon. Last month, Chahine was also charged in the Eastern District of Michigan, along with a senior ICE official in Detroit and others in a bribery and extortion conspiracy in which federal immigration benefits were allegedly awarded to illegal aliens in exchange for money.

Employment at FBI and CIA

In April 1999, through a series of false representations and use of her fraudulently procured proof
of U.S. citizenship, Prouty, then known as "Nada
Nadim Alley," obtained employment as a special
agent of the FBI. It was a prerequisite to FBI employment that she be a U.S. citizen. As a special agent
with the FBI, Prouty was granted a security clear-
ance and assigned to the FBI's Washington Field
Office to work on an extraterritorial squad investigating crimes against U.S. persons overseas. During
her tenure with the FBI, Prouty was not assigned to
work on investigations involving the international
terrorist group Hizballah.

In August 2000, Prouty's sister, Elfat El Aouar,
entered into a marriage with Talal Khalil Chahine,
the owner of La Shish Inc. In September 2000, Prouty,
while employed as an FBI special agent, used the FBI's
computerized Automated Case System (ACS), without
authorization, to query her own name, her sister's
name, and that of her brother-in-law, Talal Khalil
Chahine. In addition, on or about June 4, 2003,
Prouty accessed the FBI's ACS and obtained information from a national security investigation into Hizballah that was being conducted by the FBI's Detroit
Field Office.

According to court documents, in August 2002,
Prouty's sister, Elfat El Aouar, and her brother-in-law,
Talal Khalil Chahine, attended a fundraising event in
Lebanon where the keynote speakers were Chahine

himself and Sheikh Muhammad Hussein Fadlallah. Sheikh Fadlallah had previously been designated by the U.S. government as a Specially Designated Global Terrorist based upon his status as a leading ideological figure with Hizballah.

In June 2003, through a series of false representations and use of her fraudulently procured proof of U.S. citizenship, Prouty, then known as "Nada Nadim Prouty," voluntarily left her position with the FBI and obtained employment with the CIA. It was also a prerequisite to CIA employment that she be a U.S. citizen.

On Nov. 6, 2007, Prouty resigned her position at the CIA. Pursuant to the terms of her plea agreement, she has agreed to fully and truthfully cooperate with the CIA on any matters the CIA deems necessary to transition Prouty out of its employment in a manner consistent with safeguarding the national security of the United States. This cooperation includes participation in debriefing and polygraph interviews.

The ongoing investigation into this matter is being conducted by the FBI and ICE, with assistance from the U.S. Department of State, Diplomatic Security Service, and the Internal Revenue Service.

The case is being prosecuted by Eric M. Straus, Chief of the National Security Unit, and Kenneth R. Chadwell, Assistant U.S. Attorney, from the U.S. Attorney's office for the Eastern District of Michigan, as well as Mark J. Jebson, Special Assistant U.S. Attorney and Senior Assistant Chief Counsel for U.S. Immigration and Customs Enforcement.[15]

Prouty, who has since written a book about her saga, maintains that she is an American patriot. Subsequent investigations did not yield evidence that suggested she ever turned over any information to Chahine or Hezbollah. Moreover, it is unlikely that she would support a Muslim terrorist group like Hezbollah because she was born Druze—a religion whose adherents are persecuted by Islamic fundamentalists—and is now a practicing Christian. Still, her mistake—being dragged into the sphere of Chahine in her attempt to gain U.S. citizenship—was grave. It cost her a livelihood and almost her right to remain in the United States. In the end, she was not deported.

I asked locals in the Yemeni cafe in Hamtramck what they thought of this story. Based on the reactions I got, it left a bitter taste in the mouths of Michiganders.

"How do I know when I go in here that I'm not funding a terrorist organization down the line?" one said.

I replied, "I'm not sure your chicken schwarma is going to make a huge difference as a one off."

We joked about this until he eventually changed the subject. He pointed out—more out of intrigue than hostility—women in pairs shuffling down Joseph Campau street wearing full niqabs. I'll be honest, this sight disgusts me every time I encounter it. Not only is it an outward sign of Sharia, it is also an atrocious practice. No woman should ever feel compelled—by a culture or a religion—to drape herself in black from head to toe and hide herself in public. Whenever I see a niqabed woman, it makes me deeply sad.

Unfortunately, there are plenty of places in Hamtramck where women can buy their latest cover-alls. "What happens is everyone has their own," explains Dr. Radzilowski. He adds, "The Poles don't go to the Bangladeshi stores. They don't buy

Bangladeshi clothes. The Yemenis don't go to the Bangladeshi store. As Hamtramck always was, people have their own stores, their own sub groups in the city. It'll loosen up a little bit but there's no reason anyone would want to shop in a Muslim clothing store."

This voluntary segregation interested me. I asked him if there were any local issues surrounding the latest wave of migrants. He replied,

> A thing that bothers people more [is] that we have a lot of charter schools that are either associated with Yemenis or Bangladeshis. Some of them are very successful. Frontier. It's primarily a Yemeni school. The issue is, are they running parochial schools? Are they praying when they shouldn't be praying in schools? It's alright if it's not part of the school curriculum— that's a distinction often lost on people. You hear that quite often.
>
> More than the issue of dress, it would be the issue of Muslim parochial schools.
>
> The charter schools—some of them, Frontier is the best example—are the best schools, according to state standards. They're obviously doing well in terms of an American curriculum.

Hearing this gave me hope for America. Children who attend excellent schools in America are inundated with patriotism. The flag, the anthem, and the pledge of allegiance all help to preserve some semblance of the nation state and command the loyalty of its inhabitants, whether they're aware of this or not. Patriotism is one of the surest pathways to integration.

Anything that stunts the growth of patriotism in an area that is at risk of becoming a No Go Zone concerns me. This concern is always roused when I see satellite dishes adorning the rooftops and balconies of houses and apartment buildings in such areas. Language barriers stymie integration like nothing else.

"I don't know how many families would be getting channels from overseas," Radzilowski says. I discovered he had some interesting experiences in Europe related to this matter. He revealed, "I was in Germany about seven or eight years ago at a summit meeting on the German problem on migrant groups. That was a big complaint about the Turkish minority. The third generation born in Germany know less German than their parents." He continued, "About 25 years ago I was at a conference. An elderly Belgian professor was talking about the first modern forms of Islam evolving in Belgium and the Netherlands."

"It's quite the opposite," I said.

"Exactly," he shot back, without a second thought.

He then compared this experience to that of Polish-Americans in Hamtramck. I think this comparison is misplaced in terms of culture and variegated dynamics like race, religiosity, politics, and more. Different groups simply behave differently. It shouldn't be controversial to say that. But I am sure I will take some heat for writing it in this book, so let me clarify by saying people aren't the same the world over. They don't have the same instincts or tendencies because they don't have the same life experiences or histories to inform their behavior.

Nevertheless, the story of the Turkish-Germans still reminds Radzilowski of the Polish-Americans' story:

> One of the things I've noticed, I was the acting director
> of the Immigration Research Center at the University

of Minnesota for a number of years, and I worked there for decades, we made the distinction between the immigrants and the ethnics. Once you become an ethnic American...first most came here with only a most rudimentary national identity. They became Polish and American at the same time. The second generation created the identity. I'm third generation and I grew up speaking Polish. This was a very insular community. It was institutionally complete. Except for being able to provide employment, and Dodge provided a lot of that employment.

There was no question we were loyal Americans. That appears very early. Poles had the per capita largest enlistment in the U.S. Army [during WWII]. They had a chance [in WWI] to join a Polish Army but they chose to serve in the American Army. Right from the beginning they were Americans.

As early as 1905 a local Polish paper was carrying detailed descriptions of the Detroit Tigers games. They were very proud of their city, the buildings they built here. Next to African Americans they were the next most discriminated against group.

Again, I think the Polish-Americans saga in Hamtramck is unique. No other wave of immigrants in the area has a story like this.

———

One of my most jarring experiences of Michigan occurred in the Arab American National Museum (located in Dearborn), which is affiliated with the Smithsonian group of museums and mostly funded by the Rockefeller Foundation, local corporations, and the governments of Saudi Arabia and Qatar. The museum building is unassuming. But scattered throughout its lackadaisical exhibits is a vicious Arab nationalism that aims its ire at Israel and even President Trump.

On the ground floor, a temporary exhibit funded by the local, Troy-based Kresge Foundation offers insight into the "Arab American" mind. The "Activist Wall," which has a Lear Corporation plaque beside it, sports hand-written Post-It notes with statements such as "I make sure people know ISRAEL IS AN APARTHEID STATE" and "Free Palestine" and "Viva falasteen!" and "I am a black nationalist." But upstairs, on the museum's third (and most tedious) floor, there is an entire wall dedicated to anti-President-Trump activism.

A few scraps of paper, taped together and dog-eared at the edges, recreate a tweet from then Governor Mike Pence decrying a Muslim ban for the United States. I wondered why there wasn't a placard somewhere nearby explaining that the Trump (and Pence) administration has clarified the "ban," instead pressing for a far more reasonable temporary travel restriction combined with extreme vetting. It seemed like the Saudi-funded museum was propagating old, and therefore fake, news to its visitors, ostensibly to whip up resistance against the U.S. government.

Pictures from anti-Trump marches in Washington, DC; Baltimore, Maryland; and Oakland, California adorn the walls around the tweet. Aside from photos of the marches, the backbone of this "exhibit" seems to be quotes from hijab-clad march attendees and the glorification of nonsensical placards that read "Palestinian Justice is a Feminist Value." (Side note: any of these "activists" want to head to Gaza and tell Hamas about Palestinian feminism? Thought not.)

Back downstairs, cartoons on the walls depict Israelis as monsters, demons, aggressors, and rapists. There are also stories from first and second generation "Palestinians" that describe the "Nakba" (catastrophe), which is what Arabs consider the founding of the State of Israel. Nakba Day is May 15. In 2011, it was the rationale behind attacks on Israel's borders and reciprocal defensive measures by the Israeli army.

Perhaps these exhibits would all be completely normal in the Arab world. But this was Detroit, not Damascus. Dearborn, not Doha.

I left the museum with a sense of disgust. Witnessing foreign government funding being used for anti-American activism in the heart of the United States filled me with an impending sense of doom. It was just as Marion Le Pen and my guide in Brussels told me: they're using Western liberties—in this case the First Amendment—against us.

NINE

FROM AMERICA, WITH RADICAL ISLAM

I believe that Sharia is the best way of life, I believe one day it will come to America and the rest of the world.

—**ANJEM CHOUDARY,** RADICAL IMAM, SPEAKING ON FOX NEWS WITH SEAN HANNITY

This book took me across the Western world. It led me to people I should have had no business meeting. I, a West London boy who studied politics at the University of Westminster, arguably should not be the one telling these stories from the United States, or Belgium, or France, or Sweden. But the failure of the mainstream media to produce real reporting on No Go Zones has left me with no other choice than to bring this topic to light.

In retrospect, I suppose this project found me. After all, Mohammed Emwazi ("Jihadi John") attended my alma mater just two years after me. No, I never met him. But coincidences like this are more of a predictable eventuality when we consider the governments across the Western world that have not only failed to tackle radical Islam but have also allowed the conditions in which it flourishes to fester and grow.

As we draw to the end of this book, I suppose the last crucial question that must be answered is "What now?"

I remember sitting in a pitch meeting with the wonderful folks at Regnery Publishing discussing the timetable for the release of this book. It was just after the U.S. presidential election, and they were concerned that the book may not be relevant if President Trump managed to defeat radical Islam quickly enough, as he hyperbolically alluded to on the campaign trail. I chuckled to myself.

I suppose I shouldn't have. No Go Zones are an incredibly serious subject. However, the notion that radical Islam can be exterminated in a few months, or even in one presidential term, is hopeful nonsense. Realistically, it will take a long time to accomplish this goal. We need to understand and acknowledge the issues surrounding No Go Zones in Europe, heed the warnings they represent, and implement policies that will ensure these issues do not migrate to the United States—though, in my estimation, they already have.

I am aware of how vague and political that proposal seems. It is meant to be vague because at this point in the dilemma, a solution can only be an aim, a goal, or an aspiration. There are so many impediments standing in our way. A lasting solution to this problem requires so much hard work and humble collaboration that preparing for the war will be just as difficult as winning it.

First, of course, we will have to address the political Left's opposition to solving the problems stemming from radical Islam, which is an issue it likes to keep handy for its electoral and philosophical aims. The Left knows that if one group or religion or nation is targeted by extreme vetting or even a travel ban, its entire concept of the universal free movement of people and completely open borders—its ultimate aim—will be destroyed.

Second, we will have to embolden law enforcement and security and intelligence communities to tackle the unique issues that arise in places like Dearborn, California, or New York—another place I visited on my trip that displayed signs of closed communities. If these three communities continue to be reticent when addressing these issues, these areas will continue to produce the most heinous and worrisome outgrowth of No Go Zones: terrorism.

Unfortunately, the first hurdle, created by the Left, is especially difficult to clear. It cannot stomach the idea of curtailing behavior that encourages jihadism. When pressed on this issue, the Left frequently points to religious groups like the Amish and Jews who have religious liberty protections secured by the First Amendment. When you clarify that Jews aren't jumping in SUVs and mowing down civilians on Westminster Bridge, you are immediately met with the third problem we must overcome before we can effectively deal with the developing threat of No Go Zones: "Islamophobia."

Let's address these three things in reverse order.

As we have already learned in this book, the word Islamophobia is, in effect, a popularized Muslim Brotherhood term now habitually bandied about by often well-meaning, though embarrassingly naive, leftists or "moderates." In reality, these "useful idiots" are toeing the line of institutions and organizations that, on a 50,000-foot level, want to force the Islamic principle of fitna on the Western world. Why else would there be such vicious reactions to some satirical, French cartoons of Muhammad?

"Behead all those who insult the Prophet," the placards in London have read. This is the enforcement of fitna. Phil Haney had some choice words for me on this issue:

> To me the word Islamophobia is a secular political term for a Quranic concept: Fitna.
>
> Fitna is the opposition to the advancement of Islam. It's also translated quite frequently as oppression. It also means resistance, interference with, a lot of different adjectives. But basically understand the concept of Islam advancing forward and anybody who stands in the way of that—whether it be in the social, political, or law enforcement arena—it's causing the Islamic community fitna.
>
> It's a capital offense according to them. So for me Islamophobia...this is by Muslims who know the concept of fitna and in their mind I'm sure are thinking: "You are causing the Islamic community opposition or oppression or resistance. You're committing Fitna."
>
> And the catalyst for that—two verbs in the Quran, that are more violent than verbs you have that only occur 40 times.
>
> The first verb, Qital, which means slaughter. The other is Kharaj which means to violently displace. Which means when fitna is encountered by the forward movement of Islam, resistance, then the Quran authorizes the use of these two operative verbs—they occur four times more frequently in the Quran than jihad. About 170–180 times. So for me Islamophobia

is a disguise word. When they say Islamophobia, they're thinking Fitna.

[Quranic verses] 5:32 and 5:33: For those who cause mischief in the land their left hand or their right foot will be cut off, they will be crucified, or killed. Such is the fate of those who cause mischief.

Yes, [fitna is mischief].

This is a war because the authorized response according to the Quran...2:191–193: "Kill them. Slaughter them."

The Western world is trying to hold back the tide...just the act of trying to hold it back is Fitna.

You can see it occurring, if you look closely enough, across the Western media. Islamophobia has become an obsession, as evidenced by the conclusions that are leapt to when Ahmadiyya Muslims are attacked. But there are other more telling incidents of this nature that are worth noticing in local and national media in the United States.

In June 2015, a Muslim teacher claimed that he had to change his name from Hamid Mahmood to Harry Mason in order to get more job interviews. Lazy journalists jumped on the story, quoting Mahmood at length, propagating his victimhood status.

"Last year, in May, I sent off an application and cover letter to Langdon Academy via email and through the official application system," Mahmood told *BuzzFeed*, adding, "I didn't receive any sort of response. I rang them up to ask them about the progress of the application, and the school said it would get back to me. Two weeks later, I was told I didn't get shortlisted."

"I wondered if it was something about myself that was the reason I didn't get shortlisted," he said. "So I did something that would test my assumption that I was rejected because of racism or Islamophobia."

He submitted his resume under the name Harry Mason instead and claims he received many more positive responses than he did when his resume was submitted under the name Hamid Mahmood. Mahmood's revised resume also omitted his experience working at the Islamic Institute of Education. He was upfront about this. But the media never reported that this school is attached to the Deobandi Markazi Masjid in Dewsbury, the Tablighi Jamaat headquarters.

It is likely someone advised Mahmood to omit this affiliation from his resume. Why? Perhaps this person was afraid that whoever reviewed his application would know what the Deobandi Markazi Masjid actually is. All a potential employer would have to do is Google the term to discover that in 2006, the *Daily Mail* linked the mosque, and a "Muslim rights activist" in the news, to the 7/7 bombers who committed terrorist atrocities in London. "The mosque is run by Tablighi Jamaat, a radical Islamic movement believed by intelligence agencies to be a fertile source for recruiting young extremists," the report stated.

In fact, it's possible that the employers who reviewed Mahmood's unrevised resume read the 2006 *Times of London* report that stated, "Several of the suspects arrested in August over the alleged plot to blow up transatlantic airliners had attended meetings of Tablighi Jamaat, which French intelligence has labelled an 'antechamber of fundamentalism.' The FBI says it is a fertile breeding ground for al-Qaeda." Or perhaps they read the 2007 *Times of London* report, which said, "One of the suicide bombers who attacked London in July 2005,

Shehzad Tanweer, studied at the Deobandi seminary in Dews-bury and Mohammad Sidique Khan, the leader of the 7/7 terror plot, was a regular worshipper at the adjoining mosque. Richard Reid, the shoe bomber, was said to have been influenced by Tablighi Jamaat, several of whose adherents were also among those arrested last year over an alleged plot to blow up transat-lantic airliners."

Mr. Mahmood never replied to me when I approached him for a comment on this story in 2015. Just one month later, national news outlets reported that despite its sterling rating from Britain's Office for Standards in Education, the Islamic Institute of Education threatened to expel students who mixed with non-Muslims or "outsiders."

Whether Mahmood knew what he was doing—maybe some-one else put him up to it—or not, he is responsible for perpetuat-ing a trend in which Islamophobia is used as a tool to fool the national media and the public into believing that there is a rag-ing, institutional, xenophobia across Britain. The Mahmood incident is a prime example of how the word Islamophobia has begun to lose whatever scant meaning it ever had. That being said, discrimination against some Muslims certainly exists. I've experienced it myself, from across the political spectrum, too. But it scarcely exists to the degree that those who seek to benefit from it claim it does.

Another great example of this trend is how one group called Tell MAMA—long regarded as an expert on the subject of Islamophobia in the United Kingdom—lost its government funding (yep, UK tax payers were subsidizing this nonsense) after it was discovered that the group inflated the number of Islamophobic-fueled hate crimes. Andrew Gilligan at the *Tele-graph* reported the story:

A controversial project claiming to measure anti-Muslim attacks will not have its government grant renewed after police and civil servants raised concerns about its methods.

The project, called Tell Mama, claimed that there had been a "sustained wave of attacks and intimidation" against British Muslims after the killing of Drummer Lee Rigby, with 193 "Islamophobic incidents" reported to it, rising to 212 by last weekend.

The group's founder, Fiyaz Mughal, said he saw "no end to this cycle of violence," describing it as "unprecedented." The claims were unquestioningly repeated in the media.

Tell Mama and Mr Mughal did not mention, however, that 57 percent of the 212 reports referred to activity that took place only online, mainly offensive postings on Twitter and Facebook, or that a further 16 percent of the 212 reports had not been verified. Not all the online abuse even originated in Britain.

Contrary to the group's claim of a "cycle of violence" and a "sustained wave of attacks," only 17 of the 212 incidents, 8 percent, involved the physical targeting of people and there were no attacks on anyone serious enough to require medical treatment. [1]

My advice regarding this issue is to view anyone who speaks on behalf of all Muslims—American or otherwise—with suspicion, especially if they do so to "speak out" against Islamophobia. It's likely that such a spokesman isn't a jihadist, or Islamist, or Muslim Brotherhood operative. He or she is probably just a "useful idiot," which is why we should always research his or her claims and reliability as a source. None of us should blindly trust the premise of Islamophobia because the term stems from what is basically a blasphemy law.

For advice about how to address the inability or unwillingness of law enforcement to manage issues that come from Islamism in America, I spoke with the Clarion Project's Ryan Mauro.

America's experiences with radical Islamic terrorism are well documented. Well, mostly.

We hear a lot about 9/11, San Bernardino, Orlando, the threat of the Muslim Brotherhood, and so on. But, to the frustration of some national security practitioners, we rarely hear about a little known group by the name of Jamaat al Fuqra. Fuqra (for short) was classified as a terror group in a 1999 State Department document, but it isn't formally proscribed in the United States. It is, however, banned in Pakistan.

Mauro told me, "Jamaat al Fuqra goes by the name Muslims of the Americas in the U.S., but they have various fronts such as the International Quranic Open University and they have an interfaith front, the United Muslim-Christian forum that they established as part of their image makeover when enough information about their extremism came out.

"They are led by a radical cleric in Pakistan named Sheikh Gilani, the name if it sounds familiar, that's the guy Daniel Pearl was going to interview when he was beheaded." Pearl was an Israeli-American working at the *Wall Street Journal* when he was beheaded by Muslim terrorists in 2002.

"The power of the leadership has been transferred somewhat to leader[s] in the U.S. including Gilani's sons," Mauro added, noting that the transfer was made in order to carry on the organization's leadership after Gilani, who is now a doddery, eighty-year-old man, dies.

"[It] could be at any moment," says Mauro. He adds, "They're more of a jihadi cult. They're not your typical jihadist group. They're a cult because they view their leader to being an essential, end time, prophetic figure that's involved in this great big war at the end of time, and whoever he appoints as his successor is also part of those prophecies."

"The membership is primarily African American," he explains, noting that "a lot of prison converts" make up a large portion of Fuqra's membership base.

"[T]hey first got established in the 1980s when they started…what they call Islamic villages around the U.S. Compounds that are dozens of acres large, private property, beginning with the one that is most famous which is the Islamberg headquarters in Hancock, New York. It's about 70 acres large," he reveals.

Islamberg, if you can believe it, is in the United States of America. Yes, it is private property, but it is still astonishing. It is also alarming that the establishment media is starting to recognize areas like these as genuine "towns." Here is a snippet from *The Guardian*'s 2016 report on another compound called Islamville in South Carolina: "Ramadan Saeed Shakir is the mayor of Islamville, an all-Muslim town of about 300 people located in the northern woodland of South Carolina."

Sorry, the mayor? Of a private compound? The media is already giving the cover of electoral legitimacy to this guy, who simply presides as a figurehead over a small enclave of cult followers.

"It's very sad that one of our national presidential candidates is speaking so much ill will about Islam and Muslims. Not just American Muslims but around the world," one of the residents of Islamville, Shakir, tells the paper. He continues, "It's unfortunate that the media is giving him that platform. He's no different from Jon Ritzheimer, the KKK, any of these bigots."

Interesting reporting. If I were given access to a Fuqra camp, I'm not sure I'd be asking the residents what they think about Trump. Surely, given the wealth of information amassed by the likes of Mauro and others like him, it might be more prudent to ask them about their links to Gilani and the guerilla training, whippings, and lashings that are conducted in their camps. Instead of reporting these things, the *Guardian* made Islamophobia the focus of the entire piece.

"We have video of guerilla warfare training going on," Mauro told me.

The videos have actually been aired a number of times by local and national media. Under the auspices of defense, Gilani has even produced YouTube videos urging Muslims to get in touch with Fuqra.

"Somewhere around 2001/2 of the women, sources inside the group say that stuff like that continues to go on but they won't wear the military fatigues anymore. The number two compound is Islamville in South Carolina which was defended by Mick Mulvaney who is now the leader of [the Office for Budget Management]," Mauro also explains.

The Trump appointee Mick Mulvaney met with the group in 2015, posing for pictures and declaring that the group posed no terror threat. But others disagree. A 2009 investigation led by WLTX News 19 quoted York County Sheriff Bruce Bryant, who said this about the group: "Absolutely it concerns me." He divulged his concerns about jihadism and the fact that the group had been linked to a number of terrorist attacks and plots, according to a 2006 report conducted by the government-funded Regional Organized Crime Information Center.

The report states, "Gilani is now known as an international terrorist. In Khartoum, in December 1993, at a major jihadist gathering, or 'terrorist roundtable,' Gilani and other terrorist leaders, such as Osama bin Laden, were caught on film by the Canadian Broadcasting Company chanting, 'Down, down USA! Down, down CIA!' and 'Death to the Jews!'"[2]

With such radical views stemming from the leadership of these groups, one would assume their memberships would be low. Sadly, that is not the case.

"According to the published estimates, [membership] is somewhere between 1,500 and 3,000," says Mauro. He adds,

> We hear different accounts as to how many people still strictly follow Gilani as their cult leader. Some may not follow Gilani but are jihadist. Some have fallen out of the group and are actually moderate but afraid to leave. If you include the kids, because they have a lot of kids, some estimates put it as high as 15,000.
>
> A lot of the members will say they follow Sharia law but don't. By a lot of hard line interpretations they violate Islam. Such as them putting Gilani essentially on the same level as Allah. Giving him the attributes of Allah is considered "shirk" (idolatry) in Islam. It's one of those sins you can't be forgiven for. They would argue that they're following Islamic jurisprudence, Sharia law. It's a hard line Sufi group. They call themselves Sufi-Sunni, a fusion of both.

After characterizing the groups' "demographics," Mauro reveals something far more disturbing about them. Mauro explains the links between Fuqra and the Tablighi Jamaat movement: "Yes [they're like the Deobandis], and there's been some links between them and Tablighi Jamaat. It looks like it'll be trips that Tablighi Jamaat will arrange and some MOA members will go to the mosque, on the trip itself. It doesn't look like an organizational agreement but there has been some links there, as well as links to Al Qaeda." In light of the reports about Gilani's support for the Afghan mujahideen (later the Taliban), it is unsurprising that Mauro is able to draw these connections.

In an interview with me, Phil Haney confirmed at least theoretical links (i.e. connections between the two groups' world views). "Probably the greatest incorrect premise about Deobandi Tablighis," he says, "first of all...they're very pro-jihad, they're just called a different name: they're called the Taliban. The Taliban is a Deobandi movement. Taliban just means plural for student. So if I tell you I'm a student, what's your natural question going to be?"

"What are you studying?" I reply.

"Deobandi Islam," he responds. He adds,

> And when I interviewed the madrassa boys, sometimes they would travel themselves from South Africa to Pakistan. On the walkabouts. They would go to different masjids and madrassas in Pakistan...I'd ask them if they ran into any Taliban when they were out and about over there: "Oh yeah." Well what'd you do? "Well, we pray. That's what they'd say to us. You pray, we'll shoot."
>
> And that's pretty much what summed it up for me. The difference between Tablighi and Taliban was the Taliban say "We'll shoot, you pray, Tablighis," while they're standing in the same foxhole.

So they're like fingers on the same hand. Lashkar-e-Taiba, Taliban, Tablighi Jamaat, they're all part of the same macro Deobandi movement which emerged in the 1860s and then allied with Saudi Arabia because they found out they're essentially pashtun/Urdu-speaking Wahhabis.

There are other sources that support the links between Fuqra and Tablighi Jamaat. A 2009 NYPD report reveals that Fuqra was the subject of a Terrorism Enterprise Investigation (TEI #14/03) and that one member was under surveillance as part of the Terrorism Enterprise Investigation into the Tablighi Jamaat group.[3] The Fuqra Files website also notes, "Fuqra/MOA is linked to TJ, according to B. Raman, [of] the counter-terrorism division of India's Research and Analysis Wing intelligence agency from 1988 to 1994. He went so far as to say that Fuqra is a 'front organization' for the TJ movement."

After discussing these links, Mauro told me, "You'll be met with hostility [if you visit]. They've said in the past that anyone who shows up will be welcomed in to see how peaceful and moderate [they] are. But now, as someone who has actually tried to take them up on their offer, I can tell you you'll be met with hostility, aggression, what looks like will often happen now is you'll show up and then they'll actually block your car in. You have a car behind you, seems like they have spotters outside the village. And you'll have a car in front of you. It's just an intimidation tactic."

I told him that scenario sounded like the Louis Theroux documentary on the Church of Scientology. He replied,

Right, yeah [it does sound like Scientology]. It has a lot of cultish, weird things. I've been followed. I attended one of their interfaith events and they were following me into the bathroom, asking a lot of questions. Being overly nice to the point where it gets uncomfortable, getting in your personal space. If it's a public event that is how they'll intimidate you. If you show up at the camp like Islamberg, they'll be like, "Who are you, what are you doing," probably call the cops, but that's happened to a few people I know now where they block in your car so you feel uncomfortable and leave.

Perhaps I spoke too soon. Mauro's experience sounds worse than Theroux's.

Now that we've learned all we need to know to determine that these groups' communities demonstrate telltale characteristics of No Go Zones, we need to determine if private property can be considered a true No Go Zone. Mauro thinks so, and I agree.

"The closest match for a No Go Zone in the United States would be the Fuqra lands," says Mauro. He continues,

They've been around since the early 1980s, their own publications have boasted about enforcing Shariah law in the lands. They've got pictures in their own publications saying how they'll whip someone but it's a voluntary whipping. They agree to the whipping because they're a member of the organization and they agree they have sinned and so they agree to the punishment.

Yes they have a Shariah court that will come in and enforce, if they find you with alcohol. Sometimes if they find you with a television. They banned that in some cases because someone was caught with pornography.

This is interesting. Surely there can be no greater authority in America than that of the U.S. government, even on private property. This doesn't seem to be the case in Fuqra lands. Mauro confirms this:

> [If someone says there isn't Sharia in the United States] they haven't researched Fuqra.
>
> When people say there are no radical Islamic communities in the United States. I remember Ted Cruz was attacked for this. They didn't look into the issue. I was on the *O'Reilly Factor* and a high level official for the Clinton administration was on with me and she said there are no radical Islamic communities to monitor because Ted Cruz has said that's the type of thing you need to monitor. And I said, I have a map of where they're at. She had no response to that but what was more alarming was that it was under the Clinton administration, where she served, that the State Department was saying this is [a] terror-linked group.
>
> So you even have people that criticize, that these groups being radical exist in the United States, unaware of what their own administration did.

I asked him if all of this was going on outside the knowledge of law enforcement and national policy makers. Mauro replied,

> There have been investigations into individual members. You have to have evidence of criminal activity

to launch an investigation. And you have to have evidence of ongoing criminal activity and success in your investigation to continue it. It can't go on indefinitely. We have declassified documents, many of them, thousands of them, showing that there are investigations going on in the United States and then they get closed. It's not an investigation of the group as a whole as far as we can tell.

This group engages in enough criminal activity...that has been the way law enforcement has handled the group. But regardless as to whether you shut down criminal revenue, you still have these camps across the United States with thousands of cult-like, fanatical followers that believe in jihad. That believe their leader is one day going to command them to commit jihad, and so the law enforcement actions that you see of them going after drug traffickers and their revenue is just not enough.

The camp in Colorado, one of the first ones which shut down in 1992. That was 101 acres large when the authorities raided it. They found weapons and tunnels underneath. Most people don't know that there was an actual terrorist training camp raided and shut down on U.S. soil in Colorado in 1992. But the rest of the network remained.

The other camp that was shut down—actually abandoned before it was raided—was Baladullah (Land of Allah) in California, which was shut down in 2001.

We have pictures that show they were shooting into cars that they had as target practice. That was a massive camp, some accounts put it as big as 400 acres. But if you look at the overhead footage of it, the thing was just massive. You wouldn't believe this thing existed in the United States.

In light of this, I asked Mauro if he thought the group's practices could be curtailed under the auspices of tackling Sharia law in the United States. I also reminded him Sharia practices include halal meat, the wearing of the niqab, and so forth. He replied,

> I think if you were to have a law against Shariah compliance, I'm not sure that it would pass, constitutionally, and it could go to court because what do we care the way someone eats food? I wouldn't want to go so far as banning Islamic customs and practices that don't threaten me. My focus is on national security and human rights.
>
> I'm concerned about the children that are not being educated in these camps, I'm concerned about the women that are being whipped. Even the men that are being punished in some of these camps. According to sources that we have inside the organization they've locked people up in trailers, they've lashed them, they've done physical beatings, they have something that is referred to as the hole where they actually put someone underground and they give you minimal food and water to survive and you're down there for—depending on your offence—30 days. These are stories we hear from multiple sources and I'm especially heartbroken for

the children that are being brainwashed and in some cases kids that are malnourished, not treated well, and a lot of them are poor because what jobs they do have, most of the revenue is going to Gilani.

I am not concerned with someone wearing the niqab in principle but I do also feel that an individual business should have the right to say "we are uncomfortable with someone coming in when we can't identify your face." Government institutions should be able to say that as well, whether it is a subway or an airport, you don't want to have the security risk of someone coming in and having their face covered. But if someone wants to wear the niqab out somewhere, in principle I have no issue with it.

Looping back to the issue of the lack of U.S. law enforcement in these areas, Mauro paints an ugly and disturbing picture of how little "attention" these groups receive from the authorities:

Fuqra does not seem to be a priority at all among the authorities. I do a lot of training of law enforcement and there have been many occasions where I tell a member of law enforcement about one of these Islamic villages that's near them and they never even knew about it. In some cases they've asked their superiors, or people in the FBI, "hey what information do you have on this group" and they say "we're not going to share it with you" or "don't worry there's no threat there" but then the declassified documents I have show that that is a lie.

Local officials appear not to be briefed accurately and fully by the federal authorities about this group and on the federal level, when I talk to personnel working for the FBI or Homeland Security, they'll frankly admit: "Look we don't want to cause up to 22 Wacos. Do we want to raid one village and then have all of these explode at once, particularly when the group isn't carrying out terrorist attacks on American soil, at least not yet, is it worth it?"

So there's a certain level of fear on the part of the federal government—amongst those that understand it. But there's also a lack of interest. I've had it said to me repeatedly: "We are focused on Al Qaeda and ISIS, we consider it to be a bigger threat, we are short on resources, so our attention is going to go on who is setting off a bomb right now and we don't consider Fuqra to be a part of that."

There's also been an issue of arguably overconfidence on the part of authorities. I know sources that have dealt with the authorities on this issue and been a source of information for them and they said they felt they haven't been taken seriously or there was a lack of communication that they interpreted as a lack of interest.

Haney has a different view when it comes to Sharia, though his experiences with the authorities on the issue of Tablighi Jamaat is strikingly similar. He states,

I've told this story 55 times just before Congress alone in the past 5 years. Hundreds and hundreds of times…on the radio, on the TV…I took a vow as a law enforcement officer to help protect our country from threats both foreign and domestic. And even though I'm now retired from federal law enforcement my vow is still in effect. I'm not at the place in my life where I can just turn my back on it and walk away. When I see the same trends that I talked about five and ten and fifteen years ago not only growing stronger but growing wider across not only the world but here in America, then it's my duty that I have to speak out.

I gave the Department of Homeland Security and the Customs and Border Protection department a chance to tell their side of this story. Essentially, they said Haney was overstepping his responsibilities, but they didn't attempt to deny any specific details of his story.

Unfortunately, the government hasn't just passively remained silent about these concerning trends Haney believes are spreading and "growing stronger." Both Haney and Mauro claim that the Obama administration ordered records pertaining to radical Muslim groups to be scrubbed. Why? Purportedly, the information in the records wasn't yielding anything useful. Perhaps it would have if the right people had been studying it. Haney's op-ed for *The Hill* in 2016 concludes,

It is very plausible that one or more of the subsequent terror attacks on the homeland could have been prevented if more subject matter experts in the Department of Homeland Security had been allowed to do our jobs back in late 2009. It is demoralizing—and infuriating—that today, those elusive dots are even harder to find, and harder to connect, than they were during the winter of 2009.

Obviously, the first step we must take to change the way the law enforcement and security and intelligence communities address radical Islam and No Go Zones in America is heed Haney's words and allow the practitioners to do their jobs. The second step is to convince these communities that the two issues should be just as much of a priority to them as Al Qaeda and ISIS. More resources need to be directed toward rooting out the influence radical Islam has on areas in America like Fuqra lands.

With that strategy in mind, let's turn our attention back to the hardest hurdle we'll have to clear to solve the growing problem of radical Islam and No Go Zones in America: the political Left.

When one considers the reliance the Democrat Party has on minority votes, it's easy to imagine that the party wouldn't be above pursuing an agenda that either excuses or lends legitimacy to a lot of problematic groups, including "under the radar" radical Islamists. By doing this, of course, Democrats create bigger problems for the nation and the minorities they claim to serve, like average American Muslims. For some reason, the alternative—retracting support from these groups and acknowledging the threats they pose to America—is not appealing to them. Actually, the reason is pretty evident.

Think about it. Democrats lost over 1,000 seats—at the state and federal level—under President Obama. The party is in dire straits, with few encouraging or promising figureheads on the horizon. How can they be convinced to drop desperately needed support and deal with this issue properly? To support an agenda that tackles radical Islam?

First, the Left needs to realize that its tactics to gain support are self-defeating. By propping up Islamophobia and using it to mask extremist groups, radical Islam is able to grow and function in America. This, in turn, has a devastating consequence that affects not only those who support the Left, but all Americans: it tills American soil for Sharia law, which seeks to supplant the "supreme Law of the Land."

Second, the Left needs to answer the following question: how can it destroy the footholds it has created for radical Islam in America? My advice would be to listen to Phil Haney and "Start with the Constitution."

Haney points out, "Article VI of the Constitution says that the U.S. Constitution is the supreme law of the land. We need to take the clicker and change the channel. It's not just a First Amendment issue. It has to do with Article VI."

Here is the article of the Constitution Haney references:

> This Constitution, and the Laws of the United States which shall be made in Pursuance thereof; and all Treaties made, or which shall be made, under the Authority of the United States, shall be the supreme Law of the Land; and the Judges in every State shall be bound thereby, any Thing in the Constitution or Laws of any State to the Contrary notwithstanding.
>
> The Senators and Representatives before mentioned, and the Members of the several State Legislatures, and all executive and judicial Officers, both of the United States and of the several States, shall be bound by Oath or Affirmation, to support this Constitution; but no religious Test shall ever be required

as a Qualification to any Office or public Trust under the United States.

Haney continues,

> We already do [have Sharia law in the United States]. We see places where men are married to more than one wife. We see the hijab. That is the canary in the coalmine. When you see women covering up it is the first indication of the existence of Sharia law.
>
> Five or ten years ago you virtually saw no one in America with hijab. What's happened? It's the gravitational force of Sharia law. Because what women who wear the hijab might not realise that they're advertising is that their husbands can marry up to four women, that they can be divorced at any moment at the whim of their husband and there's virtually nothing they can do about it. Plus if they are divorced they receive nothing from their husbands apart from possible care.
>
> But those are all contrary to civil law here in America. There's no state that allows polygamy, but there are people coming here—not to mention other things like female genital mutilation, which is occurring more and more frequently now.

I think it is a crying shame that the Obama administration and his higher ups in Customs and Border Protection and the Department of Homeland Security ignored Haney. He has a great plan for defending America from the effects of Sharia law. It is the same solution that should be used to combat issues that stem from radical Islam or "rituals" like female genital mutilation: upholding the Constitution. The laws of the United States in the form of the Constitution can be used to pursue anyone anywhere, even in No Go Zones where people pretend U.S. law is not supreme.

President Trump's administration should learn from the mistakes of Obama's administration and adopt a zero-tolerance policy toward communities that live outside U.S. law. Call yourself a "mayor" when you're not? Lashing your women? Sharia courts? The U.S. government must crack down fast. The backlash from adopting this policy might be difficult to weather at first. But I believe that there are many Muslims like Zuhdi Jasser and Raheel Raza who would defend this policy and counter predictable cries of "Islamophobia." They, like Ryan Mauro, would agree that No Go Zones cannot be allowed to exist in America because such places pose an immediate threat to national security and human rights.

EPILOGUE

I'll keep this brief.

At the start of this project, I hoped my investigation into No Go Zones would be fruitless. Instead, it has yielded enough alarming information to fill a book. Honestly, I could have traveled for another six months and presented another six hundred pages to my editors. From riots to language barriers, from massive deprivation to voter fraud, from extremism and terrorist links to authorities who no longer enter certain areas, it would be incredibly naive and dishonest of me to pretend that there are not serious problems stemming from these areas. But in keeping with my desire to be brutally honest about all of this, I want to make two things clear.

First, most of the areas I've discussed in this book are not aflame (for the most part) with radical Islam. If you visit them, you won't be flogged, and you're unlikely to encounter screeching Islamist imams on their street corners. As I said in the first chapter, an accurate representation of these places needs to reflect reality, not parody.

Second, I want this book to serve as a warning to the United States so that such areas are not allowed to flourish in America. To ensure that never happens, there are many things we must do.

The Left needs to stop fixating on re-running the 2016 presidential election and start supporting the government and its function. This will make societal divisions and cultural discord easier to overcome. The Left's alternative—its default *modus operandi*—to politically "divide and conquer" Western nations will only create breeding grounds for closed communities like No Go Zones.

It is also crucial that the Left finally recognizes and acknowledges that No Go Zones are not the same as "Little Poland" in Detroit or Little Italy in New York. They are closed communities of immigrants who are not interested in integrating into the cultures they migrate to. When Polish immigrants dominated Hamtramck, the city streets were not filled with a call to pray at Catholic altars. So why are they now filled five times a day with a call to pray at the many new mosques scattered across the city despite complaints? The answer lies in the key difference between the latest wave of migrants to this city and their predecessors: Islam.

It is naive to ignore the impact Islam has had on the areas where it is allowed to supplant native cultures. Sevran's cafes and coffee shops were not always devoid of women. Today, however, they are almost exclusively populated by men who claim, "Women are not banned here but this is a place for men. A practicing Muslim woman who knows her religion would not come here." The more closed the communities in these areas are, the more inundated they become with foreign customs that are counterintuitive to modern Western civilization. They also become more susceptible to foreign governance like Sharia law as is evidenced by the disturbing links between radical Islam and Fuqra communes, such as Islamville in South Carolina.

Encouraging integration is one way to stymie the progress of these alarming cultural trends in No Go Zones. To that end, we need to address the problem created by giant satellite dishes that provide television in foreign languages to residents in No Go Zones. These satellites enable a language barrier to grow between natives and immigrants, which prevents integration.

Another way to keep No Go Zones "in check" is to solve the problem of the state-sponsored ghettoization of these areas. Especially in dangerous areas like Rinkeby, the only solution to this problem may be to raze mass tenement buildings to the ground and create new housing programs for immigrants and refugees that encourage integration. In my experience, many of the people living in these areas really don't want to ghettoize. They also don't seem overly concerned about it. It doesn't eat away at them. They do, however, express a preference for nicer living conditions. This will be difficult to implement in places like Sweden, which would require an overhaul of its welfarist policies.

We can also encourage assimilation in No Go Zones if residents of these area are rewarded for keeping crime low and their streets clean. Implementing the model Mayor Robert Ménard established in Beziers for this reward system may not be a bad place to start.

Finally, we can no longer afford to turn a blind eye to the seeds of radical Islam that are growing in the Western world. It is time to start policing our borders again. It is time to start demanding, like Roosevelt did, that there are no divided allegiances. And it is time to insist that our national institutions, from democratic organizations to media outlets, start tackling these issues with realism, not idealism.

I am not insinuating that there will ever be an Islamic Caliphate of Britain or a black Islamic State flag flying above the White House. But if we do not change the way we address No Go Zones, within the next ten or fifty years, our nations will host expanding enclaves policed by those whose first loyalties are not to the British Crown or the American Constitution.

We can be polite with it, if it makes you feel better.

No Go Zones? No, thank you.

ACKNOWLEDGMENTS

The research for this book took me to many cities around the Western world, and it would be impossible to list the number of people—for fear of their safety, as well as just the sheer number of people—who helped me with navigating and researching in the areas covered.

I hope they'll forgive me for not being able to list them all by name, but I want to express my sincerest thanks to them all for their unflinching support and bravery, some of them traversing hostile weather conditions, taking time off work, driving me around for hours on end, and kindly hosting me in their homes. I am, and I know all this book's readers are, eternally grateful for their support.

On a more personal level, there are a great many people without whom I would have never had the fortitude to put this piece of work together.

While they may not realize it, my parents and my brother instilled in me my contrarian nature and hard-headedness that has given me the ability to do what I do. Thank you to Yasmin, Jamaludin, and Jamil for everything you've given me over the years.

I want to thank some bosses and mentors of mine, without whom my worldview could have been far more accepting of the injustices and iniquities pointed out in this book. To Nigel Farage, MEP, Steve Bannon, Matthew Richardson, and Benjamin Harris-Quinney, from the bottom of my heart...thank you.

My first bosses at my earliest jobs taught me there was nothing quite like hard work and rolling up your sleeves. Thank you to them: Kevin and Sonya Clynes and their son Kevin, one of my best friends growing up. Thank you to Paul Dixon, my old manager when I used to sell video games part-time for a few dollars an hour. Without your guidance, I may have been another lazy millennial!

There are people who supported me emotionally and professionally throughout what I found to be a very tough process in pulling all this information together, including Michelle and Kimberly Moons, Oliver Lane, Victoria Friedman, Arron Banks, Dr. Alan Mendoza, Dr. Sebastian Gorka, Andy Wigmore, Dan Jukes, George, Joe Jenkins, Liam Deacon, Simon Kent, Nick Hallett, Jack Montgomery, Patrick Christys, Alex Marlow, Larry Solov, Jon Kahn, Chris Tomlinson, Ezra Dulis, Rebecca Mansour, Caroline Magyarits, Beth Reardon, Greg Sahakian, Liz Aiello, Paul DeMilio, Angela Barrett, Matthew Boyle, Senator Rand Paul, Congressman Louie Gohmert, Congressman Dana Rohrabacher, Jack Abramoff, Nina Rosenwald, Mimi Perlman, Alexandra Preate, Daniel Pipes, Pamela Geller, Robert Spencer, Dr. Zuhdi Jasser, Ryan Mauro, Melissa Galatas, Lauren

Scirocco, Nathalie Tamam, Sarah Hylander, Ed and Meaghan Kozak, Rachel Megawhat, Erica Elliott, Chris Bruni Lowe, Glynis Williams, Ani Tramblian, Mhairi and Lauren Fraser, Rob Towner, Dmitry Shapiro, Adam Kredo, Eli Morse, Ana Barrera and so, so many more people...thank you all.

To those who helped interpret my notes and often hastily written copy, thank you. Marji Ross, Harry Crocker, Tom Spence, Alyssa Cordova, Elizabeth Dobak, Merritt Corrigan, and all those at Regnery and those who helped with dotting the i's and crossing the t's, thank you.

Finally, to all my supporters and benefactors, my Facebook fans, my Twitter followers who have been like an army of common sense, defending me against routine abuse for telling the truth...to all those who have donated to my work and who continue to support the causes of liberty and conservatism around the world...you are MY heroes. Thank you.

To anyone I've forgotten...sorry...I'll buy you a pint!

NOTES

ONE: THE UNSETTLED DEBATE

1. Carmen Fishwick, "Fox News Man Is 'Idiot' for Birmingham Muslim Comments—David Cameron," *The Guardian,* January 12, 2015, https://www.theguardian.com/media/2015/jan/12/fox-news-expert-ridiculed-over-birmingham-is-totally-muslim-city-claims.

2. Natasha Adkins, "Steve Emerson: More Ludicrous Statements Made by 'Expert' Who Claimed Everyone in Birmingham Is a Muslim," *Mirror,* January 12, 2015, http://www.mirror.co.uk/news/uk-news/steve-emerson-more-ludicrous-statements-4966090.

3. Patrick Hennessy and Melissa Kite, "Poll Reveals 40pc of Muslims Want Sharia Law in UK," *The Telegraph,* February 19, 2006, http://www.telegraph.co.uk/news/uknews/1510866/Poll-reveals-40pc-of-Muslims-want-sharia-law-in-UK.html.

4. Raheem Kassam, "Data: Young Muslims In the West Are a Ticking Time Bomb, Increasingly Sympathising with Radicals, Terror," *Breitbart,* March 22, 2016, http://www.breitbart.com/london/2016/03/22/polling-muslims-in-the-west-increasingly-sympathise-with-extremism-terror/.

5. Esther Addley, "BBC Defends Extremist's Presence on Muslim Reality Show," *The Guardian,* December 9, 2016, https://www.theguardian.com/media/2016/dec/09/bbc-defends-extremists-presence-on-muslim-reality-show.

6. Danny Shaw, "Why the Surge in Muslim Prisoners?" *BBC News,* March 11, 2015, http://www.bbc.com/news/uk-31794599.

7. Conrad Hackett, "5 Facts About the Muslim Population in Europe," Pew Research Center, July 19, 2016, http://www.pewresearch.org/fact-tank/2016/07/19/5-facts-about-the-muslim-population-in-europe/.

8. Alex Nowrasteh, "Muslim Assimilation: Demographics, Education, Income, and Opinions of Violence," Cato Institute, August 24, 2016, https://www.cato.org/blog/muslim-assimilation-demographic-education-income-opinions-violence.

9. Center for Security Policy, "Poll of U.S. Muslims Reveals Ominous Levels of Support for Islamic Supremacists' Doctrine of Shariah, Jihad," Press Release, June 23, 2015, https://www.centerforsecuritypolicy.org/2015/06/23/nationwide-poll-of-us-muslims-shows-thousands-support-shariah-jihad/.

10. Adam Withnall, "Saudi Arabia Offers Germany 200 Mosques—One for Every 100 Refugees Who Arrived Last Weekend," *Independent,* September 10, 2015, http://www.independent.co.uk/news/world/europe/saudi-arabia-offers-germany-200-mosques-one-for-every-100-refugees-who-arrived-last-weekend-10495082.html.

11. Rick Noack, "Leaked Document Says 2,000 Men Allegedly Assaulted 1,200 German Women on New Year's Eve," *The Washington Post,* July 11, 2016, https://www.washingtonpost.com/news/worldviews/wp/2016/07/10/leaked-document-says-2000-men-allegedly-assaulted-1200-german-women-on-new-years-eve/?utm_term=.d30539270a81.

12. Lee Stranahan, " 'Hawaii's George Soros': The Hidden Donor Funding the Illegal Immigration, #BlackLivesMatter Activists," *Breitbart,* December 9, 2015, http://www.breitbart.com/big-government/2015/12/09/hawaiis-george-soros-hidden-donor-funding-illegal-immigration-blacklivesmatter-activists/.

13. Mark Townsend, "Anti-Muslim Prejudice 'Is Moving to the Mainstream,'" *The Guardian,* December 5, 2015, https://www.theguardian.com/world/2015/dec/05/far-right-muslim-cultural-civil-war.

14. Kimiko De Freytas-Tamura and Milan Schreuer, "Paris Attacks: The Violence, Its Victims and How the Investigation Unfolded," *The New York Times,* November 15, 2015, https://www.nytimes.com/live/paris-attacks-live-updates/belgium-doesnt-have-control-over-molenbeek-interior-minister-says/.

15. "German Court Lets off 'Sharia Police' Patrol in Wuppertal," *BBC News,* December 10, 2015, http://www.bbc.com/news/world-europe-35059488.

16. Andrew Gilligan, "Tower Hamlets Mayor Lutfur Rahman Is Sacked for 'Corrupt Practices,'" *The Telegraph,* April 23, 2015, http://www.telegraph.co.uk/news/uknews/crime/11559926/Muslim-mayor-is-sacked-for-corrupt-practices.html.

17. Erik Wemple, "Bobby Jindal Remarks: Does Two-Year-Old CNN Report Prove Existence of 'No-Go Zones'?" *The Washington Post,* January 20, 2015, https://www.washingtonpost.com/blogs/

erik-wemple/wp/2015/01/20/bobby-jindal-remarks-does-two-year-old-cnn-report-prove-existence-of-no-go-zones/?utm_term=.
b7ebdca004aa.

TWO: WHAT HAPPENS IN EUROPE

1. Kara Pendleton, "Fox News Is Being Sued by France. No, Really.",
   Independent Journal Review, 2015, http://ijr.com/2015/01/235834-
   2-paris-mayor-threatens-to-sue-this-group-for-insulting-the-image-
   of-paris/.
2. Carol Matlack, "Debunking the Myth of Muslim-Only Zones in
   Major European Cities," *Bloomberg,* January 14, 2015, https://
   www.bloomberg.com/news/articles/2015-01-14/debunking-the-
   muslim-nogo-zone-myth.
3. David Graham, "Why the Muslim 'No-Go-Zone' Myth Won't
   Die," *The Atlantic,* January 20, 2015, https://www.theatlantic.
   com/international/archive/2015/01/paris-mayor-to-sue-fox-over-
   no-go-zone-comments/384656/.
4. Daniel Pipes, "Muslim 'No-Go Zones in Europe?" Daniel Pipes
   Middle East Forum, December 2, 2015, http://www.danielpipes.
   org/16322/muslim-no-go-zones-in-europe.
5. https://clarionproject.org/exclusive-clarion-project-discovers-
   texas-terror-enclave/.
6. Meira Svirsky, "Exclusive: Islamist Terror Enclave Discovered in
   Texas," Clarion Project, February 18, 2014, https://clarionproject.
   org/exclusive-sanders-delegate-member-fuqra-terror-cult/.
7. Brian Stone, "What If America Looked Like Dearborn,
   Michigan?" *HuffPost,* February 26, 2016, http://www.
   huffingtonpost.com/brian-stone/what-if-america-looked-like-
   dearborn_b_9328288.html.
8. London Borough of Tower Hamlets, "2011 Census Headline
   Analysis: Demography, Households and Health," December 2012,

http://www.towerhamlets.gov.uk/Documents/Borough_statistics/
Ward_profiles/Census-2011/RB-Census2011-Headline-analysis-
Demography-Households-Health-2012-12.pdf.

9. Dave Hill, "Tower Hamlets: The Rise and Fall of Lutfur Rahman,"
    The Guardian, June 10, 2015, https://www.theguardian.com/
    uk-news/davehillblog/2015/jun/10/tower-hamlets-the-rise-and-
    fall-lutfur-rahman.

10. Kris Maher, "Muslim-Majority City Council Elected in
    Michigan," *The Wall Street Journal,* November 9, 2015, https://
    www.wsj.com/articles/muslim-majority-city-council-elected-in-
    michigan-1447111581.

11. Raheem Kassam, "Data: Young Muslims in the West Are a
    Ticking Time Bomb, Increasingly Sympathising with Radicals,
    Terror," *Breitbart,* March 22, 2016, http://www.breitbart.com/
    london/2016/03/22/polling-muslims-in-the-west-increasingly-
    sympathise-with-extremism-terror/.

12. Breitbart London, "Breaking: Lutfur Rahman Guilty of
    Corruption, Bribery and Making False Statements," *Breitbart,*
    April 23, 2015, http://www.breitbart.com/london/2015/04/23/
    breaking-lutfur-rahman-guilty-of-corruption-and-bribery/.

13. Full text of the court judgment annulling the election of Lutfur
    Rahman as mayor of Tower Hamlets, pg. 199, https://www.scribd.
    com/doc/263636225/Tower-Hamlets-Judgement#from_embed.

14. Ibid.

THREE: FROM MOLENBEEK, WITH TERROR

1. Kimiko De Freytas-Tamura and Milan Schreuer, "Paris Attacks:
    The Violence, Its Victims and How the Investigation Unfolded,"
    The New York Times, November 15, 2015, https://www.nytimes.
    com/live/paris-attacks-live-updates/belgium-doesnt-have-control-
    over-molenbeek-interior-minister-says/.

2. Roger Cohen, "The Islamic State of Molenbeek," *The New York Times*, April 11, 2016, https://www.nytimes.com/2016/04/12/opinion/the-islamic-state-of-molenbeek.html?_r=0.

3. Danielle Ziri, "Molenbeek: Europe's Terrorism Capital," *GQ*, November 16, 2015, http://www.gq.com/story/molenbeek-europes-terrorism-capital.

4. Johan Leman, "Is Molenbeek Europe's Jihadi Central? It's Not That Simple," *The Guardian*, November 17, 2015, https://www.theguardian.com/commentisfree/2015/nov/17/molenbeek-jihadi-isis-belgian-paris-attacks-belgium.

5. Population.City, "Molenbeek-Saint-Jean: Population," http://population.city/belgium/molenbeek-saint-jean/.

6. "Reportage Petit-Journal : Molenbeek, Attentat et Désinformation," YouTube video, posted by Malouxa, February 17, 2017, https://www.youtube.com/watch?v=kHNYFm3Po8I.

7. Matthew Goodwin, Thomas Raines, and David Cutts, "What Do Europeans Think About Muslim Immigration?" Chatham House, February 7, 2017, https://www.chathamhouse.org/expert/comment/what-do-europeans-think-about-muslim-immigration#.

8. "Transcript: President Donald Trump's Rally in Melbourne, Florida," updated by Jacob Gardenswartz, *Vox*, February 18, 2017, https://www.vox.com/2017/2/18/14659952/trump-transcript-rally-melbourne-florida.

9. Teun Voeten, "Molenbeek Broke My Heart," *POLITICO*, November 21, 2015, http://www.politico.eu/article/molenbeek-broke-my-heart-radicalization-suburb-brussels-gentrification/.

10. Rachel Browne, "The 'Heart of Jihadism' in Europe Is More Complicated Than You Think," *Vice News*, November 17, 2015, https://news.vice.com/article/the-heart-of-jihadism-in-europe-is-more-complicated-than-you-think.

11. Ian Traynor, "Molenbeek: The Brussels Borough Becoming Known as Europe's Jihadi Central," *The Guardian,* November 15, 2015, https://www.theguardian.com/world/2015/nov/15/molenbeek-the-brussels-borough-in-the-spotlight-after-paris-attacks.

12. Voeten, "Molenbeek Broke My Heart."

FOUR: FROM SWEDEN, WITH RAPE

1. Oliver Lane, "Sweden Top Cop on No Go Zones: Europe's Open Borders 'Has Brought Crime Here,'" *Breitbart,* February 23, 2017, http://www.breitbart.com/london/2017/02/23/sweden-top-cop-europes-open-borders-brought-crime/.

2. Statistiska Centralbryan, "Population Surveys," http://www.scb.se/en/finding-statistics/statistics-by-subject-area/population/.

3. Ibid.

4. Miriam Valverde, "What the Statistics Say About Sweden, Immigration and Crime," Politifact, February 20, 2017, http://www.politifact.com/truth-o-meter/article/2017/feb/20/what-statistics-say-about-immigration-and-sweden/.

5. Swedish Migration Agency, "History," https://www.migrationsverket.se/English/About-the-Migration-Agency/Facts-and-statistics-/Facts-on-migration/History.html.

6. Karin Fallenius, "162.000 kom till Sverige—500 fick job," SVT Nyheter, May 31, 2016, https://www.svt.se/nyheter/inrikes/162-000-kom-till-sverige-500-fick-jobb.

7. John-David Ritz and Aretha Bergdahl, "People in Sweden's Alleged 'No-Go Zones' Talk About What It's Like to Live There," *Vice,* November 2, 2016, https://www.vice.com/en_au/article/people-of-the-no-go-zones-talk-about-what-its-like-to-live-in-no-go-zones-726.

8. Anders Magnus and Mohammad Alayoubi, "Krise i svensk politi:—Satses det ikke skikkelig nå, ender det i katastrofe," Norsk Rikskringkasting, September 17, 2016, https://www.nrk.no/urix/svenske-politifolk-frykter-at-de-taper-kampen-mot-kriminelle-1.13138829.

9. Ibid.

10. Oliver Lane, "Sweden Ambulence Boss: Paramedics Banned from 'No Go Zones,' Need Military Equipment," *Breitbart,* February 28, 2017, http://www.breitbart.com/london/2017/02/28/sweden-ambulance-boss-paramedics-banned-from-no-go-zones-need-military-equipment/.

11. "Media LAUGED When Trump Talked About Muslims in Sweden, Then THIS Was Revealed," *The Washington Feed*, http://washingtonfeed.com/media-laughed-when-trump-talked-about-muslims-in-sweden-then-this-was-revealed.html.

12. Chris Tomlinson, "Left Wing Swedish Newspaper Journalist Attacked in 'No Go Zone,'" *Breitbart,* February 21, 2017, http://www.breitbart.com/london/2017/02/21/swedish-newspaper-photographer-attacked-no-go-zone/.

13. David Crouch, "Sweden Shooting Puts Focus on Life in 'Ghettoes without Hope,'" *The Guardian*, March 20, 2015, https://www.theguardian.com/world/2015/mar/20/gothenburg-shooting-sweden-ghettoes-gangs-varvadersligan-klas-friberg.

14. Peter R. Neumann, "Foreign Fighter Total in Syria/Iraq Now Exceeds 20,000; Surpasses Afghanistan Conflict in the 1980s," International Centre for the Study of Radicalisation and Political Violence, January 26, 2015, http://icsr.info/2015/01/foreign-fighter-total-syriairaq-now-exceeds-20000-surpasses-afghanistan-conflict-1980s/.

15. " 'Honour' Culture Common in Stockholm," *The Local*, April 14, 2009, https://www.thelocal.se/20090414/18828.

16. Sarah Lyall, "Lost in Sweden: A Kurdish Daughter is Sacrificed," *The New York Times,* July 23, 2002, http://www.nytimes.com/2002/07/23/world/lost-in-sweden-a-kurdish-daughter-is-sacrificed.html.

17. "Hogsby Retrial Brings 'Honour' Killings Back Into Focus" *The Local,* June 17, 2011, https://www.thelocal.se/20110617/34496.

18. "Father Draws Prison for Honor Killing," UPI, March 22, 2011, http://www.upi.com/Top_News/World-News/2011/03/22/Father-draws-prison-for-honor-killing/19461300798941/?spt=su.

19. Agence France-Press, "Teen in Sweden Jailed Eight Years for Honour Killing," NDTV, January 29, 2013, http://www.webcitation.org/query?url=http://www.ndtv.com/article/world/teen-in-sweden-jailed-eight-years-for-honour-killing-323857&date=2013-02-03.

20. Lizzie Dearden, "Swedish City to Offer Returning Isis Fighters Housing and Benefits in Reintegration Programme," *Independent,* October 20, 2016, http://www.independent.co.uk/news/world/europe/sweden-isis-fighters-city-lund-returning-jihadis-housing-job-education-benefits-reintegration-a7371266.html.

21. Richard Orange, " 'Child Migrant Who Killed Asylum Centre Worker Is an Adult, Swedish Migration Rules," *The Telegraph,* February 12m, 2016, http://www.telegraph.co.uk/news/worldnews/europe/sweden/12153428/Child-migrant-who-killed-asylum-centre-worker-is-an-adult-Swedish-migration-rules.html.

22. Virginia Hale, "Germany: 80 Per Cent of Migrants Paperless, Many Lie for More Welfare," *Breitbart,* August 13, 2016, http://www.breitbart.com/london/2016/08/13/80-migrants-paperless-lie-welfare/.

23. Tino Sanandaji, "What Is the Truth About Crime and Immigration in Sweden?" *National Review,* February 25, 2017, http://www.

nationalreview.com/article/445237/sweden-crime-rates-statistics-immigration-trump-fox-news.

24. Philip Connor, "Number of Refugees to Europe Surges to Record 1.3 Million in 2015," Pew Research Center, August 2, 2016, http://www.pewglobal.org/2016/08/02/number-of-refugees-to-europe-surges-to-record-1-3-million-in-2015/.

25. "Behörden können mehr als 130 000 Asylsuchende nicht mehr auffinden," Suddeutsche Zeitung, February 29, 2016, http://www.sueddeutsche.de/politik/fluechtlingspolitik-mehr-als-jeder-zehnte-asylsuchende-ist-verschwunden-1.2881071.

26. "European Agenda on Migration: Commission Presents New Measures for an Efficient and Credible EU Return Policy," European Commission Press Release, March 2, 2017, http://europa.eu/rapid/press-release_IP-17-350_en.htm.

27. "EU Migrant Crisis: Sweden May Reject 80,000 Asylum Claims," BBC, January 28, 2016, http://www.bbc.com/news/world-europe-35425735.

28. Mona Charen, "What's Up with Rape in Sweden?" *National Review,* February 23, 2017, http://www.nationalreview.com/article/445169/sweden-rape-sexual-assault-non-muslim-immigrants.

29. "Swedish Police to Hand Out anti-Groping Armbands," *The Local,* June 29, 2016, https://www.thelocal.se/20160629/swedish-police-to-hand-out-anti-groping-armbands.

30. Lee Roden, "Why Sweden is NOT the 'Rape Capital of the World,'" *The Local,* February 21, 2017, https://www.thelocal.se/20170221/why-sweden-is-not-the-rape-capital-of-the-world.

31. Ruth Alexander, "Sweden's Rape Rate Under the Spotlight," BBC, September 15, 2012, http://www.bbc.com/news/magazine-19592372.

32. Alexander, "Sweden's Rape Rate Under the Spotlight."

33. Brå, "Rape and Sexual Offences," http://www.bra.se/bra-in-english/home/crime-and-statistics/rape-and-sex-offences.html.

34. Rape, Abuse & Incest National Network, "Statistics," https://www.rainn.org/statistics.

35. Brå, "Rape and Sexual Offences," http://www.bra.se/bra-in-english/home/crime-and-statistics/rape-and-sex-offences.html.

36. Ibid.

37. Brå, "The Swedish Crime Survey," http://www.bra.se/bra/bra-in-english/home/crime-and-statistics/swedish-crime-survey.html.

38. Ibid.

39. "Swedish Minister Does U-Turn on Comments About Sweden's Sex Crimes," *The Local,* March 4, 2017, https://www.thelocal.se/20170304/fake-news-minister-does-u-turn-on-comments-about-swedens-sex-crimes.

40. Doug Saunders, "Sweden's Rape Crisis Isn't What It Seems," *The Globe and Mail,* May 14, 2016, http://www.theglobeandmail.com/opinion/swedens-rape-crisis-isnt-what-it-seems/article30019623/.

41. Kevin Drum, "We Should Practice Truth in Statistics, Even When It Hurts," *Mother Jones,* February 19, 2017, http://www.motherjones.com/kevin-drum/2017/02/we-should-practice-truth-statistics-even-when-it-hurts.

42. Ivar Arpi, "It's Not Only Germany That Covers Up Mass Sex Attacks by Migrant Men...Sweden's Record is Shameful," *The Spectator Australia,* January 6, 2016, https://spectator.com.au/2016/01/its-not-only-germany-that-covers-up-mass-sex-attacks-by-migrant-men-swedens-record-is-shameful/.

43. Caspar Opitz, "Questions and Answers on DN's Handling of Events in the Kungsträdgården," *Dagens Nyheter,* January 11, 2016, http://www.dn.se/nyheter/sverige/questions-and-answers-on-dns-handling-of-events-in-the-kungstradgarden/.

44. Andrew Brown, "This Cover-Up of Sex Assaults in Sweden Is a Gift for Xenophobes," *The Guardian,* January 13, 2016, https:// www.theguardian.com/commentisfree/2016/jan/13/sex-assaults-sweden-stockholm-music-festival.

45. Oliver Lane, "Malmo: The Ghost Town of Migrant Children," *Breitbart,* September 17, 2015, http://www.breitbart.com/ london/2015/09/17/malmo-ghost-town-migrant-children/.

46. Virginia Hale, "Leaked Report: Sweden Sees More Than 50 Per Cent Rise in 'No-Go Zones,'" *Breitbart London,* June 13, 2017, http://www.breitbart.com/london/2017/06/13/sweden-50-per-cent-rise-no-go-zones/.

FIVE: FROM FRANCE, WITH HATE

1. Reuters France, "Enquête pour discrimination sur le Quick halal de Roubaix," February 19, 2010, http://fr.reuters.com/article/ topNews/idFRPAE61I0ID20100219.

2. "Banlieue de la République," Institut Montaigne, http://www. banlieue-de-la-republique.fr; Soeren Kern, "France Goes Halal," Gatestone Institute, February 28, 2012, https://www. gatestoneinstitute.org/2886/france-halal.

3. Open Society Institute, *Profiling Minorities: A Study of Stop-and-Search Practices in Paris,* 2009, https://www.opensocietyfoundations. org/reports/profiling-minorities-study-stop-and-search-practices-paris.

4. "Mass Rally in Paris Against Police Brutality," *Al Jazeera,* March 19, 2017, http://www.aljazeera.com/news/2017/03/thousands-march-paris-police-violence-170319205028094.html.

5. "Caged Fervour," *The Economist,* September 17, 2016, http:// www.economist.com/news/europe/21707230-should-jails-segregate-jihadists-caged-fervour.

6. Harriet Alexander, "What Is Going Wrong in France's Prisons?" *The Telegraph,* January 17, 2015, http://www.telegraph.co.uk/news/worldnews/europe/france/11352268/What-is-going-wrong-in-Frances-prisons.html.

7. "Caged Fervour."

8. Molly Moore, "In France, Prisons Filled with Muslims," *The Washington Post,* April 29 2008, http://www.washingtonpost.com/wp-dyn/content/article/2008/04/28/AR2008042802560.html.

9. Farhad Khosrokhavar, "The Mill of Muslim Radicalism in France," *The New York Times,* January 25, 2015, https://www.nytimes.com/2015/01/26/opinion/the-mill-of-muslim-radicalism-in-france.html?_r=0.

10. Open Society Initiative, *Profiling Minorities,* 10.

11. Ibid., 49.

12. Craig Considine, "The Paris Attacks and My Racist Facebook 'Friends,'" *HuffPost,* November 16, 2015, http://www.huffingtonpost.com/craig-considine/the-paris-attack-and-my-racist-facebook-friends_b_8568322.html.

13. Manisha Krishnan, "The Racist Backlash to the Paris Attacks Is Helping the Islamic State," *Vice,* November 17, 2015, https://www.vice.com/en_us/article/the-racist-backlash-to-the-paris-attacks-is-helping-isis.

14. Eliana Dockterman, "George Takei Releases Powerful Statement Against Racism After Paris Terror Attacks," *Time,* November 14, 2015, http://time.com/4113040/george-takei-releases-powerful-statement-against-racism-after-paris-terror-attacks/.

15. Pascal Bruckner, "The Invention of Islamophobia," signandsight.com, March 1, 2011, http://www.signandsight.com/features/2123.html. Originally published in *Libération,* November 23, 2010,

http://www.liberation.fr/societe/2010/11/23/l-invention-de-l-islamophobie_695512.

16. "Full Text: Writers' Statement on Cartoons," *BBC News,* March 1, 2006, http://news.bbc.co.uk/2/hi/europe/4764730.stm.

17. Rob Parsons, "How a White Schoolboy with Anti-Muslim Views Was Lured Away From Far-Right Extremism," *Harrogate Advertiser,* January 3, 2017, http://www.harrogateadvertiser.co.uk/news/crime/how-a-white-yorkshire-schoolboy-with-anti-muslim-views-was-lured-away-from-far-right-extremism-1-8314040.

18. Emmanuelle Saliba, "Paris Killer Cherif Kouachi Gave Interview to TV Channel Before He Died," NBC News, January 9, 2015, http://www.nbcnews.com/storyline/paris-magazine-attack/paris-killer-cherif-kouachi-gave-interview-tv-channel-he-died-n283206.

19. Gilles Kepel, *Terror in France: The Rise of Jihad in the West* (Princeton: Princeton University Press, 2017), 78.

20. Emma-Kate Symons, "Meet the Founder of the French Jihad-Busting Mothers' Brigade," New York Times, September 21, 2016, https://nytlive.nytimes.com/womenintheworld/2016/09/21/meet-the-founder-of-the-french-jihad-busting-mothers-brigade/.

SIX: FROM THE UNITED KINGDOM, WITH SHARIA

1. Occupy London Facebook Post, June 17, 2016, https://www.facebook.com/permalink.php?story_fbid=866898896748546&id=124563204315456.

2. Innes Bowen, "Who Runs Our Mosques?" *The Spectator,* June 14, 2014, https://www.spectator.co.uk/2014/06/who-runs-our-mosques/; "Indian Muslim Welfare Society Trustees' Report and Audited Financial Statements for the Year Ended 30 September 2013, http://apps.charitycommission.gov.uk/Accounts/Ends46/0001067746_AC_20130930_E_C.PDF.

3. Kurt Barling, "London Mosque Accused of Links to 'Terror' in Pakistan," BBC News, September 22, 2011, http://www.bbc.com/news/uk-england-london-15021073..

4. Libby Brooks, "Murder Accused Says He Killed Asad Shah Disrespecting Islam," *The Guardian,* Wednesday 6, 2016, https://www.theguardian.com/uk-news/2016/apr/06/asad-shah-murder-accused-says-killed-disrespected-islam.

5. "Jalal Uddin Murder: Syeedy Guilty Over Rochdale Imam Death," BBC News, September 16, 2016, http://www.bbc.com/news/uk-england-manchester-37388073.

6. Craig S. Smith, "French Islamic Group Offers Rich Soil for Militancy," *The New York Times,* April 29, 2005, https://web.archive.org/web/20120904013458/http://www.nytimes.com/2005/04/28/world/europe/28iht-muslim.html.

7. "Muslim Group Avoids Holocaust Day," BBC News, January 5, 2006, http://news.bbc.co.uk/2/hi/4582736.stm; Jamie Doward, "British Muslim Leader Urged to Quit Over Gaza," *The Guardian,* March 7, 2009, https://www.theguardian.com/world/2009/mar/08/daud-abdullah-gaza-middle-east.

8. Denis M. MacEoin, *Sharia Law or 'One Law for All'?* (London: Civitas, 2009), https://www.amazon.co.uk/Sharia-Law-One-All/dp/1906837082/ref=sr_1_1?ie=UTF8&s=books&qid=1245844843&sr=8-1.

9. Michael Curtis, "The Problem of Sharia Law in Britain," Gatestone Institute, February 10, 2012, https://www.gatestoneinstitute.org/2839/sharia-law-britain.

10. Kate Ferguson, "One Female Genital Mutilation Case Reported Every Hour in the UK," *Independent,* February 6, 2017, http://www.independent.co.uk/life-style/health-and-families/health-news/female-genital-mutilation-fgm-case-per-hour-uk-nhs-circumcision-a7564571.html.

11. Inayat Bunglawala, "Front-Page Incitement," *The Guardian*, April 30, 2007, https://www.theguardian.com/commentisfree/2007/apr/30/frontpageincitement1
12. Ibid.
13. "UK's 'Youngest Terrorist' Jailed," *Reuters*, September 19, 2008, http://www.reuters.com/article/us-britain-munshi-idUSLJ44015720080919.
14. Josh Halliday and Jamie Grierson, "Fears Grow for Friend of Dewsbury Boy Believed to Be Latest ISIS Suicide Bomber," *The Guardian*, June 15, 2015, https://www.theguardian.com/world/2015/jun/15/fears-grow-for-friend-of-dewsbury-boy-believed-to-be-latest-isis-suicide-bomber.
15. Sue Reid, " 'Go Away, You Shouldn't Be Here. Don't Come Back': The Corner of Yorkshire that Has Almost No White Residents," *Daily Mail*, November 2, 2016, http://www.dailymail.co.uk/news/article-3899540/Go-away-shouldn-t-Don-t-come-corner-Yorkshire-no-white-residents.html.
16. Danny Lockwood, *The Islamic Republic of Dewsbury* (The Press News Ltd, 2011).
17. Robert Winnett and Gordon Rayner, "Shahid Malik, His House and the Slum Landlord: MPs' Expenses," *The Telegraph*, May 14, 2009, http://www.telegraph.co.uk/news/newstopics/mps-expenses/5326333/Shahid-Malik-his-house-and-the-slum-landlord-MPs-expenses.html.
18. "Donald Trump: Full of Hate, Contempt and Intolerance," *Urban Echo*, December 4, 2016, http://urban-echo.co.uk/donald-trump-full-of-hate-contempt-and-intolerance/.
19. Liam Deacon and Raheem Kassam, "UK Armed Forces 'Pray' at Terror-Linked 'Army of Darkness' Mosque," *Breitbart*, May 17, 2016, http://www.breitbart.com/london/2016/05/17/british-army-pray-army-darkness-tablighi-jamaat-radical-mosque/.

20. Giulio Meotti, "Londonistan: 423 New Mosques; 500 Closed Churches," Gatestone Institute, April 2, 2017, https://www.gatestoneinstitute.org/10124/london-mosques-churches.

21. "NOP Poll of British Muslims," UK Polling Report, August 8, 2006, http://ukpollingreport.co.uk/blog/archives/291.

22. Patrick Hennessy and Melissa Kite, "Poll Reveals 40pc of Muslims Want Sharia Law in UK," *The Telegraph*, February 19, 2006, http://www.telegraph.co.uk/news/uknews/1510866/Poll-reveals-40pc-of-Muslims-want-sharia-law-in-UK.html.

23. Kassam, "Data: Young Muslims in the West Are a Ticking Time Bomb, Increasingly Sympathising with Radicals, Terror."

24. David Morgan, "Poll Finds Some U.S. Muslim Support for Suicide Attacks," *Reuters,* May 22, 2007, http://www.reuters.com/article/us-usa-muslims-poll-idUSN2244293620070522.

25. Kassam, "Data: Young Muslims in the West Are a Ticking Time Bomb, Increasingly Sympathising with Radicals, Terror."

26. "British Muslims Poll: Key Points," BBC News, January 29, 2007, http://news.bbc.co.uk/2/hi/6309983.stm.

27. Ewan Palmer, "Al-Qaeda Terror Magazine Inspire Urging Lone Wolf Attacks Downloaded 55,000 Times in UK," *International Business Times,* March 23, 2017, http://www.ibtimes.co.uk/al-qaeda-terror-magazine-inspire-urging-lone-wolf-attacks-downloaded-55000-times-uk-1483954.

28. Bowen, "Who Runs Our Mosques?"

SEVEN: FROM SAN BERNARDINO, WITH LIES

1. "Transcript: President Obama's Address to the Nation on the San Bernardino Terror Attack and the War on ISIS," CNN, December 6, 2015, http://www.cnn.com/2015/12/06/politics/transcript-obama-san-bernardino-isis-address/index.html.

2. Matt Kwong, "At Syed Farook's Mosque, San Bernardino Shooting a Trauma for all Muslims," CBC News, December 5, 2015, http://www.cbc.ca/m/touch/world/story/1.3352154.

3. Ibid.

4. "Home," Al-Shifa Clinic, http://www.alshifafreeclinic.org.

5. Erick Stakelbeck, "Ex-Muslim Speaks Out about 'The Koran Dilemma,'" CBN News, May 11, 2012, http://www.cbn.com/ cbnnews/us/2011/september/ex-muslim-speaks-out-about-the-koran-dilemma/?mobile=false.

6. "Remarks by the President at Islamic Society of Baltimore," The White House, February 3, 2016, https://obamawhitehouse. archives.gov/the-press-office/2016/02/03/remarks-president-islamic-society-baltimore.

7. "Chris Murphy on the Roots of Radical Extremism," Council on Foreign Relations, January 29, 2016, https://www.cfr.org/event/ chris-murphy-roots-radical-extremism.

8. Paul Sperry, "The Purge of a Report on Radical Islam Has Put NYC at Risk," New York Post, April 15, 2017, http://nypost. com/2017/04/15/the-purge-of-a-report-on-radical-islam-has-put-nyc-at-risk/.

EIGHT: FROM DETROIT, WITH THE CALL TO PRAYER

1. New York Correspondent, "Ballots for US Presidential Election Available in Bangla," bdnews24.com, October 10, 2016, http:// bdnews24.com/world/2016/10/29/ballots-for-us-presidential-election-available-in-bangla.

2. Lowell, "Discuss Detroit Message Board," November 9, 2006, http://www.atdetroit.net/forum/messages/76017/86968. html?1164003862.

3. Marla Scafe and Kurt Metzger, The Chaldeans in Metropolitan Detroit: 2008 Household Survey Results, Chaldean American

Chamber of Commerce, http://www.chaldeanfoundation.org/ wp-content/uploads/2014/06/CACC_Household_Survey_Results. pdf.

4. Ahmed Afzaal, "Is Islam a Religion of Peace?" New Clear Vision, January 24, 2011, http://www.newclearvision.com/2011/01/24/ is-islam-a-religion-of-peace/.

5. Melanie Elturk, "Modesty and Hijab," Iona Masjid, http://www. ionamasjid.org/about-us/19-publications/articles/articles/308-modesty-and-hijab.

6. Steve Mustapha Elturk, "Shariah," Read the Spirit, http://www. readthespirit.com/explore/dispelling-myths-about-islamic-law-shariah-explained/.

7. Aftab Borka, " 'Enough Is Enough' Says Muslim Leader about Trump's Remarks," Oakland Press, December 8, 2015, http://www. theoaklandpress.com/article/OP/20151208/NEWS/151209607.

8. Hasna Begum, "Hera Food 2 Go," Restaurant Guru, April 2017, https://restaurantguru.com/Hera-Food-Mart-Warren/reviews/ google.

9. "2016 US Grantmaking/2016 UK Grantmaking," Unbound Philanthropy, https://www.unboundphilanthropy.org/who-we-fund.

10. Letter from Theodore Roosevelt to Richard Hurd, Library of Congress Manuscript Division, http://www.snopes.com/politics/ graphics/troosevelt.pdf.

11. "Theodore Roosevelt on Immigration," Snopes, http://www. snopes.com/politics/quotes/troosevelt.asp.

12. Ellen Wulfhorst, "U.S. Girls, Women at Risk of Genital Mutilation Has Tripled: Study," Reuters, January 14, 2016, http://www. reuters.com/article/us-usa-mutilation-women-idUSKCN0US30Q20160114.

13. Allie Gross, "Hamtramck's Mayor Is on CNN Talking Muslims. It's, Well, Interesting," *Detroit Metro Times*, November 23, 2015, https://www.metrotimes.com/news-hits/archives/2015/11/23/hamtramcks-mayor-is-on-cnn-talking-muslims-its-well-interesting.

14. E.A. Torriero, "They're 100% American, and Pro-Hezbollah," *Chicago Tribune*, July 27, 2006, http://articles.chicagotribune.com/2006-07-27/news/0607270148_1_hezbollah-israeli-terrorist-organization.

15. Department of Justice, "Former Employee of CIA and FBI Pleads Guilty to Conspiracy, Unauthorized Computer Access and Naturalization Fraud," November 13, 2007, https://www.justice.gov/archive/opa/pr/2007/November/07_nsd_910.htm.

NINE: FROM AMERICA, WITH RADICAL ISLAM

1. Andrew Gilligan, "Muslim Hate Monitor to Lose Backing," *The Telegraph*, June 9, 2013, http://www.telegraph.co.uk/journalists/andrew-gilligan/10108098/Muslim-hate-monitor-to-lose-backing.html.

2. Regional Organized Crime Information Center, *Jamaat ul-Fuqra: Gilani Followers Conducting Paramilitary Training in U.S.*, 2006, https://info.publicintelligence.net/ROCICjamaatulfuqra.pdf.

3. "New York," Fuqra Files, The Clarion Project, http://www.fuqrafiles.com/knowledgebase/new-york/.